Artists with PhDs

Published and Forthcoming by New Academia Publishing

Visual Culture / Popular culture / Cinema

PERSPECTIVES ON CONNOISSEURSHIP OF CHINESE PAINTING, edited by Jason C. Kuo.

VISUAL CULTURE IN SHANGHAI, 1850s-1930s, edited by Jason C. Kuo.

HERETICAL EMPIRICISM, by Pier Paolo Pasolini. Ben Lawton and Louise K. Barnett, trs., eds. With Ben Lawton's new Introduction and the first approved English-language translation of Pasolini's essay, "The Repudiation of the 'Trilogy of Life'."

PIER PAOLO PASOLINI: In Living Memory, edited by Ben Lawton and Maura Bergonzoni.

SHOPPING FOR JESUS: Visual Culture and the Marketing of Christianity Dominic Janes, ed.

SUPER HEROES: From Hercules to Superman, edited by Wendy Haslem, Angela Ndalianis, and Chris Mackie.

EVERY STEP A STRUGGLE: Interviews with Seven Who Shaped the African-American Image in Movies, by Frank Manchel.

IMAGING RUSSIA 2000: Film and Facts, by Anna Lawton.

BEFORE THE FALL: Soviet Cinema in the Gorbachev Years, by Anna Lawton.

Literature: History / Theory / Criticism

RUSSIAN FUTURISM: A History, by Vladimir Markov.

WORDS IN REVOLUTION: Russian Futurist Manifestoes 1912-1928, A. Lawton and H. Eagle, eds., trs.

THE MAFIA IN SICILIAN LITERATURE, by Corinna del Greco Lobner.

RIVERS OF FIRE: Mythic Themes in Homer's Iliad, by C.J. Mackie.

ON THE ROAD TO BAGHDAD, or TRAVELING BICULTURALISM: Theorizing a Bicultural Approach to Contemporary World Fiction, Gönul Pultar, ed.

SHAKESPEARE'S THEATER OF LIKENESS, by R. Allen Shoaf.

To read an excerpt, visit: www.newacademia.com

Artists with PhDs

On the New Doctoral Degree in Studio Art

Edited by James Elkins

NEW ACADEMIA
PUBLISHING

Washington, DC

Copyright © 2009 by James Elkins

New Academia Publishing, 2009

Printed in the United States of America

Library of Congress Control Number: 2008940921
ISBN 978-0-9818654-5-4, paperback (alk. paper)

Contents

Part Two: Examples

Introduction

If you're a young artist, and you are wondering about how to land a secure teaching job, there is an interesting—I should really say frightening—new possibility. It appears that before too long, employers will be looking for artists with PhDs rather than Masters or college degrees. For the best jobs, it will no longer be enough to have an MA or an MFA. The best universities and art schools will increasingly be looking for candidates with one of the new, PhD-level degrees, sometimes called "creative-art doctorates" or "practice-based doctorates." It may even happen that the PhD degrees become the standard minimum requirement for teaching jobs at the college level.

That may seem unlikely, but consider what happened in the United States after the Second World War: returning soldiers signed on for the new Master's in Fine Arts degrees, and by the 1960s those degrees had become standard across the country. At first the MFA provoked resistance. It was said that it would lead to the academization of fine art, turning artists into scholars, and requiring that they produce impossible amounts of writing. Now, at the start of the twenty-first century, MFAs are ubiquitous and effectively devalued. A recent job search for a plum position at the University of North Carolina at Chapel Hill attracted almost 700 candidates, the vast majority of whom would have had MFAs. The degree, by itself, has come to be little more than a requirement for competition on the job market, somewhat akin to the requirement of a high school or college diploma. To compete, job candidates need to have the MFA *and something else,* such as an exhibition record or a second field of expertise.

If history has a lesson to teach here, and I think it does, then the PhD in studio art will spread the way the MFA did a half-century ago. The resistance to it will subside, and it will become the baseline requirement for a competitive job teaching studio art. The MFA will continue, and will still be sufficient for jobs in secondary schools and smaller colleges, but the PhD will increasingly be a necessity for competition at the highest levels.

As I write this, in the autumn of 2008, it hardly seems likely that the creative-art PhD will become a standard requirement in the United States and Canada. At the moment there are PhD-granting programs in Maine (the program started by George Smith, represented in this book), Virginia Commonwealth, University of California at San Diego, York University (Toronto), the University of Western Ontario at London, Texas Tech, Ohio University, Concordia, New York University (reviving an older program there), and Montréal; and programs are planned in Carnegie Mellon, CalArts, Ryerson University in Toronto, the School of the Art Institute of Chicago, Parsons, the University of Rochester, and elsewhere. In Latin America there is a program at the University of São Paulo. (That is not counting design PhDs or music PhDs, which have been around for several decades and have different structures.) That may not seem like too many schools, but when I wrote the first draft of this Preface, in 2004, there were only two institutions on the list. At this rate there will be 127 programs by 2012.

In fall 2003 there was a conference session in Los Angeles on the subject of PhDs in studio art. I gave a paper there, along with Timothy Emlyn Jones, two of whose essays also appear in this book. The audience, comprised of deans and presidents of North American art schools and art departments, was by turns astonished, unconvinced, dismissive, and paranoid.

"How can you expect art students to write 50,000-word dissertations, when my students can barely write a short Master's thesis?" one asked.

"This is a horrible idea," another person said, "it makes art into a hothouse flower. It makes it into philosophy, or literary criticism."

"Why should artists do research like scientists?" a third wanted to know. "That is simply not how art is made." Others asked how students would pay for such degrees, and who would be qualified to assess them (surely instructors with MFAs could not supervise PhD theses).

The audience in Los Angeles could afford to be skeptical, because the United States has no consistent history of PhDs in studio art. Since the 1970s there have been a handful of universities that offer such degrees, but in my experience they do not command much attention or turn out high on the lists of desirable programs. I have heard it said that they are just extensions of the MFA—two or three more years in the studio, to no clear purpose. (One person in the Los Angeles meeting said she thought the PhD would be a waste of time, a way of "hanging around" in school after the Masters is complete.)

But the crowd in that conference in 2003 was unsettled, especially when they heard Tim Jones say that there were currently two thousand students in the UK enrolled in programs that could result in the PhD.[1] Another panelist, David Williams, said that within two years, Australia would have ten universities that offer the PhD degree. Since then I have heard that in Malaysia, art teachers at college level are required to have PhDs. Clearly, in the UK and in countries influenced by their university system, the PhD is fast becoming a standard.

Since that conference, there have been at least ten other sessions in the US on the subject. (Most are documented in the chapters of this book.[2]) So far, the PhD in studio art has two bibliographies: a scattered and (I think) mainly unhelpful series of papers published from the 1970s onward, principally aimed at justifying the creation of new programs in the UK; and seven recent books including this one. The seven books are, in order:

1) an Irish publication I edited called *Printed Project*, from which this book grew (that was the first publication on this subject)

2) *Thinking Through Art*, another edited volume (it is discussed in Chapter 9)

3) a collection called *Artistic Research*, edited by Annette Balkema and Henk Slager[3]

4) Graeme Sullivan's *Art Practice as Research*[4]

5) an e-book called *Thinking Through Practice: Art as Research in the Academy*[5]

6) a collection of essays on PhDs in Finland,[6] and

7) this book.[7]

So the literature is not difficult to master—a good thing, given the masses of administrative literature that are likely to be produced when this subject is seriously debated in the US. I predict that in twenty years most larger art schools and university art departments in North America will offer such degrees. The question is not whether the new programs are coming, but how rigorously they will be conceptualized.

The philosophy of this book is simply that it is best to try to understand something that is coming, rather than inveighing against it.[8] The PhD in studio art has many problems, and if the MFA is an indication they won't all be solved before the programs are in place. (Or, if you're cynical, the problems will never be solved, and the programs will be put in place anyway.) Students *will* have to pay more, and they will stay in school longer, and write more. There will be new pressures on the job market. Some kinds of art will probably be influenced by the new degree, and art as a whole may even become more academic and intellectual—more involved with theory, possibly even more alienated from skill and technique. But it is best to consider the new degree as a potential feature on the academic landscape, and try to understand it, rather than writing polemics against it.

In this book, I offer several tools to promote discussion of the new degree. Part One sets the stage and gives relevant facts; Part Two, offers excerpts from studio-art PhD dissertations to show the kind of work that has been done.

I begin with some homework. Judith Mottram's essay, Chapter 1, is a mass of quantitative information that will help you see the shape of things in the UK, which is the place the new degrees got started. Mottram's contribution may seem long and detailed if you are new to the subject, but it is the most accurate history of the degree in the UK: skim it, at least, if you're coming at this subject for the first time. She meditates on what a PhD means in any field, and shows how certain influential models of the PhD, such as Christopher Frayling's, began.

(A note about Frayling: he wrote an influential paper distinguishing kinds of PhD research; it is alluded to and quoted in several chapters of this book. It is not reprinted here because it is available online, but it is useful background reading. If you are not familiar with it, you might want to download a copy before reading the chapters of this book.[9] Alternately, Frayling's claims are summarized in Chapters 8 and 9.)

Chapter 2 is a revision of Jones's paper from the 2003 conference. In this essay you will be introduced to the literature that has grown up in the UK to justify the new degrees. Again it's a long essay, with detail that will be unfamiliar to US readers, but his meditation on research remains one of the best, and best-documented, defenses of the concept of research in the arts and advanced degrees "by research."

From there things get more polemical.

In the 1990s a literature grew up that reacted against the stultifying terms proposed in the UK. Some of it is informed by poststructural ideas of dialogism that come from sources such as Levinas, Derrida, Deleuze, and Nicolas Bourriaud; and some is associated with subaltern studies and postcolonial theory (for example, essays on the PhD by Sarat Maharaj). In this book, I exemplify this tendency with an essay by Henk Slager, who directs the first PhD-granting institution in the Netherlands (Chapter 3). Slager draws on various poststructural paradigms to argue for a sense of art research that is transdisciplinary, post-humanistic, mobile, and unquantitative. This kind of argument is often made in support of the idea that art research is different in kind from other research, with its own often difficult and ambiguous characteristics.

Writing about the studio-art PhD tends to draw on a shallow sense of its own history; it shares that historical amnesia, to some degree, with the sometimes allied field of visual studies. Mick Wilson's contribution, Chapter 4, is a reminder that some central terms in the subject, such as the idea of research and the idea of the PhD, have deeper histories. Wilson draws on some of the literature of the history of European universities to remind would-be innovators that their apparent innovations spring from unseen roots.

Victor Burgin's essay, Chapter 5, is lucid and succinct on the problems of invoking research to justify the new programs. I wholly agree with the first three-quarters of the essay. His proposals for three kinds of PhD programs are brief but cogent. As he says, the real issue is how to assess the new programs: a problem no one knows how to solve.

Tim Jones's second essay, Chapter 6, gives some hints and instructions to US institutions interested in learning from the UK example. An earlier version of the essay was also published in the *Art Journal*, one of the CAA's two official journals, in 2006: an early signal of the emerging interest in the new degree.

Chapter 7 was written by George Smith, who started the first PhD program in the United States influenced by international developments.[10] Smith has taken an unusual step, which is unique, I think, in the entire world: he has decided not to teach studio art in his program. Instead he wants to provide the theoretical instruction that he finds missing at the MFA level, and in universities.

Chapter 8, by two scholars working in Leuven, reports on the collaboration of Belgian universities in practice-based PhDs. The essay is a wide-ranging, theoretically- and historically informed article, which also includes a review of pertinent senses of *research,* and a speculative section on the possibility of PhDs for creative writers (which already exist in the United States) and even art critics.

I am not a neutral editor here, and I will not hide the fact that I think a great deal of theorizing about research and the production of new knowledge is nonsense. I just don't think it makes enough sense to say that art research is "mobile," "dialogic," "contextual," "topical," "unquantitative," "between zones," "nomadic," or "implicated in poststructural paradigms" — to quote a few authors who have written on the subject. This kind of theorizing, I think, either tortures the concepts of *research* and *new knowledge* to make them answer to fine art practice, or abandons them for an uncertain celebration of complexity. Dialogic, Deleuzian, postcolonial, and other poststructural approaches *could* make the kind of sense that would allow the PhD in studio art to be accepted throughout the university, but at the moment they don't, and I don't think it helps the visual arts to be packaging their initiative in this way. Nor does it help to continue tweaking the UK ideas of research and new knowledge so they can continue to make sense. Chapter 9 is my contribution to the discussion of the concepts "research" and "new knowledge." I have collected the principal meanings that have been given to the two concepts, and the major attempts that have been made to get away from them. The chapter is polemic, but it is also intended as a reference to the current state of theorizing on the subject.

What is needed, I think — and Burgin says as much in Chapter 5, and Jones in Chapter 6 — is a ground-up rethinking of the possible conceptualizations of the PhD in studio art that does not need to rely on notions of research or the production of new knowledge. Chapter 10 is a brief but wonderfully lucid essay on the same issue by Charles Harrison—one of his few forays into this subject. I include it here because its clarity and succinctness makes it especially amenable to discussion.

Like Burgin and Wilson, I think one of the most interesting things about the new degree is the opportunity it affords to rethink the supervisor's role. In a word, no one knows how to supervise these degrees. Chapter 11 is an attempt to consider the new degree as an abstract possibility: I want to know what could be made of it in the best of all possible worlds, aside from all its national historians, its conceptual entanglements, and its half-forgotten histories. This is my own "position paper," and sets out my own interests in the field. (The two chapters I have contributed to this book take an unusual editorial license: I cite and comment on the other chapters in the book. I hope that will make the book more useful by bringing the contributors into dialogue.)

That's Part One. Then the book changes direction, and in Part Two, I have excerpted some examples of PhD dissertations and PhD-level artwork, to show what can be accomplished. Most of the examples comes from Australia, because the UK examples are more commonly seen and discussed. A great deal of interesting work is being done by students in the new programs in Australia; these are just a sample.

The book ends with some brief conclusions and a challenge.

Navan, Co Meath, Ireland - Chicago, Illinois - Ithaca, New York
April 2004–January 2009

Notes

1 For exact figures see the section "The Size and Shape of the Research Art Community" in Judith Mottram's essay, Chapter 1.

2 See the notes in Chapters 1, 2, and 6, and in general, the *Journal of Visual Arts Practice*; further Thierry de Duve, "When Form Has Become Attitude — and Beyond." in *The Artist and the Academy, Issues in Fine Art Education and the Wider Cultural Context*, edited by Nicholas de Ville and Stephen Foster (Southampton: John Hansard Gallery, University of Southampton, 1994).

3 In the series *Lier en Bloog* [Dutch Society for Aesthetics], vol. 18 (Amsterdam: Rodopi, 2004), ISBN 90 420 1097-5.

4 Sullivan, *Art Practice as Research: Inquiry in the Visual Arts* (London: Sage, 2005).

5 Published online by RMIT University (Melbourne), October 2007, at search. informit.com.au/browsePublication;isbn=9781921166679;res=E-LIBRARY; published in printed form in 2008; ISBN 978-0-9804679-0-1.

6 *The Artist's Knowledge: Research at the Finnish Academy of Fine Arts*, edited by Jan Kaila (Helsinki: Finnish Academy of Fine Arts, 2006). ISBN 951-53-2879-9.

7 This is not counting *Practice-based PhD in the Creative and Performing Arts and Design*, edited by Hilde Van Gelder, e-publication (CD ROM), proceedings of an international conference on the subject at STUK, Leuven (10 September 2004); see Van Gelder and Baetens's chapter in this book.

8 This is the burden of my "Ten Reasons to Mistrust the New PhD in Studio Art," *Art in America* (May 2007): 108-9, which summarizes my take on the concerns voiced this book.

9 Frayling, "Research in Art and Design," for example at www.constellations.co.nz/index.php?sec=3&ssec=7&r=687#687, accessed September 2008. The essay is discussed in a wide range of sources, including Victor Margolin, *The Politics of the Artificial: Essays on Design and Design Studies* (Chicago: University of Chicago Press, 2002), 259; Darren Newbury, "Knowledge and Research in Art and Design" (Birmingham Institute of Art and Design, n.d.), online at www.biad.uce.ac.uk/research/rti/rtrc/pdfArchive/da8.PDF, accessed September 2008; Roy Prentice, "The Place of Practical Knowledge in Art and Design Education," *Teaching in Higher Education* 5 no. 4 (2000): 521–34; Nigan Bayazit, "Investigating Design: A Review of Forty Years of Design Research," *DesignIssues* 20 no. 1 (2004): 16–29; and many others.

10 As with all firsts, this one is contentious. It could be added that Virginia Commonwealth's program, begun the year before, is the first program that was made with awareness of developments in the UK and elsewhere; and it could also be argued that Smith's program is not a studio-art PhD at all, because it does not involve studio instruction. (More on this below, and in Smith's chapter.)

Acknowledgments

First I owe thanks to Jason Oakley, who invited me, on June 22, 2004, to edit an issue of the publication called *Printed Project*, the occasional publication of the Sculptors' Society of Ireland (now the Visual Arts Society of Ireland). Thanks to Jason and to Toby Dennett, then Director of the Sculptors' Society, for putting in all the work on that publication. (For this book, I have added eight essays in Part One, and rewritten the Introduction and Conclusion, but Part Two remains the same.)

Thanks, too, to the many people who advised me along the way: Tim Jones, Dean of the Burren College of Art in Ballyvaughan, Ireland, and my co-conspirator in studio-art PhDs when I worked at the University College Cork, Ireland, from 2004 through 2006; Richard Woodfield, who shared many sources with me; Michael Newman in Chicago and Nigel Lendon in ANU Canberra, who recommended interesting recent PhDs for Part Two; and the many authors who participated (some of whom did not, for reasons of space, make the final book), including Michael Biggs, Sarat Maharaj, Anke Bangma, and Graham Eadie. Thanks, too, to Katy Macleod, Lin Holdridge, David Williams, Tony Jones, Christa-Mia Lerm Hayes, and Slavka Sverakova, for various kinds of help and encouragement. And thanks to the unruly crowd at that conference in Los Angeles in 2003: without a show of resistance like that, I might not have concluded this is a subject worth pursuing.

A brief note to readers who may know my *Why Art Cannot Be Taught* (University of Illinois Press, 2001): I still think that art can't be taught. But on the way to not teaching, a lot of interesting things can happen.

A Glossary of Terms

The UK, Australia, New Zealand, and Scandinavia, where these degrees are most widespread, use slightly but confusingly different words for many of the concepts under discussion.

The expression "PhD in studio art," which I tend to prefer, is not neutral, and from a UK perspective it implies new possibilities. (Jones notes this in Chapter 6.) The usual expression in the UK is "practice-based doctorate," and there are a number of variants, including for example the DCA or Doctorate in Creative Arts, the DFA or Doctorate in Fine Art (a more studio-based alternative to the PhD), "creative practice research," and the "interdisciplinary creative-arts PhD." For the DCA, see Chapter 6, point number 10.

For some authors, those distinctions are at issue, and I have left them intact. In other places, I have substituted US for UK usage. I refer to the written component of the degree using both its US name, "dissertation," and its UK appellation, "thesis." A dissertation is assumed to be a "written dissertation," as it is sometimes called. The artwork itself, together with its accompanying exhibition and statement, is also sometimes called the "thesis": that is a radical possibility, which I mention in Chapter 11; usually a dissertation is a written text that follows some protocols of scholarly research. In the UK, a "dissertation" is usually a research paper written by an undergraduate, or a paper written on the way to another degree. a "thesis" is what is called a "dissertation" in the US: PhD students write them.

One term that has no US synonym is the Research Assessment Exercise (RAE), which appears many times in these pages, especially in Chapter 10. Mention it to someone in the UK, and you will probably get a big sigh, and then—if you're unlucky—an excruciating litany of complaints. The RAE is a hugely time-consuming series of reports that quantify a department's performance. It leads to meetings upon meetings, and issues in recommendations intended to improve the department, and in the allocation of funds for such things as new lecturers. In Ireland in 2004, I prepared a 300-page report, followed by a 60-page abbreviation, followed by a 20-page survey about how I found the experience of writing the 60-page abbreviation, followed by two 3-page summaries; that took most of two years and entailed something over 20 meetings—all for a department with only 3.4 full-time faculty in it. The practical results of the report, as far as I can see, will be actually, absolutely zero. The starred recommendation on the final distillation of the Department's response to the university's response to the External Committee's response—that the secretary have her Xerox machine moved to a different room—was not implemented. That's an extreme instance, but the RAE is the albatross, or the whipping-post, of the UK academic system; its pale, harmless North American equivalent is the periodic departmental review. For the UK authors in this book, the RAE looms large, and shadows every aspect of departmental life, including the language used to justify the new PhD programs.

Another such term with no parallel is External Examiner: a scholar signed by by every department in Ireland and the UK, whose job is to vet examination questions before they are printed, and later to visit the department in order to read borderline examination answers and essays, help with the adjustment of students' grades, and comment on the teaching and organization of the department. No such thing exists, for better or worse, in the US.

Some other terms: for "postgraduate student" (the UK usage for students who stay at university after their BA or BS) I use "graduate student"; for "postdoctoral" I use "postgraduate" (i.e., something after the PhD); for "module" I use "class" or "course"; for "course" "major"; for "programme" "program"; for "MPhil" nothing (no such degree exists in the US; it is an "untaught" graduate-level degree, done by tutorials, sometimes leading to the PhD). Such are some of the minor and major confusions of the two systems.

Part One

Essays

1

Researching Research in Art and Design
Judith Mottram

"Research culture" is a phrase used to indicate an intangible state of being that we might have within an academic community such as a department in a university. A research culture, I imagine, could be a Petri dish of sticky goo in which fertile memes come together with emerging questions and pressing issues. It could also be a set of interconnected comings together of interesting and interested people who talk about their academic inquiries, sharing references to other work in the field, reach consensus on what sort of questions need to be asked to further understanding in the field, and who then find the resources and get on with it. A third iteration of a research culture might be the corridor of closed doors, where no one actually knows much about what their colleagues are doing, and certainly never gets the time to read or see their work, but there is intense competition to be known to be getting the grants, or being invited to give keynote presentations, or getting that publishing deal. Within the art and design sphere, that could translate to getting that gallery show, selling to that collection, or getting a contract with that manufacturer.

So: is research culture a place, a context, a set of values, or a mode of operation? and are we automatically assuming "culture" to be a value-added commodity, a "good thing"? My suggestion is that the culture is what we make it, and when talking about research cultures in academia, it is the academics that have the responsibility for determining the specifics of that cultural environment in which they might wriggle and grow. We also have the responsibility for careful and sensible consideration of new opportunities and challenges.

The Art and Design Index to Theses

This is a long way around to introducing the background to the Art and Design Index to Theses (ADIT) project, but sets the scene for how that particular body of work originated. ADIT comprises a database of information on all research degrees awarded by UK universities in the subject fields of art and design. The background for why we undertook to build the database provides a useful context for considering the key questions that could arise when considering the PhD in relation to studio subjects like fine art. An initial analysis of the database itself may provide useful material for developing arguments about different ways to move the debate about advanced degrees in art and design subjects forward. Finally, reflection upon the perspectives offered by the ADIT material when seen in conjunction with an analysis of the research field drawn from the data compiled for the 2001 Research Assessment Exercise, may give some clear pointers for additional questions needing further address in the field.[1]

A few years ago, while visiting Leeds Metropolitan University as an External Examiner for their Masters programs in art and design, the discussion between the other External Examiner, Tom Fisher of Sheffield Hallam University, members of the Leeds Met staff, and myself, turned to the imperative to come to some sort of consensus on the research agenda for our subjects.[2] We thought this would be beneficial to counter the range and particularity of doctoral projects being undertaken by research students we knew, and would provide a benchmark against which to reflect upon the usefulness of specific contributions to subject knowledge in the field. Such clarification of an agenda might also suggest strategic topics for ring-fenced funding. One of the concerns we explored was the resistance shown by some doctoral students to locating their inquiry within its context—otherwise known as "doing the literature search."

We mapped some of the factors that might form a background to this tendency, speculating upon the impact of a model whereby the framing of a doctoral project within art and design was, more often than not, based entirely upon the individual student's area of interest. We noted how this differed from the model used in many other academic subjects, where a student doctoral study might be part of, or tightly related to, an area of inquiry articulated by the Supervisor or Principal Investigator of a major research project. We conjectured on the importance of the individual "voice" within art and design practice, and the influence of that dominant model on emerging research practice. On occasions, creative practitioners assert importance, or originality, based only upon the evidence that they "know" or "feel" that what they have produced is creative, original, or novel. The argument might go as follows: "I created it, thus this expression of my individual experience/being/creativity/voice has value." It is clear that this sort of value model does not sit comfortably alongside with the well-established model of verification and replicability that forms the backbone of generic understandings of research within the university system and more widely throughout industry, commerce and general society.

A more pragmatic explanation for the lack of reference to previously completed doctoral work within the literature reviews of research students was the difficulty of getting access to this material. We shared the experience of advising students to look at this thesis or that thesis from a particular university, that we might have heard about at a conference or other discussion with peers, but which the student was then unable to locate. It was concluded that this fairly common experience in our little Petri dish could result from institutions not passing completed theses to the central Index to Theses, or that students were not aware of or were overwhelmed by the mass of material contained within that Index. It was recognized that the subject classifications of the full Index did not usefully reflect the range of activity that we were aware of and there were clearly omissions within it. All of these latter issues could be dealt with, but the reasons for not passing material to the national repository were beyond speculation.

The conversation moved on, exploring the need to develop a consensus on the important questions for our subjects. In part, we were developing a consensus that doctoral study had an important part to play in building the knowledge base of art and design, in a way in which it had not previously been possible. The potential to influence or direct the selection of questions or avenues for inquiry was considered worthy of further consideration. But we were also grappling with the chicken and egg question: does the agenda derive from activity in the field, or do the "gatekeepers" or "stake holders" determine that agenda? The Arts and Humanities Research Council (still a "Board" at that point) had been fairly open to the subject fields in relation to its priorities.[3] It had not been identifying and ring-fencing funding for strategic subject initiatives, as was fairly standard among the other research councils. It was however starting to develop funding streams tackling specific infrastructure issues. A particular initiative, the Collaborative Doctoral Training scheme, appeared to provide us with a useful vehicle through which we could explore the topic of research agenda development while addressing the way in which information on doctoral theses could be accessed in the future. So, in the spirit of my second iteration of a research culture, we prepared and won a bid for a collaborative project, led by Tom Fisher at Sheffield Hallam University, to set up a database of research theses in art and design that could be used as a resource for training future doctoral students. We determined that an important part of the groundwork for developing research agendas in the field should be an analysis of the sorts of questions and approaches that had figured in doctoral work to date. The data collected would be interrogated for dominant or emerging themes, and careful attention would be paid to the claims for methodological innovation or precedence.

The core of the raw data already existed within the Index to Theses, which is drawn from records sent to them by university registrars.[4] However relevant records in this database were not categorised in a way which reflects current practice in art and design. Potential records were cross-referenced against the Allison Research Index to Art and Design[5], which covered subject-specific material from early art education studies at Leicester Polytechnic up to the mid-1990s, and additional material was drawn directly from university Registrars and Art and Design departments. A working version of the ADIT database of art and design PhD records up to those awarded in the first few months of 2005 was completed by December 2005.

The subject spread of the database reflected our focus on disciplines where engagement in art or design practice could be a viable component of investigation. Criteria were established to determine inclusion or exclusion. The project covers the fields of design, including architecture, and fine art, but excludes technical studies of materials, historical studies, museology, consumer studies or philosophical studies that do not focus on contemporary creative practice. The main focus was on research where the title or abstract (if available) made it apparent that the study or speciality came from within the art and design field, rather than inquiry from outside looking inwards. The Joint Academic Classification System (JACS) was used by the Researcher to code the records, to enable future users to identify records of interest by subject.[6] It was acknowledged that any project of this nature, requiring the categorisation of complex material, could be open to different interpretation, and testing how we apply coding schemes might well be an appropriate area of further work. For the purposes of the analysis reported here, the JACS codes are grouped into seven sets under the headings Fine Arts, Architecture, Design Subjects, Textiles/Fashion, Visual Communication, Crafts, and Film and Photo.

1957 to 1975: The Early Theses

Key questions that the database allows us to address include the growth of activity within the field. When were the first PhDs in art and design awarded, what subjects were they in, and what methods did they use? The very first record in the database comes from

1957: Chew's "Some Recent British sculptors: A Critical Review," undertaken at the University of Manchester.[7] From then until 1975, twenty-six of the thirty-eight PhDs awarded by UK universities were in architectural subjects. That year, 1975, saw the first PhD awarded by the Council for National Academic Awards, to a candidate from the polytechnic sector. There were only another three Fine Arts PhDs during this first period from 1957 to 1975: Pal's Cambridge University PhD on the sculpture and painting of Nepal,[8] Wilkinson's Courtauld study of Henry Moore's drawings,[9] and Sleigh's "Learning to Paint: A Case Study of a School of Fine Art" at the Institute of Education.[10]

From 1976 to 1985, one hundred PhDs were awarded by UK universities (see Table 1). Forty-four of these were in architectural subjects, six in visual communications (three of these at the Royal College of Art) and twenty-one in Fine Arts subjects. Eight of these Fine Arts PhDs were in polytechnics with studio courses in Fine Art. An indication of the focus or approach can be inferred from the titles of some of these studies, but most of the records drawn from the British Index to Theses or ARIAD of pre-1984 PhDs in art and design do not include abstracts. Seven of the records indicate a focus on childhood learning about art or upon art education questions.[11] Another five records indicate studies of a more historical or anthropological nature.[12]

	Archi-tecture	Creative art and design	Design subjects	Fine art	Photo, film	Textiles, fashion	Vis com	Totals
1976	2		3	1				6
1977	2		2					4
1978	6			1	1			8
1979	9			3		1	1	14
1980	2		3	3			1	9
1981	3		5	1		1	1	11
1982	6	2	2	2			1	13
1983	5	1	4	7			1	18
1984	4			1		1	1	7
1985	5		3	2				10
Totals	44	3	22	21	1	3	6	100

Table 1: PhDs by subject group, 1976 to 1985

The remaining nine PhDs awarded during this period do appear to focus upon the processes of art-making from the perspective of the practitioner, rather than being historical, anthropological, educational or developmental studies, and were generally undertaken in polytechnic departments. The focus upon questions arising out of practice was a perspective that informed the framing of my own doctoral work in the mid-1980s, and several of this following group were among the few models available for doctoral students in art and design studio disciplines at that time.[13]

The subject foci of the remaining doctoral projects in the period 1975 to 1985 were Design Subjects (22 projects including industrial and product design), Textiles (3 projects), Photography (1 project) and three in Other Creative Arts and Design. In each year during this period there were between four and eighteen PhDs awarded. Even in 1985, the year after I started my own doctoral study, there were only ten doctoral awards made, and only two in my own subject, Fine Art.

1985 to 1995: Emerging Models for Research in Art and Design

Twenty years later, some important assumptions formed the backdrop to the initial discussions and the emergence of the ADIT project. The members of the collaborative team[14] were already involved in the supervision of doctoral students. There was "buy-in" to the core concept that we were responsible for providing training for the students undertaking doctoral research, and that understanding of the context for research was an important part of what doctorates were about. The origins of the way in which we frame our position on such topics developed in part as a result of the way the new university sector responded to the opportunity to engage in research degree study during the ten years from 1986 through to the mid-1990s. In the context of thinking about a new PhD in Studio Art, the following exploration of the background to emerging research practices makes links to some specific events, before looking at the characteristics of more recent doctoral activity.

The question of what a PhD is for continues to exercise parts of the academic community, but implicit in the framing of the ADIT project was clear recognition that in part, doctoral research is about finding out a lot about a particular field or topic. Doing a PhD is about becoming an expert in something that there are few other experts in. Generally, that finding out a lot part is what might take place in the initial stages of the doctoral project—the Master of Philosophy or MPhil bit. During this "finding out" part, the researcher formulates, or reinforces, the argument that we (the academic community?) need to know much more about a particular question, and that we might best go about that by using specific tools, or methods. This leads to what I consider the other two main points of doing a PhD. These are: first, the development of knowledge about and aptitude in the application of specific tools or research methods that are appropriate for finding out things in that subject field; second, that such knowledge be demonstrated through the address to a particular and specific question or problem, using appropriate tools, generating some new perspective, understanding or knowledge of interest or useful to that subject field.

The framing of these two latter stages of the doctoral project is my interpretation of the explicit direction enshrined within the UK Quality Assurance Agency (QAA) level descriptors.[15] I would not necessarily impose my reading upon colleagues, but it is, however, a fairly widespread understanding within the academic community more generally and is enshrined within the generic definitions of a PhD provided by the research degree regulations of those institutions with a Royal Charter to award research degrees. It also provides a useful background for thinking about what the purpose of doing a PhD might be. Beyond satisfying the intellectual curiosity of the individual, a PhD has been described as providing the experience that can provide a basis for high-level problem finding and problem solving. The QAA asserts that holders of this degree would be able to "make informed judgements on complex issues in specialist fields... and be able to communicate their ideas and conclusions clearly and effectively to specialist and non-specialist audiences." Within the university context, the PhD has more generally been seen as providing the appropriate training for further research, which the QAA level descriptor describes as the ability to "continue to undertake pure and/or applied research and development at an advanced level, contributing substantially to the development of new techniques, ideas, or approaches." It is also seen in some subjects as a useful introduction to academic life, and within research supervision training, the idea that one is supervising ones "colleague of the future" is a key concept. At times it can be difficult to maintain certainty in the extent to which these cultural models are shared, as indicated in the following two anecdotes.

When asked by former colleagues working as fine art lecturers and technicians about what she was currently working upon, a recently completed PhD student, whose first degree was in painting, responded that she was developing ideas for a research project that would investigate the relationships between aesthetics and neuroscience. "What," her interrogators inquired, "are you not doing anything in the studio?" She felt that their valuing of engagement "in the studio" was so strongly held that they were belittling her aspirations to find out more about the subject that they were all involved with. This reflects my own experience almost twenty years ago, when, as a recently completed PhD student myself, I was asked at an interview for a lecturing job why I hadn't been working in my studio. I gave up trying to get a job within academia for another six years. What both of us actually had to offer was knowledge of our particular field of contemporary art that was of greater breadth and depth than could have been achieved through study at Masters level, which had previously been viewed as the terminal degree within art and design. We also had the capacity to undertake further research in subjects both close to and at a remove from our core interests, potentially enabling us to prepare teaching materials for a range of undergraduate or more advanced courses. Perhaps we should continue to view the Masters degree as the terminal degree within art and design practice, and consider, for a moment, whether more advanced inquiry might necessarily mean a broader field of activity than provided by practical engagement within a creative art or design field. Looking at the evidence provided by doctoral projects that have been completed within the context of practice might enable a clearer position to emerge on this question.

The key issue does continue to be uncertainty about what we could, or should, be doing with this fairly new opportunity to do research degrees. I would suggest that posing the question this way is a more appropriate framing than asking "what can we get from this new opportunity to award research degrees?" This second model may be more appealing to colleagues who are engaged in advanced studio work, but is not one that I have come across with colleagues who have themselves completed doctoral study. It is important to keep reminding ourselves of how recently the opportunity became clearly apparent to the art and design subject fields. Key events include the inclusion of the subject fields within the academic degree-awarding systems in the UK in the 1960s, and the establishment of the Council for National Academic Awards (CNAA). Up to 1992, most research degrees were awarded by universities, although the CNAA was keen to stimulate activity in this area. Among the one hundred PhDs awarded between 1976 and 1985, only twenty-three were from the CNAA. After 1992, awareness of the opportunity to engage in doctoral study became more widespread in art and design, when the former polytechnics, home to most art and design schools, became part of new university system and were given the power to award their own degrees. It is not absolutely clear what stimulated the emergence of research degree activity, but the following notes indicate some factors that may be implicated.

Prior to 1992, the CNAA Research Committee for Art and Design had supported the emergence of research degree activity, and a series of conferences had reported on some of the early work in the field and explored some of the emerging issues of infrastructure and scope.[16] In 1984, the CNAA made a statement which noted that as an important part of staff development, it was important for lecturers to be involved in research and related activities which infused teaching with a sense of critical inquiry. They saw such activities as including the following: "academic research, applied research, consultancy, professional practice, scholarship, creative work, curriculum and pedagogic research, and the development of applied, interdisciplinary and collaborative activities that are responsive to industrial and community needs."[17] Inaccurate reporting or obtuse interpretation of this clear articulation of activities that support subject health could be considered a key reason why there has been some confusion about the relationship of research and creative practice within the English-speaking world. The statement was about "research," and "related activities," which infuse teaching. A sensible interpretation might be that those activities to which the authors appended the word "research" might be understood as that particular sort of academic inquiry, and that those that did not include the word "research" might be understood as "related activities." That appears to be what the CNAA intended, if we look at subsequent statements.

The 1988 Matrix conference publication included a 1989 statement from the CNAA Art and Design Committee, which clearly stated that they did not accept creative work as legitimate scholarly activity, but recognized rapid growth in the reporting of such activity.[18] The Committee reinforced recognition of the breadth of activities that they considered was needed to support healthy subjects and debated whether we needed alternative awards to recognize advanced creative work. The Committee was clearly making a distinction between advanced creative work, which has long been held as an important component in the teaching of the creative arts, and the growing interest in research degrees. It would appear that there was recognition that the sector might be starting to confuse research with creative practice, although the conference itself evidences some sensitive consideration of how the sector might develop its approach to research. The papers stressed the need to look at what we could usefully investigate within the discipline, rather than leaving it up to people from other disciplines to tell us what was special and distinctive about our activities, and an important point made by Alan Livingstone was that we were mistaken to believe that "analysis leads to paralysis."[19]

By 1992, the rapid growth of creative activity being reported under the research and related activities performance indicator of the CNAA (but not accepted by them as "legitimate scholarly activity') was entered into the UK Research Assessment Exercise (RAE). Art and Design, as the "new kids on the research-block,"[20] were the saviours of the new universities. The volume of activity submitted by art and design rather skewed the projections made by the Higher Education Funding Council (HEFCE) about how far the research money would go, but did create a climate in which the activities and outcomes the art and design departments submitted as research did generate significant income streams for several universities. Brown Gough and Roddis note that a lot of the activity reported at that 1992 RAE was applied work undertaken within commercial or industrial contexts, and note that it was the sort of activity described mostly as "professional practice." Thus it was probably the sort of activity the by-now disbanded CNAA would have described as "related activities" and possibly not as legitimate scholarly activity in their terms.

What we can see in this account of the CNAA's comments on research and the 1992 RAE is a sudden about turn. In the late 1980s, a clear distinction was being made between research activity and creative professional activity. Suddenly, post-1992, the equivalence card was played and funding proved to be a convincing part of the argument. But in terms of working out what we should be doing with the development of advanced-level inquiry within the subject fields, it is uncertain whether this helps or hinders progress.

All of this confusion gives an interesting backdrop to the growth in the numbers of students undertaking research degrees in art and design (see Table 2). The total number of completing PhD students in Art and Design in the UK during the ten year period from 1986 to 1995 was 181, against 100 during the previous ten year period. Numbers are still small in many of the subject fields, with just one or two completions each year in photography, crafts, visual communications and textiles. The volume of Fine Art and Design completions continues to remain similar over the period, together accounting for almost a third of the activity. Architectural subjects remain the most prevalent during this period as during preceding years.

	Archi-tecture	Craft	Design subjects	Fine art	Photo, film	Textile, fashion	Vis com	Total
1986	12	1	1	3	1	1		19
1987	7		3	2		1	1	14
1988	6		3	6			1	16
1989	5		2	2		1		10
1990	9	1	2	6		1		19
1991	8		5	2				15
1992	8	4	4	6		1		23
1993	6		6	4		2	1	19
1994	9	2	5	6	1	2	1	26
1995	11		2	3	1	2	1	20
Totals	81	8	33	40	3	11	5	181

Table 2: PhDs by subject group, 1986 to 1995

Defining Research in Art and Design

In 1993, Christopher Frayling, then Rector of the Royal College of Art, first applied Herbert Read's model of teaching for, through and into a discipline to the subject of research.[21] He noted that research could be for practice, as in Picasso gathering source material for the making of a painting such as *Les Desmoiselles d'Avignon*. He saw research through practice as being exemplified by the interative process of making a working prototype, testing and amending that model, and research into practice as including observations of practicing artists at work. The particularly tricky thing about this triad when thinking about research degree programs is the emphasis placed within undergraduate programs upon research for practice. There is a search which forms an integral part of many creative processes, but the extent to which this becomes more than the compilation of a "research file" of material that is intended to stimulate studio work may be questionable. Is it the same sort of intentional data gathering or data generation undertaken in order to address a research question? The collection of "stuff" indicates very little about the capacity to organise, evaluate or interpret, although the counter-argument would be that it is the resulting art object that articulates this evaluation and interpretation. In 1993, Frayling saw the goal of this collection of stuff as art, rather than knowledge or understanding, and more about autobiography and personal development than about communicable knowledge.[22] Buchler, in 2000, also considered that "the aim of academic research is the production of expert knowledge; the aim of art is the expression of understanding as an account of experience."[23]

An additional complication that started to emerge during this period was a bit of a hang-up about wanting to show creative work as a part of the research degree submission. This opportunity had been enshrined within CNAA regulations since the late 1970s, but making that operational within the new university structures of the 1990s required some adroit argumentation with colleagues beyond the subject domain. Given that the preceding period had also seen the emergence of cultural models that privileged the audience over author in terms of meaning-making, deeply held beliefs that the work "speaks for itself" start to become unravelled. A key factor may be that within the art and design world we are too used to "show and tell" as our main means of exchange within the professional context. But as Frayling has said, "no scientist would ever say that contents of a test-tube changing colour 'speaks for itself.'"[24]

From the evidence of the forty records coded as "fine art," "drawing," "painting" and "sculpture" from the period 1986 to 1995, the abstracts indicate that the outcomes of creative practice were particularly important for two submissions. It is apparent that a visual record of the creative practice forms a central part of Douglas," "Structure and Improvisation: The Making Aspect of Sculpture," undertaken at the University of Sunderland. Gilhespy's "appraisal and artistic response" to Soviet sculpture, while indicating in the abstract that one chapter documents his own artistic practices, does not make it clear whether the sculptures produced formed part of the actual submission. On balance, this particular PhD appears to be predominantly an appraisal into Soviet sculpture of a more historical nature. Seven of the forty awards made in this subject group during this period appear to fall within Frayling's notion of research "through" practice, including that Douglas's. What is particularly interesting about these projects is the indication that experimental methods provided the dominant strategy for investigation, and there was a clear concentration on issues of media or process. Pepper makes unambiguous reference to experiments in his investigation of display holography, while Akyuz refers to "testing several instruments" before producing his "standard atlas of 2-dimensional pencil marks." Douglas also makes explicit reference to experiments with materials, noting that she initially drew her methods from Materials Science. She recorded "the relationship between different aspects of the material through one and two parameter testing: colour to texture, texture to form" and so on. Testing was also part of the strategy employed by Watson's exploration of chance "as a stimulus to the creative activity known as sculpture."

This project included the development of a device, an exploration of the use of chance by other artists, and a review of models for understanding creativity. Bennett more emphatically focuses on the use of reflection upon practice in what was described as an "art teacher research report" that "connects research to painting," but this reflection upon ones own practice is an emerging strand in this set of records[25].

Many of the inquiries continued to look at the work of others, and all apart from the above seven fit into Frayling's model of research into practice. Of these, five fit the model of inquiries into the processes of making art or the media used, with three of these from the Royal College of Art.[26] The remaining twenty-eight PhDs in the fine art subject group during this period are a combination of more historical, anthropological or education-orientated studies. A significant proportion of these, twenty-one of them, continue to come from the long-established universities that generally did not have studio practice programs within their portfolios.[27]

In the mid-1990s it appeared that the dominant model for doctoral activity within the fine art subject field continued to be that provided by art history, but that there were emerging strands of experimental studies through practice, and of studies into the processes of contemporary practice. What had not yet appeared were studies that fit Frayling's notion of research "for" practice, which he had considered the most problematic, but probably the closest to our understanding of the normal day-to-day practices of professional artists.

1996 to 2005: The Growing Research Population

What comes over the next ten years is a significant increase in activity. The total number of theses recorded in this period is 406, up until the first few months of 2005. There appears to be a steady rate of successful completions, with over forty doctoral projects being awarded each year.[28] During this period, the Arts and Humanities Research Board (AHRB) was established, in 1998. This body took over the responsibility for providing bursaries for postgraduate education across a range of arts and humanities disciplines, and reframed these resources as national competitions. Since then, they have adjusted the balance of funding between the support of Masters and Doctoral awards year-on-year, increasing provision of bursaries for the more advanced projects. Their reports on the 2005 competition[29] indicate that they funded ninety-eight doctoral projects through their Visual Arts Postgraduate Panel, of which only fourteen are in fine art and design fields. In addition to these, the

Panel funded forty-three awards for studies in the History of Art, Architecture and Design, fourteen in Cultural Studies, and twenty-one in Film Studies. Perhaps it is more useful to consider the number of actual applications. There were sixty-seven applications for bursaries for fine art PhD study, and twenty six for design doctoral funding, indicating perhaps that the interest is there if not the quality applications that could be funded. Whatever the numbers applying to or funded by the AHRC, total annual completions do start to make it meaningful to consider PhDs awarded in relation to the total population of research active academics in the art and design sector, and in relation to the total number of undergraduate students. We are starting to have a population of researchers and research supervisors who do form a community of research practitioners, and who may start to generate common understandings and shared agendas as a part of their research culture.

The Size and Shape of the Research Art Community

The research and teaching community is made up of academic staff, research students, and undergraduate and other postgraduate students. The most accessible and reasonably precise indicators of the size of the student community can be found through the Higher Education Statistics Agency.[30] Data for undergraduate enrolments for the 2004-2005 academic year indicates that there were 11,285 full-time undergraduate architecture students, 13,500 on fine art programs, 1,205 on craft courses and at least 50,425 on design courses.[31] This gives a total of 76,415 undergraduate students in art, architecture and design within the UK, excluding part-time students. The nationally available statistics on staff numbers do not break neatly into subject fields,[32] but on the basis of undergraduate numbers, the total number of academic staff by "full-time equivalent" (recognising that many staff work part-time in these fields) could be calculated on the basis of a fairly normal staff:student ratio of 1:20. This suggests there may be about 3,800 academics working in these subjects. On the basis of most doctoral programs taking three to four years, with between forty to fifty completions each year, it is reasonable to speculate that a conservative estimate of the annual population of UK doctoral students in art and design may be around 200, out of a national total in all subjects of 91,605.[33]

We can also look at research-active staff numbers through the record of research activity occurring in UK universities as reported in the last Research Assessment Exercise (RAE). According to the RAE records,[34] 2,523 academic and researchers were submitted to the 2001 RAE from Art and Design departments. In architecture, it is more difficult to determine exact numbers, as some departments submitted the work of their architects to the Art and Design panel, and some to the panel looking at a range of subjects under the label "Built Environment." There were 691 academic staff and researchers submitted to this panel, but many of them were structural or civil engineers, or other subject academics working within property and construction departments. This RAE data suggests that there may be around 3000 academics actively engaged in research and possibly supervising research degrees. We thus have a ratio in art and design subject fields of staff to doctoral researchers of about 15:1, based on a doctoral student population of 200. The total number of academics in UK universities is 106,900. If we assume 50% of staff nationally are research active, with a research student population of 90,605, we get a ratio of 1:1.7 for staff to research students across the academic community in the UK. It appears that significant growth in the research student population would be required to reach national norms. But at least the fifty or so doctorates each year at present could contribute to the model where research students are our colleagues of the future.

Current figures suggest that 50% of successful doctoral candidates do progress to careers within the education sector, as researchers or lecturers in higher education, or within the primary and secondary sectors.[35] What may be an issue is subject spread, as in many of the subject fields within art and design, the number of successfully completed doctorates each year is still in single figures. It is only in design subjects (industrial and product design), fine art and architecture where the numbers of completions each year exceeds ten per annum in two or more of the years in the period from 1996 to 2005.

Volume and Dissemination of Research Activity

In relation to the research activities of staff, the high proportion of PhDs in fine art subjects is reflected in the volume of research outputs submitted by their supervisors and others to RAE 2001.[36] Almost forty per cent of the outputs were the outcomes of fine art research and practice, although these subjects only make up about 20% of the staff and students in UK higher education. The outputs from the fine artists included a high proportion of exhibition-type outputs, at 80% (1,907) of the 2,398 examples of work from this subject field. Just 4% of the fine art outcomes were books, and several of these were books by other authors that illustrated the work of the artist. There was a similar proportion of journal articles (114, or 5% of the fine art subject outputs) and about half that of conference papers (52, or 2% of the fine art subject outputs). It should be noted that the type of outputs submitted by academics and other researchers in fine art subjects shows a different pattern to those submitted by their colleagues in design. The range of outputs from the design disciplines is much more evenly spread, with a ratio of 1.48:1 of text-based to practical outputs, compared to a ratio of 1:5.45 for the fine art subject academics.[37] The imbalance of in types of research activity and the particular nature of prevalent outputs might influence the growth of doctoral activity in the design subjects, and is likely to impact upon perceptions of the type of outcome expected from research activity for all subjects in the art and design domain.

In comparison to other subject groupings such as Built Environment, or General Engineering, the different patterns of output type are even more distinctive. These subject fields have a much greater reliance on publication within journals as the dominant mode of dissemination. In the 2001 RAE, the proportion of research outputs published by the "General Engineers" through journal publications was 93%. For the architects and other researchers covered by the Panel for the Built Environment, journal articles were the method of dissemination for 60% of the research activity reported. What we need to note here is that it is largely the academic community itself that runs these journals—they are one of the fundamental building blocks of the research culture in those disciplines.

Before picking up again on the issue of subject spread, this data on the sorts of outputs being recorded by the research assessment exercise gives us an opportunity to reflect on who is undertaking the gate-keeping function for research and professional practice within the art and design subject fields. A positive aspect to the range of output types used by the design subjects is that researchers in those fields, particularly if they are involved in refereeing for journals or conferences, may be able to have more influence than their fine art colleagues, who may be dependent upon gallery directors or curators or commissioning bodies, on disseminating and assessing the quality of new thinking. It is important to recognize who gets to decide what gets disseminated within different fields. The reason that the engineers focus so single-mindedly on journal articles for dissemination of research results may be partly because there is no "professional" world of engineering exhibitions or books about engineering for the broader populace. Art and design are different—our "products" may hit a commercial market and it may be qualities that are far removed from research rigour or research impact that determine whether they get to the front page of *Vogue* or *Elle Decoration* or set new records at auction. The decision to exhibit work in the Waddington Galleries or the Lisson, or to include objects in an exhibition at the Hayward or Documenta, has very little to do with its research value, and is made largely by individuals with very little interest in or understanding of the academic world. In short, the scholarly community has little or no influence over the gallery world or over the design market.

When looking at PhD completions within the period 1996 to 2005 in relation to the proportion of research outputs submitted to the 2001 RAE Panel for Art and Design, there are some interesting imbalances. What is in balance is the proportion of the total number of doctorates awarded in fine art, and the volume of activity by subject academics in fine art—both sit at over 35% of the total activity. Of greater concern is the gap in some of the other subjects where the total volume of activity is much smaller. In particular, it appears that there is a very low proportion of doctoral activity within the craft disciplines (3.93% of all doctorates awarded in the period), compared to these fields making up 8.11% of all outputs returned to RAE 2001 by academics in these subjects. Similarly, visual communications PhDs are less than 5% of the total, with the outputs returned by potential supervisors running at 12.48%. Inverse ratios are present in the figures for architectural subjects, which may be explained by some outputs being returned to the Built Environment Panel. The data on staff research activity in design subjects such as product and industrial design paints a surprising picture. Of the outputs in the 2001 RAE submission that have been coded, only 194 fall into this subject group, although this has been one of the stronger subjects in terms of doctoral awards over the past twenty years. We may be right to express concern about the levels of engagement by supervisory staff in product and industrial design in their own research. At least the fine art doctoral students are in a context in which potential supervisory staff are more likely to be visibly engaged in some sort of research or professional activity in the public domain.

Outputs and completed PhDs	% of RAE, 2001 outputs	% of PhDs, 1996-2005
Textiles/fashion	8.67	7.86
Architecture	5.87	19.90
Design subjects	10.04	16.46
Vis com	12.48	4.91
Fine art	39.54	36.36
Craft	8.11	3.93

Table 3: Comparison of outputs and PhD completions by subject groups

Emerging Characteristics of Recent PhDs

Of the 406 doctoral theses in art and design awarded in the ten year period from 1995 to 2005, the largest group are in fine art. These 148 awards account for 36% of all successful completions in the period (see Table 3). Fine Art theses had accounted for 22% of all art and design theses in the preceding ten year period of 1986 to 1995, so not only had the overall number more than doubled, but projects focusing on fine art subjects now also accounted for a larger proportion of the activity. Architectural projects account for the next largest group, continuing the model seen in the preceding twenty years, with eighty-one completions. There were sixty-seven awards for design subjects, including industrial and product design, and thirty-two in textiles and fashion.

The majority of the fine art studies (55%) continue to adopt approaches that could be described as largely historical, anthropological or educational. The defining characteristic of these studies is that they are looking into the subject by looking at the practices of others. An emerging tendency is for these projects to engage with re-visiting theoretical and philosophical models, as in Park Chun's journey "through melancholia, feminine difference and Paul Cezanne,"[38] or Crawford's "Figuring Death: The Phantom of presence in art."[39] This PhD claims to analyse "Hegel's master/slave dialectic and de Man's notion of "prosopoeia," to "demonstrate how modernist discourses construct a figure [face] of/for the artist and cover up [entomb] the recalcitrance of his or her corporeal body to be the [ontological] site of meaning." The anthropological focus is turned on subjects as diverse as the Irish, the Senegalese, Korean and Aboriginal women artists.[40]

Investigations of process continue to provide a counterpoint to the historical studies, bringing inquiry closer to the subject as practiced in the contemporary world. Thirty of the projects receiving awards in the period from 1996 to 2005 appear to be investigations into the processes of making or apprehending contemporary art practice. At times, the influence of models of thinking from other subject areas is strong, such as in Hand's consideration of "the peculiar problem for interpretation" presented by the "material and temporal conjuring" of artworks, in *What's Happening With Das Ding? Psychoanalysis, Aesthetics And Temporality In Art.*[41] At times projects focusing on process can be largely descriptive, highlighting clear questions that could also usefully be investigated by other researchers. A particular example of an abstract opening up a range of possibilities for further work is Hogarth's account of his practice.[42] There are also examples of theses which are apparently written to accompany studio work,[43] but it is uncertain at times whether the contribution to knowledge is enshrined within the art works or within the thesis. Another eleven projects that focus on the processes of art practice appear to be undertaking this through art practice.[44] There is some indication that the methods employed do occasionally extend to include experiments,[45] or other analytical methods. The abstracts of these theses indicate a fairly strong emphasis on literary argumentation.

Practical questions about the use of specific media and specific practices have been addressed through eleven projects,[46] which could be described as investigations into or through media, as distinct from the inquiries into process already mentioned. One study makes a clear claim for being practice-led, but the meaningfulness of that particular label might be questioned.[47] The particular project appears to adopt a multi-method approach that included "questionnaire, quantitative tests of materials, participation in, and initiation, of collaborative case studies, documenting workshop practice and visual development of printed art works, and exhibition for peer review." If this model were to be applied to many other disciplines, it might be true to say that any applied research could be described as practice-led. Despite this small issue of nomenclature, the theses in this group include a number of straightforward studies that are generally characterised by their usefulness to day-to-day professional practice within the field.

It is clear from immersion within the abstracts of theses awarded by UK universities that there has been a great variety in the work completed. It is becoming more various, and some very interesting models are emerging. The quality of the language used to describe the activities undertaken is uneven, and some abstracts slip more towards the language of the catalogue essay rather than adopting academic precision. The need to ensure that all institutions regularly forward abstracts as well as core bibliographic details to the British Library or other repositories is clear. One major postgraduate institution that has supervised more doctoral work than any other in the UK has only provided abstracts for one third of the eighty-seven projects awarded PhD. This omission makes work such as this paper difficult, particularly given the overall small number of examples that are currently open to investigation.

Summary and Conclusions

I have attempted to convey the outcomes of some simple analysis of data available about a range of activities within the academic arena of art and design. The report on the initial analysis of the

ADIT database can only provide a taster of the sort of search that can be carried out by interested individuals, and that should be carried out by future research students. Any codification of data as dense as the material covered here is bound to be open to some differences in interpretation, but as the research culture develops in our fields, it is important to develop consensus on the labels we use. This opening work is carried out in that spirit, of attempting to initiate discussion of the usefulness of different categorisation systems.

It is intended that the inclusion of definitions from the Quality Assurance Agency and of references to the previous gatekeepers of academic standards in the UK polytechnic system, the CNAA, can provide a useful record of benchmarks. The inclusion of data on staff and student numbers is also intended to provide measures, both of the current situation, and for projecting future targets. Comparisons of subject field activity in doctoral work and in that carried out by the supervisory community again gives us benchmarks that we can use to establish target ratios for future activity.

The volume of material generated by doctoral students over the past ten years has grown to the extent that it is a daunting task to begin to survey. The coding work that has been a part of the ADIT project is an important contribution to the field in terms of enabling easier access to subject specific subsets of that material. The completion of "tidying-up" the records accumulated to date, and the establishment of a secure and accessible home for the database is underway, and the ADIT team are looking at the possibility of extending the scope of the project to cover the research degree activity of other countries.

The material I have surveyed has been of variable quality and covers a wide range of approaches. The abstracts consulted range from the minimal one-liner, through straightforward and well-constructed summaries, to mini-essays of extreme richness and complexity. It is clear that the work undertaken was motivated by some very different objectives. It would appear that we now have a reasonable volume of material that can provide a basis for the academic community to review how we intend to develop activity at this level in the future.

I would suggest that we do need to understand a bit more about the notion of visual knowledge and its transmission with intentionality, if we are to continue to assert any central role for the art or design object in doctoral (or any other) research. It might also be useful for us to consider the quality of our evidence, visual or otherwise, and the way it might be accessed in the future.

As well as clarifying the extent to which we have a consensus on the veracity of sorts of visual knowledge, the position that might be taken on subject knowledge is also open to discussion. I have suggested in an earlier paper[48] that the academic community "has the responsibility for knowledge transfer, and for determining benchmarks and values for the subjects for which it is responsible and for which it confers degrees." I went on to suggest that the "domain knowledge and strategic knowledge within art and art education would be the appropriate focus for the academics that are part of the field." By domain knowledge I was referring to knowledge about past achievements within the domain—that which might be enshrined in all those artefacts and records of past activity, and might come to be embodied or recorded in artefacts or records of future activity. By strategic knowledge, I was referring to the active understanding of how to operate within the domain—how to undertake meaningful action. Either of these, or a combination, would seem to be appropriate arenas for inquiry by doctoral research students, if they are to demonstrate advanced understanding and knowledge of their field, and the survey reported here indicates that this is what has been attempted to date.

When considering doctoral projects, I would argue that it is particularly important not to deny the power of that set of really important texts that are built up when doing a PhD, which form the basis of ones mature intellectual framework. Effectively these references form a mini-canon of subject knowledge for that project, which will hopefully overlap to some extent with that of peers. How different is the combination of these to the notion of a body of knowledge within a subject field? Can we seriously say we are doing research if we reject the idea of a body of knowledge? We may need to be cautious about the extent to which we rely on the records of artists themselves, whether in the form of studio notebooks, monologues or interview transcripts because, as Elkins warns us, "history would seem to indicate that artists have been consistently misguided about what they do."[49] A research culture does need its benchmarks and its resources on which to base further work. Innovation cannot take place in a knowledge vacuum.

But there is in some parts of the art and art education sector a rejection of the idea of a body of knowledge, which some would label our "cultural inheritance."[50] There is also an over-emphasis on strategic knowledge. This is partly a result of recognising the importance of tacit knowledge, that understanding of how it "feels" to wield the chisel/drape the fabric/draw the connection. Within art and design, this tacit knowledge is special stuff, our stuff, and the bit that current teaching generations see less and less of. It is, though, the site of some rich questions that we may need to answer before we can claim the potential for studio activity to provide an opportunity for the development of skills and knowledge at a level commensurate with the descriptors for PhD study enshrined in university Royal charters and the QAA. What is more invasive in the culture of the studio at present, is knowledge about how to "be" an artist or a designer (or even how to "be" a student). This strategic knowledge is sometimes confused with tacit knowledge. It is fairly easily communicated by the practitioner academic or visiting lecturer with little pre-preparation, but it is more difficult to enshrine this expertise in a way that can be accessed without recourse to individual show and tell.

I would like to think that antipathy to the notion of a body of knowledge is merely a holdover from the rejection of over-arching meta-narratives that characterised the post-modern transition. It seems quite viable to me for us to recognize that we have to take on the challenge of mapping the multiplicity of information that might need to be accommodated within a domain, without falling foul of imposing partisan world views. The opportunity technology now gives us to encompass the knowledge quotient of "all the diverse practices" and the "many cultural positions from which art is made" is clear.[51] The evidence of doctoral studies completed to date suggests we are growing some interesting models in our Petri dishes, but we may wish to reflect further on whether we want to identify particular questions and approaches that might warrant prioritising in future activity. We do now have non-linear and non-hierarchical repositories for information which can be accessed and utilised in a variety of ways, and we can build new ones. The ADIT project is a clear marker that the research culture within art and design in the UK is becoming a responsible teenager—still gawky in places and prone to making some daft claims—but starting to look after our own data.

Notes

1 For the Research Assessment Exercise see "A Glossary of Terms" at the beginning of this book, and also Charles Harrison's essay, Chapter 10. [— J.E.]

2 For a definition of External Examiner see "A Glossary of Terms" at the beginning of this book. [— J.E.]

3 For the AHRC see Charles Harrison's essay, Chapter 10. [— J.E.]

4 *Index to Theses in Great Britain and Ireland*, www.theses.com, accessed 26 March 2006.

5 Brian Allison, *Allison Research Index to Art and Design*, second edition (Leicester: ARIAD Associates, 1995).

6 JACS is used in all UK universities and the University and College Admissions Service (UCAS), for the identification and coding of academic programs by subject. See www.hesa.ac.uk/jacs/jacs.htm, accessed 28 March 2006.

7 B. A. Chew, *Some recent British sculptors: a critical review* (University of Manchester, 1957).

8 P. Pal, *Studies in the Painting and Sculpture of Nepal* (University of Cambridge, 1966).

9 A.G. Wilkinson, *The drawings of Henry Moore* (University of London, Courtauld Institute, 1975).

10 H. C. Sleigh, *Learning to paint: a case study of a school of fine art* (University of London, Institute of Education, 1975).

11 E. M-R. andrews, *The innovation process of culturally-based art education* (University of Bradford, 1983); D. Davis, *Imagery in thought: nature and function of complexual thinking in art education* (CNAA, 1980); R.V. Dunning, *Language in art education: a theoretical and empirical study of the relations between the visual and the verbal in art and art education* (University of London, Institute of Education, 1983); B. Fakhoury, *Art education in Lebanon* (University of London, Institute of Education, 1983); S. M. Mather, *The drawings of C andida: one child's graphic development from her first to her thirteenth year* (University of London, Institute of Education, 1983); G. C. Millard, *The relationship between image and language in the drawings of young children: the evaluation of a structured teaching program* (CNAA, 1979); and John Swift, *The role of drawing and memory-drawing in English art education 1800-1980* (CNAA [now University of Central England, Birmingham Institute of Art and Design], 1984).

12 J. Aulich, The human clay: R.B. Kitaj, 1932-1980: the evolution of a figurative aesthetic (University of Manchester, 1985); D. J. Clarke, The influence of oriental thought on postwar American painting and sculpture (University of London, Courtauld Institute, 1983); Keith Clements, Henry Lamb 1883-1960 (CNAA (now University of Brighton), 1983); S.L. Kasfir, Visual arts of the Idoma of Central Nigeria (University of London, School of Oriental and African Studies, 1979); and Mahmoud Zarringhalam, The nature of islamic art and its relationship with abstraction (Royal College of Art, 1979).

13 G. H. Bailey, *Drawing and the drawing activity: a phenomenological investigation* (University of London, Institute of Education, 1982); P. J. Baxter, *Art, ideology and one film: The Blue Angel* (University of London, University College, 1980); A. Goodwin, *Art and idea* (CNAA, 1982); Headley andrew Ironside, *An investigation into contexts relevant to understanding art production* (CNAA [now University of Brighton], 1980); P. Panton, *The Artist as Agent* (University

of Bristol, 1985); A. A. Stonyer, *The Development of Kinetic Sculpture by the Utilization of Solar Energy* (CNAA, 1978); M. Thurlby, *Transitional Sculpture in England* (University of East Anglia, 1976); A. G. M. H. Tomkins, *Art and cultural production, with special reference to cartoons and caricature* (University of London, Institute of Education, 1983); J. H. Willats, *Formal structures in drawing and painting* (CNAA, 1982).

14 The team grew to include colleagues from University of Lincoln, Manchester Metropolitan University, Birmingham Institute of Art and Design and Coventry University as well as the core project originators from Sheffield Hallam University, Leeds Metropolitan University, and Nottingham Trent University.

15 Quality Assurance Agency, 2001. Annex 1, Qualification descriptors, "The framework for higher education qualifications in England, Wales and Northern Irel and," www.qaa.ac.uk/academicinfrastucture/FHEQ/EWNI/default.asp#framework, accessed 28 March 2006.

16 The CNAA organised a series of conferences in the 1980s in conjunction with Middlesex Polytechnic, 1984, Manchester Polytechnic, 1987, and the London Institute in 1988. The conclusions from the two earlier events are reprinted in the publication of the proceedings of the 1988 event. See *The Matrix of Research in Art and Design Education: Documentation from the conference on research in art and design organised by the London Institute and the Council for National Academic Awards 1988*, edited by Bourgourd, Jeni, Evans, Stuart and Gronberg, Tag (London: London Institute, 1989).

17 The 1984 statement was referred to in a paper statement issued in 1989: Council for National Academic Awards Committee for Art and Design, May 1989 statement, "Research and Related Activities in Art and Design," in *The Matrix of Research in Art and Design Education*, Appendix 4.

18 *The Matrix of Research in Art and Design Education*, Appendix 4.

19 Livingston, Alan, "Research into the nature of the discipline," in *The Matrix of Research in Art and Design Education*, Appendix 4.

20 B. Brown, P. Gough, and J. Roddis, *Types of Research in the Creative Arts and Design* (Brighton: University of Brighton, 2004).

21 Frayling, "Research in Art and Design." *Royal College of Art Research Papers*, Vol 1 no. 1, 1993/4 (London: Royal College of Art, 1993).

22 This corresponds to the third and most problematic of Frayling's three categories, discussed in Chapters 8 and 9. [— J.E.]

23 Pavel Buchler, "New Academic Art," in *Research and the Artist: Considering the Role of the Art School*, edited by Antonia Payne (Oxford: Oxford University Press, 2001).

24 Frayling, Christopher. Transcript of Research Seminar on Practice-based Doctorates in Creative and Performing Arts and Design, held on 14 July 1998. (Surrey Institute of Art and Design University College, 1998)

25 Bennett, G., *An artist teacher's portrayal* (University of East Anglia, 1994)

Pepper, A.T., *Drawing in space: a holographic system to simultaneously display drawn images on a flat surface and in three dimensional space* (University of Reading, 1988)

Akyuz, U., *Creation of a 2-dimensional model for pencil marks* (De Montfort University Leicester, 1995)

Douglas, Anne, *Structure and Improvisation: The Making Aspect of Sculpture* (University of Sunderl and, 1992)

Watson, A., *An exploration of the principle of chance as a stimulus to the creative activity known as sculpture* (Robert Gordon University, 1992)

Leake, Irene, *Apprehending movement of the human figure through the medium of drawing, with comments on its possible relationship to computer mediated interaction* (University of Brighton, 1993)

Mathee, Jean, Art Practice as an Act of Paradoxical Creation: sublimation ex nihilo (Royal College of Art, 1994)

26 Benyon, Margaret, *How is holography art?* (Royal College of Art, 1994)

Dawe, M.Wendy., *Visual metaphor and the ironic glance: the interaction between artist and viewer* (University of Central England, Birmingham Institute of Art and Design, 1992)

Mottram, Judith A.L., *Critical concepts and change in painting: the relationship of influence to practice* (CNAA (Manchester Polytechnic), 1988)

Pizzanelli, David, *Aspects of spatial and temporal parallax in multiplex holograms, a study based on appropriated images* (Royal College of Art, 1994)

Rogers, Sheena, Representation and reality Gibson's concept of information and the problem of pictures (Royal College of Art, 1986)

27 anderson, Simon, *Re-Flux Action: the Fluxshoe exhibition tour of 1972-73, and the subsequent attempt to catalogue the residual collection, held in the Tate Gallery Archive* Royal College of Art, 1988)

Blair, L.F., *The working method of Joseph Cornell* (University of Essex, 1991)

Chaplin, R.M., *Robert Rauschenberg — between looking and longing* (University of Sussex, 1992)

Elatta, T.M, *An analysis of indigenous Sudanese graphic imagery and implications for curriculum development in art education* (De Montfort University Leicester, 1990)

Fijalkowski, C.M., *The surrealist object: proof, pleasure and reconciliation* (University of East Anglia, 1990)

Gilhespy, Tom, *A theoretical appraisal and artistic response to Soviet monumental sculpture* (University of Central England, Birmingham Institute of Art and Design, 1993)

Harada, R., *The making of an avant-garde in Japan: an assessment of Okamoto Taro's art of `counterpointism' and its debt to Europe with particular reference to Jean Arp and Georges Bataille* (University of Essex, 1993)

Harvey, J., *The visualization of religious concepts in the Welsh nonconformist tradition, with particular reference to the paintings of Nicholas Evans* (University of Wales, College of Cardiff, 1990)

Holloway, M., *Picasso: Suite 347* (University of London, Courtauld Institute, 1995)

Holt, D.A., *Art in primary education: a study of the generalist as teacher of the visual arts* (University of Exeter, 1989)

Jeffett, W.F., *Objects into sculpture; sculpture into object: a study of the sculpture of Joan Miro in the context of the Parisian and Catalan avant-gardes, 1928-1983* (University of London, Courtauld Institute, 1992)

Kaye, J.N., *The fine artist's use of theatre form since 1945* (University of Manchester, 1987)

Lewis, A., *Roger Hilton and the culture of painting* (University of Manchester, 1995)

Matthews, J.S., *Expression, representation and drawing in early childhood* (University of London, Goldsmiths College, 1990)

McGuigan, N.D., *The social context of Abelam Art: a comparison of art, religion and leadership in two Abelam communities* (New University of Ulster, 1992)

Nixon, J.W., *Francis Bacon: paintings 1959-1979. Opposites and structural rationalism* (New University of Ulster, 1986)

Oguibe, D.D., *The paintings and prints of Uzo Egonu: 20ᵗʰ century Nigerian artist* (University of London, School of Oriental and African Studies, 1992)

Ollett, M.L., *Toward a new program of art education* (University of London, Institute of Education, 1988)

Paine, S.M., *The development of drawing in the childhood and adolescence of individuals* (University of London, Institute of Education, 1986

Patrizio, A.P., *"The ugly and the useless': industry as a theme in Scottish art and aesthetics, 1880-1980* (University of Edinburgh, 1994)

René, Stephane, *Coptic iconography* (Royal College of Art, 1990)

Rhodes, C., *Primitivism re-examined: constructions of the `primitive' in modernist visual art* (University of Essex, 1993)

Smith, J.A., *An analytic sociology of art: art and society and the origins of modernist painting* (University of London, Goldsmiths College, 1989)

Smith, M.A.E., *Between poetry and painting: an exploration of visual and verbal integration and interaction in the arts of the twentieth century, with particular reference to France* (University of Reading, 1987)

Vargas, E., *Surrealism and painting within the context of the Argentine avant-garde: 1921-1987* (University of Essex, 1992)

Waugh, E.R.F., *Emergent art and national identity in Jamaica, 1920's to the present* (Queen's University at Belfast, 1988)

White, T.E.J., The use of the performative to disrupt form in the work of artists since 1960., (University of Warwick, 1994)

28 The apparent drop in numbers for 2004 and 2005 is anticipated to relate to the delay in records reaching the national repository and being included in the British Index to Theses, rather than an actual decline in number of awards being made.

29 AHRC, Table 1a, Number of applications and Awards in Doctoral Competition 2005, *Report on the AHRC's 2005 competition for postgraduate awards.* (2005) [http://www.ahrc.ac.uk/website/university_staff/postgrad/competition.asp], accessed 28 March 2006

30 HESA stats for student numbers indicate that the total number of students enrolled on undergraduate courses as 65,154. This includes Fine Art students (13,500), Design students (50,425), and craft students (1520). Architecture accounts for another 11,285, and an unknown number of photography students are within the "cinematics and photograpy' numbers (11500) www.hesa.ac.uk/holisdocs/pubinfo/studnet/subject0405.htm

31 The number counted as design could include a proportion of the students on courses coded as Cinematics and Photography, and there may be additional numbers covered by the ADIT subject coverage on courses coded "Others in creative arts and design."

32 The Higher Education Statistical Agency collects data on academic staff under the broad subject category "Design and Creative Arts' and "Architecture, built environment and planning," both of which would include staff working in other subject disciplines

33 HESA, private communication, 31 March 2006.

34 RAE 2001. [www.hero.ac.uk/rae/] accessed 28 March 2006

35 "What do PhDs Do?" (UK GRAD, 2005); www.grad.ac.uk/cms/ ShowPage/Home_page/Resources/What_Do_PhDs_Do_/p!eXccLa, accessed 28 March 2006
36 Seventy-five percent of the 9,242 research outputs (books, journal articles, exhibitions, conferences papers, designs etc.) submitted by art and design academics to RAE 2001 have been coded up by subject type to enable comparisons to be drawn between the activities of different subject fields. All books, edited books, book chapters, journal articles, conference papers and designs submitted to the Art and Design Panel for RAE 2001 have been coded by subject group. In addition, 2445 of the 3748 exhibitions have been coded.
37 Design: text outputs, 2047; practice outputs, 1385.Creative arts: text outputs, 548; practice outputs, 2987.
38 Park Chun, Young-Paik, *Melancholia, feminine difference and Paul Cezanne* (University of Leeds, 1999)
39 Crawford, Joanne, *Figuring Death: The Phantom of presence in art* (University of Leeds, 2002)
40 Chan, S.S.W., *De/centering whiteness, gender and "Irishness:" representing "race", gender and diaspora in Irish visual art* (University of Ulster at Belfast, 2002)
Dalgleish, S. H. R., *'Utopia' redefined: Aboriginal women artists in the Central Desert of Australia* (University of East Anglia, 2000)
Harney, E., *The legacy of negritude: a history of the visual arts in post-independence Senegal* (University of London, School of Oriental and African Studies, 1996)
Shin, JI-Young, Writing women's art histories: The construction of national identity in South Korea and the tradition of masculinity in abstract painting (University of Leeds, 2004)
41 J. Hand, *What's Happening With Das Ding? Psychoanalysis, Aesthetics And Temporality In Art* (Canterbury: University of Kent at Canterbury, 1998).
42 J. Hogarth, *Dislocated Landscapes: A Sculptor's Response To Contemporary Issues Within The British Landscape* (University of Sunderl and, 1998)
43 K. Meynell, *Time-Based Art In Britain Since 1980: An Account Of An Interdisciplinary Practice* (Royal College of Art, 1999)
44 Curtin, B.A., *Assuming the "feminine' position: erotic masculinities and the visual representation of sexual difference* (University of Bristol, 2000)
Dale, G., *Thesis accompanying the artworks of Guy Dale 1998-2001* (De Montfort University Leicester, 2001)
Fleming, Martha, *From Le Musee de Sciences to the Science Museum: fifteen years of evolving methodologies in the science/art interface* (Leeds Metropolitan University, 2004)
Francis, M.A., *The artist as a multifarious agent: an artist's theory of the origin of meaning* (University of London, Goldsmiths College, 2000)
Gledhill, J., *An inquiry into the simultaneous exposure of the interior and exterior of sculptural form* (University of Cheltenham and Gloucester, 2001)
Hanrahan, S., *A combined philosophic and artistic research methodology* (University of Ulster at Belfast, 1996)
Hegarty, S.P.M., *The presence of absence* (University of Southampton, 2002)
Horton, Derek, *The embodiment of histories: use values and exchange values in object-based sculpture* (Leeds Metropolitan University, 2003)

Roles, M., *Two kinds of being: an interface between photography and sculpture* (Royal College of Art, 1997)

Saorsa, Jac, *Drawing as a method of exploring and interpreting ordinary verbal interaction: an investigation through contemporary practice* (Loughborough University, 2005)

Staff, C., The construction, role and interpretation of reflexivity within contemporary non-representational painting (Nottingham Trent University, 2002)

45 Roles noted that "Experiments explored the practical application of methods and materials which would allow for the integration of the two dimensional photographic image with three dimensional sculptural form' - Roles, M., op cit

46 Adams, I.Z., *Exploration of water-based inks in fine art screenprinting* (University of Ulster at Belfast, 1998)

Aksoy, Mehmet Turan, *The Concepts and Practices of Urban Mural Painting since 1970: Artists' Perspectives* (University of Central England, Birmingham Institute of Art and Design, 1996)

Allen, K., *To investigate and demonstrate through my sculptural practice the relation between 'virtual' and 'real' sculpture* (University of Wolverhampton, 2001)

Bishop, C., *The subject of installation art: a typology* (University of Essex, 2002)

Graham, Beryl, *A Study of Audience Relationships with Interactive Computer-Based Visual Artworks in Gallery Settings, through Observation, Art Practice, and Curation* (University of Sunderl and, 1997)

Hinchcliffe, D., *Collaboration and partnership in public art in Birmingham from the 1980s to the 1990s* (University of Wolverhampton, 1998)

Pengelly, J R, *Environmentally sensitive printmaking: a framework for safe practice* (Robert Gordon University, 1996)

Povall, R.M., *Creating emotionally aware performance environments: a phenomenological exploration of inferred and invisible data space* (University of Plymouth, 2003)

Shepley, Alec, *Installation art practice and the `fluctuating frame'* (Manchester Metropolitan University, 2000)

Tung, Wei-Hsiu, *Art for Social Change: the Role of Artist-in-Residence Schemes in Challenging Taiwanese Identity* (University of Central England, Birmingham Institute of Art and Design, 2003)

Young, D., Fine art application of holography: the historical significance of light and the hologram in visual perception and artistic depiction (Liverpool John Moores University, 1997)

47 Pengelly, J R, op cit

48 Mottram, "Art Practice and Academic Responsibility," *Disciplines, Fields and Change in Art Education*, volume 4, *Soundings and Reflections*, edited by Jacqui Swift and John Swift (Birmingham: ARTicle Press, 2002).

49 James Elkins, *Why Art Cannot be Taught* (Chicago: University of Illinois Press, 2001).

50 Jones, "Art and Research Methodology," in *Disciplines, Fields and Change in Art Education*, volume 1, *Art Education and Art Practice*, edited by Jacqui Swift and John Swift (Birmingham: ARTicle Press, 1999).

51 Mottram "Art Practice and Academic Responsibility."

2

Research Degrees in Art and Design[1]
Timothy Emlyn Jones

After all one's art is not the chief end of life but an accident in one's
search for reality or rather perhaps one's method of search.
— W.B. Yeats to Ezra Pound[2]

Only fifteen or twenty years ago, when the debate of research in art
and design commenced in the UK, the idea that the generation of
new knowledge in art and design might be deemed research seemed
novel, exciting to some yet incomprehensible to many; even though
are are many historical precedents for the idea in the modern period, of which Yeats's is only one. For some artists and designers,
the idea of art or design practice being thought of as research can
still be said to be monstrous and the credibility of research degrees
in art and design seemed open to dismissal by at least one senior
figure as recently as five years ago.[3]

Higher Education in art and design has rapidly changed over
the last decade and thinking about research is fundamental to the
continuing change. The subject of where and how research thinking
sits in art and design is a large one on which, relatively speaking,
we have only just begun; although even now it is possible to suggest
that a new research paradigm for artistic production and art education is emerging. In this context any contribution to the debate has
to be recognized as provisional and conditional since to date no
comprehensive overview has yet been published. Unfortunately,
the need to review and revise the modernist project in terms of the
principles of inquiry and development leads to a topic too large to
be encompassed by this short chapter. In this chapter, however, I
tease out key issues emerging from my own experience and knowledge of the field—the only feasible terms of reference at such an
early time in the development of the subject—which have taught
me that, whatever else, there remains a great deal to be done. This
first attempt at an overview, therefore, is a sort of work in progress,

but one whose perspective is that of an artist and educationist—a practitioner—and not that of a philosopher. Philosophy and art theory have much to contribute to this field, but practitioners have an obligation to contribute to the debate of thinking through art, no matter how meagre an offering such as this.

Most art schools and art and design university faculties in the UK, Australia and New Zealand have by now developed or developing PhD programs, many with funded studentships, only the US and Ireland remain in the English-speaking world to do so, and there are already some significant initiatives in both of these countries.[4] Doctorates are also well developed in a number of European countries. There is, then, already a significant and growing number of art and design doctors in circulation. Recent graduates no longer think it strange that a doctoral program might be an option for them on graduation, or at least on completion of a masters, and many of these recognize that the doctorate is normal among their peers in other subjects. These are significant developments that are not yet widely understood and it seems to me that some misconceptions still remain. The doctorate has had a crucial position in university level education in the last five centuries and it has been a long time coming to art and design and to the other creative and performing arts. No wonder it might seem strange.[5]

Art and Design Practice Considered as Research

The problem with regarding creative practice as research seems to center on confusion about the place of knowledge in *practice* when seen in distinction from that in *theory*. That art and design as well as the performing arts are practical is self-evident, but that does not mean that they are not also and simultaneously theoretically based in ways that go beyond "know how." Donald Schon's development of the idea of the reflective practitioner involves a distinction between *knowledge on reflection* and *knowledge in action*.[6] The former involves stepping back from practical activity in a way that is widely recognized in the art and design undergraduate curriculum, conventionally, in the UK, in a ratio of 80 percent to 20 percent. But the idea of *knowledge in action* supposes that practical activity is itself intrinsically intelligent. It supposes thinking through art. It also stands against the absurdity of the theory/practice dichotomy which seems to imply that you must switch your brain off in order to make art or design (or whatever) and then switch it on again in order to reflect on what you have made. In his pursuit of an "epistemology of practice," Schon argues that "universities are not devoted to the production and distribution of fundamental knowledge in general. They are institutions committed, for the most part, to a *particular* epistemology... that fosters selective inattention to practical competence and professional artistry."[7] Schon goes some way to theorizing intuition in arguing that the mental buzz that is constant throughout creative activity—what he calls "the dialogue with the situation"—is itself crucial to the generation of new knowledge obtained through practice. This is what makes practice creative practice, and thereby this is what makes creative practice (but not all practice) research, that is to say, the programmatic generation of new knowledge in a defined field. As Paul van der Lem says, this is what distinguishes "knowledge building" from "knowledge use."[8]

That some practical activities of art and design are eligible to be counted as research activities in the UK Research Assessment Exercise (RAE) can be attributed in part to the sustained arguments of Colin Painter, the former Principal of the Wimbledon School of Art.[9] Painter's social constructivist argument was essentially that if research is a process of inquiry that generates new knowledge, then any such process of inquiry in a subject that performs that task is eligible for consideration as research, even if it doesn't look like research as it is found in other subjects.[10] This could be seen as an argument for the equivalence of art and design and research, as distinct from research proper, but it side-steps the identification and analysis of research in the realm of art and design. Painter's position does, however, provide a basis for reconsidering what is understood to be research in its constructivist requirement that we take research to be what we find it to be rather than the embodiment of some formula taken from the natural or social sciences. While it may be argued that Christopher Frayling's distinction of three kinds of research "into," "through" and "for" art and design provided some valuable distinctions, and his survey of the key issues cleared a lot of important ground, it is not yet fully clear how "practice-based" research should be articulated in relation to "theory-based" or "history-based" research or research based on other approaches.[11] Perhaps the problem is just that "practice-based" research is too loose a term to be useful. In my view we should stop using this term and just recognize that the doctorates in art and design do differ a little from that in other subjects, and that those differences should be valued by researchers in all subjects—an idea to which I return later in this chapter.

The UK Research Assessment Exercise in 2001 was more concerned by how the research content of practice is made explicit than the RAE in 1996, which seemed less interested in outcomes. The issue of how new knowledge may be embodied in or represented by art and design objects (by which I mean objects-of-attention rather than exclusively material artifacts) remains an alternative way of giving account of practice outcomes as research outcomes. Gilbert Ryle's distinction of "know how" from the knowledge described as "know that" does provide for works of art to be seen as evidence of the generation of knowledge, but that is not how we understand works of art or design, which we understand relatively in terms of their appeal, meaning or use.[12] We still need to engage with the object itself and its meaning. Paul Hirst's idea of "knowledge-of-the object" goes a long way to propose an account of knowledge appropriate to works of art and design, and such a distinction is necessary if we are to understand works of art or design as art or design and not as circumstantial evidence of something else.[13] Recently there has been increasing recognition that the characterisation of knowledge embodied in or represented by an object needs to be made explicit within a developing research culture, as evidenced by several recent and planned conferences, and more needs to be done.[14]

While much has been published on epistemology of art, both from the perspective of education theory and philosophical aesthetics, and authoritative texts such as Wollheim's are often embedded within taught courses, this material has yet to be fully drawn down to the developing art and design research paradigm.[15] There is a need for an authoritative literature review to map this. If art research and design research are not to be distorted to fit the terms of reference of some other discipline such as the humanities or social sciences, then we should be explicit about how knowledge may be generated and embodied within the practical dimension of artistic and design production. That research in our field may be forced to adapt to the conventions of other disciplines would be monstrous, but it is possible and may be even probable. There is a need for more theory about practice coming out of what artists and designers actually do methodologically. We need to know how we think through art. The requirements of the UK Arts and Humanities Research Board (AHRB) that research proposals be specified in terms of humanities and social sciences style research questions, in ways that tend to exclude open-ended curiosity, is one indication of how research in our field is being distorted.[16] I consider we need to look further afield than the humanities for useful comparisons; the natural sciences and their predisposition for experiment and "blue skies" research offer many useful points of reference. If the UK's Engineering Sciences and Physics Research Council (ESPRC) can be comfortable with this open approach to research, then so should the AHRB.

Regrettably, some art practitioners have been slow to recognize the need for art works to have to embody or represent *new* knowledge of something in order to count as research. Design does seem to be ahead of art in this respect, with the Le Clusaz Conference of 2000 and the DRS discussion list having clarified many of the necessary distinctions.[17] The need for such a forum in fine art is immense. This distinction between research-based practice and market-based practice takes us right to the center of the longstanding problem of how value judgements are made in the production and evaluation of works of art and design. An inquiry-based perspective on creative practice will have much to contribute to our larger understanding of art and design, and that is why I speak of a new paradigm for research in our subject.

Relationships of Research and Practice

Over the last decade there has been a much-argued differentiation of research and practice in which the latter is taken to imply either the conduct of a professional service in the manner of a medical or legal practitioner, or the character of art and design as being intrinsically practical as distinct from being scholarly.

Just as research implies the generation of knowledge, practice in the former sense implies the application of knowledge: a distinction that should hold true across both artistic and scientific disciplines. For example, the idea of the professional designer as practitioner as distinct from researcher is well founded, indeed it is supported by the establishment of professional bodies such as the Chartered Society of Designers in the UK in a way that begins to be comparable to the medical and legal professional bodies. It is less straightforward to consider fine art professional in this way.

In fine art the meaning of "practice" both confuses and enriches the issue. Here the idea of practice is widely seen to be normally innovative and seldom routine, an idea supported by Schon when he deliberately inter-relates and conflates ideas of practice and research in dealing with "knowledge in action." Here practice can be seen to fulfil many of the criteria of research and it is in this respect that an important distinction between fine art and design emerges.

The term "practice" has been adopted, however, by many visual artists since the 1980s in a way that mimics the professionalism just considered, but without adopting its standards or norms. When a fine artist talks of "professional practice" the standards of the professions such as medicine and law do not apply in any direct sense. This professionalistic creativity seeks to adopt the respectability but not the operational reality of professional conduct. This phenomenon has an historical basis in which fine art's purportedly radical paradigm of avant-garde bohemianism often meets and sometimes elides with that of bourgeois aestheticism and its patronage. This would seem to be a class specific phenomenon that might be better understood were a sociology of artists, artists" audiences and artistic patronage to be developed—an argument best developed elsewhere than here.

Research and Art and Design Research

In considering the problematics of research development it is worth considering the early days of physics or medical research when the idea of scientific method was worked out over a long period of time, borrowing and transforming ideas drawn from the world of letters and when minimal research ethics were sufficiently elastic as to allow systematic grave robbing. Even now scientific method is not thought unproblematic.[18]

Such a comparison validates the apparent shortcomings of art and design research as being reflective of the current state of development of the field rather than as being intrinsic to weaknesses in the subject. In this early stage of development we need to clarify what is not yet known but necessary to the further development of art and design research. Such an agenda for the development of art and design research, in my view, could usefully include the following: a full literature review; a review of examples of inquiry through artistic endeavor in modern history; a sociology of artists; a theoretical basis for intuition; an advanced theorization of how knowledge may be embodied in or represented by a work of art; an aesthetics of artistic method as distinct from one of artistic style; a comparative methodology of artistic production across cultures; and an international consensus in the definitions and boundaries of those subjects loosely bunched as art and design, so that debate of specialization and interdisciplinarity might be better facilitated. Such an agenda for thinking through art and design (as distinct from thinking about art and design) is more an indicator of the relevant state of development of art and design research than of any unsuitability of the subject as a field or research that may be asserted by those of other disciplines.

The Doctorate In Different Countries

The problem with the Doctorate is not that it is a Doctorate, but that it is relatively new to our subject. Across university education, the Doctorate is the key to understanding research-based education at both postgraduate and undergraduate levels as it distils many of its issues. It is just that this may not yet be obvious in art and design, for largely historical reasons.

Historically, the doctorate is probably the oldest degree to be awarded in European higher education, having been a licence to practice law or medicine since the thirteenth century, and in many of the ancient universities it has long been a licence to teach. The PhD developed in Germany in the nineteenth century as a research training, and it is now regarded as a pre-requisite to teaching in most Higher Education subjects world-wide. The training of teachers of undergraduate and postgraduate courses through the research methods of the PhD, with the expectation that they will then teach a simplified form of those methods, means that taught courses are imbued with an essential research flavour.

The research basis of taught courses in art and design is less easy to identify since the history of art and design research is virtually the inverse of that of the subjects conventionally identified with the ancient universities. Art schools in the UK largely (and not exclusively) grew out of the Industrial Revolution to meet the craft, design and drawing needs of the emerging industries in the nineteenth century. The initial development of art schools in the US (as distinct from liberal arts colleges) and several European countries was not dissimilar. Ours was initially a vocational education; a craft, and many of the objections to art and design doctorates are informed and limited by that craft perspective on the subject. Initial training in art and design was given degree-equivalent status in the UK only in the 1960s, this having been a turning point as it locked art and design in the UK and the US into university education in a way not taken up throughout Europe. I think there is no turning back. The British BA (Hons.) and the American BFA in studio art and design date only from the 1970s, and postgraduate courses did not proliferate in the UK beyond the London Three Schools and a smattering of provincial centers until the mid 1980s at which time the first PhDs began to emerge at the CNAA's behest. In the US doctorates in studio art were developed at the University of Ohio and at NYU much earlier but were subsequently abandoned after the MFA was determined by the College Art Association of America to be "the terminal degree," equivalent to other terminal degrees such as the PhD in 1977.[19] The validity of this position is now under question, given the emerging generation of studio-based doctorates in a number of US art schools in response to developments elsewhere in the English-speaking world. These are clearly of a different order of academic award from the MFA. Curiously, from a European point of view the American debate has been largely based on the principle of credentializing art teachers in higher education rather than that of research development and it will be interesting to see whether a credible academic debate can be sustained on that premise.[20] A further American initiative, "Re-Envisioning the PhD," unfortunately bypassed this debate and the opportunities that exist within it, but established national norms comparable to those of Europe.[21] The first cohort of ten studio-based PhD students enrolled at the Central Academy of Fine Arts in Beijing in autumn 2003, with a strongly national orientation it its research methods training which takes aesthetics and archaeology as its key components. Norway too is advancing cautiously with the state funding a pilot scheme of two doctoral students in each of the three third level art schools, at Oslo, Bergen and Trondheim, for three years. The first UK PhDs to be examined without a substantial written thesis emerged only in the late 1990s, and a DFA that is substantially different in more than name from the PhD has only recently materialised in the UK at Goldsmiths College, London, although the DFA and the DLA has developed in Australasia and in some European countries such as Hungary and the Czech Republic. In several European countries, such as France, art and design education remains outside the university system with a different provenance, different expectations and different possibilities.

As it is I do not think the French model is possible in the English speaking world given art and design's integration in university education. Given that there is no turning back towards a craft-led education, only once the doctorate is commonplace and doctors abundant in art and design schools will the development of higher education research culture within art and design education become mature.

The "Practice-Based" PhD

The PhD provides a training in research methods and methodology that is achieved through a program of inquiry, a project, that leads to new knowledge or understanding. That is to say, the learning of how to do research is as indispensable to a PhD as the new knowledge that is generated by means of it. More specifically, I would describe the project as *a self-reflective supervised program of inquiry leading to new knowledge*. Every PhD has at least the same standard four elements or ingredients: a research question or topic; a program of study enquiring into that question or topic; supervisory arrangements whereby the student's research is undertaken under the supervision of a senior researcher; and the examination of the conclusions of the program of research. Conventionally a PhD concludes with a thesis or argument which if persuasive is agreed to represent new knowledge, whatever form it may take. For art and design a particular issue arises here, for while it may be possible to explain how an object embodies new knowledge of the " knowledge-of" kind, it is less clear how an object can be said in itself to embody a thesis or argument. It may be appropriate to consider the objects that constitute the conclusions of the project as equivalent to or in lieu of a thesis rather than as a thesis in themselves. Alternatively, it might be possible to argue that an object, particularly in fine art does have such an active capacity, but such a case has yet to be argued and won.

I think it is worth filling in the outline I have just sketched, to consider in some detail the issues emerging for art and design from each of those four elements.

First, what is meant by a *research question?* A research question may inquire into a problem to be solved; a creative opportunity to be explored or exploited; or an issue to be examined, whether any of these be technical, procedural, philosophical, theoretical, or historical. Whichever of these a research question may be it must also take the form of a query such as: what; what if; how; when; why; why not; for whom; by whom; or any other form of question. How the question may be framed is the real challenge for art and design since there has historically been in taught courses a conservative separation of theory and practice, and where the idea of intrinsically intelligent practice, or praxis, is still relatively new, even if the idea of praxis goes a long way back to Gramsci. The need for clarity in the early definition of the PhD student's registration of a project becomes subsequently apparent at the time of examination when, for that process to fair and equitable, that benchmark for the measure of success is required. This should not be difficult in a subject in which most undergraduate and postgraduate learning and teaching is project based, and research degrees could well learn from and refine the idea of working to a self-set brief that is already common in taught courses.

It is also worth considering critically what is meant by a PhD *program of research.* Here too there is a fairly standard set of ingredients.

1. A *review*, sometimes called a literature review, is a scoping of the knowledge current within the field of inquiry undertaken to confirm that the research has not already been undertaken and the PhD therefore unnecessary. This is particularly problematic in art and design, notably in fine art where it is simply not possible to determine all that has been done, because not all creative practice of this kind has been externally referenced let alone refereed. We

need to develop a consensus of the kind of review that is most appropriate to our subject

2. *Research methods*, which are ways of doing something, and research methodology which is the study of methods, both being equally necessary to the research student. Often the two are conflated as if a methodology was a super-luxury method. This is especially problematic in our subjects since, while there is a great deal of literature on quantitative and qualitative research methods in the humanities and sciences, there is little consensus in art and design and other creative and performing arts. In my view this is one of the most fertile areas for development in art and design research. If we are able to devise explicit ways of describing and analysing how artists, designers, dramatists, choreographers and performers generate new knowledge from both primary and secondary sources, then we may have developed a new research-based theorization of, not only artistic production, but also intuition. In this way there is the possibility of constructing the much needed new paradigm for art; a new aesthetics of method.

3. *The inquiry* is the core of a research program. Many artists will have problems with characterising what they do as inquiry rather than expression, or social intervention, and whether it is in any way programmatic. However, if our subject is to have a place at the higher levels of higher education then it would seem a necessary pursuit to identify in what ways art and design do generate knowledge through inquiry. This issue is an extension of what I have just said about methods and methodology, but on a larger scale, what Schon calls "an epistemology of practice." It seems to me that the challenge is to make explicit that which is unique to art and design. We need to be more explicit about what is meant by an enquiring mind in our subject at university level, and this need is in itself an indictment of the subject's conservatives who argue for a tacit knowledge of theory among artists—seemingly an argument for the unintelligence of art.

4. *Recording the process* is also a standard element of the PhD and the log book or journal is a conventional means in research yet not one immediately obvious in art and design. The term journal in its eighteenth century literary sense was a day-book, or diary— a literary convention. If we return to that age of letters then the sketchbook, as a means of recording a journey such as the grand tour, may provide away of getting to grips with this idea. The purpose of the record in a PhD is to facilitate a dialogue between researcher and supervisor and a point of reference in reviewing progress and reflecting on further development of it. It enables the meta-inquiry, the way in which the process of research becomes a

means of learning about research. The challenge here is to make academic rigour explicit within our subjects in ways that have not always been the case.

5. The *conclusion* of a PhD presented in appropriate form is crucial to the examination regime. Conventionally an argument or case is described as a thesis, but that the term thesis can also mean a large number of words typed double spaced can confuse the issue. There are many precedents for the submission of practical outcomes that embody or represent new knowledge or understanding for examination demonstrates. Whether practical material should be submitted for examination as a thesis, or in lieu of a thesis is a moot point, but it should embody or represent the new knowledge or understanding in whatever form. What has been achieved should be capable, however, of being described if not summarised in text that together with the documented outcomes is presented in some form that can be accessed by future researchers. Conventionally, such a supplementary text has been described as a summary, and it may be necessary to use that term rather broadly in the case of art and design.

Once the program is complete it is subject to examination and the way in which the processes and outcomes are examined is reveals some key issues. Three elements of the PhD *examination process* may be apparent: value judgement; fulfilment of previously specified criteria; and defence of a dissertation. These three quite different forms of engagement might easily be confused. There has yet to develop sufficient custom and practice for there to be in art and design a consensus of how these elements inter-relate in a PhD examination. The conoisseurial value judgement would arguably seem out of place as in any criterion referenced educational process, yet a decision as to whether a PhD program has attained doctoral level does need to be made, and in this it is the opinion of experts in the field that is called upon. The risk that such a judgement could revert to one of taste does exist, and such a value judgement needs to be moderated by an examination for the fulfilment of the criteria specified in the initial registration of the program of research, that is to say examination of the outcomes against the benchmark of the initial intention. That the PhD student be required to defend his or her thesis provides a moderating factor for the value judgement of the attainment of level and the judgement of outcomes against intentions as specified as criteria. Here the autonomy of what has been achieved by the student is tested for its robustness, and the judgements of value and criteria-fulfilment are set into the context of the project outcomes in their own terms. Thesis defence, therefore, puts the viva-voce examination into a crucial position in the

examination process. A proper understanding of what is being examined in a PhD should resolve the perennial dilemma of the relation of material outcomes of artistic or design production to written
material.

Early "practice-based" PhDs in many universities and colleges
gave students some dispensation in the word length of the written
thesis that had to accompany the work. The requirement of a body
of work and a thesis could have the effect of requiring a double
PhD since the outcomes have to be produced and submitted for examination twice, whereas the reduced word count could have the
effect of a triple PhD in that is more difficult to produce a short text
than a long one. There is a track record in some universities of these
doctorates taking an inordinate amount of time to complete—up to
ten years in some cases.

The second generation of "practice-based" PhDs, such as those
initiated in the mid-1990's at the Wimbledon School of Art, did not
prescribe a word count as such and envisioned a sliding scale of
portfolio and text, while retaining a requirement for the written element. This resolved the duplication of effort previously required
(and still required by some universities), and it made the PhD feasible in the same sort of timescale and with the same sort of workload
as that expected of PhDs across other disciplines. Nevertheless,
some ambiguity of the purpose of the written element remained,
and the portfolio was regulated as "in lieu of a thesis" rather than
as the thesis itself. Since written material may be required either as
examinable research content, or as evidence of the research content
for the use of future researchers, or both can lead to the conflation
of the two purposes, and this may tend to compromise the epistemological character of the new knowledge generated by a PhD
project.

A third generation of "practice-based" PhDs emerged in 2000 at
the Glasgow School of Art, based on a the distinction of a number
of different possible relationships between material outcomes and
textual outcomes, and the different purposes that might be expected of the text. A distinction was also made between the material submitted for examination and the documentation of it for the
purposes of future reference to the research content. In this third
generation it was possible to say that the difference between an art
and design PhD and any other PhD is not in the type of doctorate,
but in the ways in which the research outcomes are presented for
examination.

At Glasgow four categories of submission for examination have
been identified in regulations. In providing for the different purposes that might be expected of material and text, the range of

these categories was also thought to provide for likely differences in projects in fine art, the decorative arts, and design in a wide range of subjects including visual communication, product design and architecture. These categories suppose different relationships between text and material evidence. These categories were subsequently taken up in modified form by another Scottish HEI to provide for music doctorates and they may be more widely applicable. The Glasgow categories are as follows:

1. *A written thesis* which may take any of a number of forms including a theoretical exegesis, an historical analysis, or a report of a project, or whatever. That it is written does not mean that it cannot be "practice-based" since it may be an account of research conducted by means of practice.

2. *A dissertation and portfolio* which supposes an equal weight given to the visual/material outcomes of practice and the discussion of the knowledge, suited to those instances where the knowledge is intelligible only when considered in the context of what is written, often text of a theoretical character. That there are two elements to the submission supposes that together they represent the new knowledge or understanding and that they do not each do so separately since that would be a double PhD.

3. *A portfolio with commentary* in which the new knowledge is presented largely in its own right but with a body of written information necessary to a full understanding of the portfolio, typically an account of procedural or contextual information; and *a portfolio with documentation and a summary* (all forms of submission requiring a "summary') in which the new knowledge is presented in its own right but documented sufficiently clearly, including the use of text, for there to be a record of the research process and its outcomes for future reference.[22]

One learning point across these three approaches has been that the less text that is submitted the more rigorous the thesis defence will need to be. In this way a PhD examination in which the thesis is embodied mainly in a portfolio may be harder than when it is embodied in a long text, contrary to the wishful thinking of some PhD applicants. A further point to emerge is the problem of supervision by subject experts of whom few are formally qualified to supervise. Many institutions adopt a team approach to supervision and while this does provide for the inclusion of non-qualified subject experts alongside qualified supervisors from other disciplines, it can imply the transfer into art and design of inappropriate methods from other disciplines in the name of academic responsibility.

In my view, it emerges that the PhD in art and design differs from PhDs in other subjects in terms of the way in which research topics may be defined and in the examination regime being adjusted for the inclusion of a portfolio or exhibition in lieu of a written thesis. In most other respects it is the same; a PhD is a PhD. What is needed is an examination regime that will allow for additional or alternative modes of examination of a thesis when it is represented by or embodied in works of art and design. What I have just described goes some way to providing for those differences, though in time it will no doubt be improved upon. The oral examination or *viva voce* will remain standard for all PhDs and perhaps it is this rather than the thesis or portfolio that should be seen as the core of examination rather than as an "add on." If we were to depend on the face to face engagement of the candidate and the examiners as the primary form of examination, then the whole discussion of text versus object would take secondary place and thereby lose much of its controversy.

Conclusions

In this discussion of the four elements of a PhD, I have tried to outline some of the key developmental issues for the PhD in our subject. What all these issues center on is a need for clarity in what we mean by *new knowledge* or understanding in the generation of works of art or design. I am developing the position advocated by Colin Painter and lucidly argued by Andrew Harrison, on the basis of Kant, that in the knowledge at stake "the medium of communication (of knowledge) must ultimately be works themselves, not descriptions of them or assertions about them."[23] This would seem to represent a basis for considering works of art as the embodiment, representation or lodgement of the knowledge that art has to bear.

The PhD and the DFA in art and design provide unique opportunities to get to grips with these issues in building such a new paradigm. In providing a foundation for practice-referenced academic standards we would have created something for the benefit of university education as a whole. What we—as a subject community in art and design, and in cognate fields such as performance, architecture and maybe literature—can most gain here is the ability to give; for it is by our relevance to other disciplines and our generosity towards them that our own disciplines will become valued within university education and by the world beyond.

Notes

1 This essay is based on a paper presented at The European League of Institutes of The Arts (ELIA) Conference Dublin, October 2002. The paper was subsequently presented at a joint conference of the Royal Academy of Fine Arts, Brussels and the Department of Philosophy and Letters, Université Libre de Bruxelles in 2003, and then as the basis of a presentation to the 2003 Symposium of the Association of Independent Colleges of Art and design at the Disney Hall in Los Angeles. It is currently being translated into Serbo-Croat for presentation at the University of the Arts, Belgrade. With each iteration of the presentation and discussion the argument of the paper has developed and I am most grateful to a number of colleagues who have assisted me in this developmental process.

2 Yeats to Ezra Pound, 15 July 1918, Yale, cited in R. F. Foster, *W.B.Yeats: A Life: Arch Poet 1915-1939* (Oxford: Oxford University Press, 2003).

3 The 7th ELIA conference, Dublin, Ireland, October 2002 took the theme "Monstrous Thinking: on practice-based research" as one of its ten conference symposia, reflecting a widespread view that this topic was in some way intrinsically controversial.

Jon Thompson, "A Case of Double Jeopardy," *Research and the Artist: Considering the Role of the Art School*, edited by Antonia Payne (Oxford: Ruskin School of Drawing and Fine Art, University of Oxford, 2000), edition of 750. The paper was presented to an invited audience at the University of Oxford, 28th May 1999.

4 [This situation has changed since the essay was written; see Jones's other essay in this volume. – J.E.]

5 In examining these issues in some detail I draw upon my own engagement with promoting, overseeing, managing, supervising and examining doctorates over two decades. In doing this I am grateful for the collaboration and wisdom of my colleagues at Stourbridge College, the University of Wolverhampton, the Wimbledon School of Art, and the Glasgow School of Art in which I have held positions of responsibility for the development of doctoral education, on which I draw in this paper. I am also grateful for the perceptions of my associates at the Hungarian Academy of Fine Art, Budapest, the Central Academy of Fine Art, Beijing, the DRS Symposium (it included Michael Biggs, John Broadbent, Richard Buchanan, Katie Bunnell, Clive Cazeaux, Rachel Cooper, Edward Cowie, Ken Friedman, Jacques Giard, Beryl Graham, Paul Gutherson, myself, Lorraine Justice, Michael Kroelinger, Malcolm LeGrice, Malcolm Miles, Alec Robertson, Chris Rust, Stephen Scrivener, Elaine Thomas, Jonathan Woodham, Martin Woolley, "'Practice-based' Doctorates in design and the Creative and Performing Arts: a Symposium," in *The "Practice-Based" PhD*, special issue of the *Journal of Design Science and Technology*, edited by David Durling, Ken Friedman, and Paul Gutherson, forthcoming; originally written 2002), the Association of Independent Colleges of Art and Design, US and the National University of Ireland, Galway with whom I am collaborating on further developments, mentioned later in this paper.

6 Schon, *The Reflective Practitioner: How Professionals Think in Action* (Ashgate Arena, 1983).

7 Schon, *The Reflective Practitioner*, vii.

8 Paul van der Lem, "The Development of the PhD for the Visual Arts," in *Exchange 2000 Conference*, Watershed Media Center, Bristol, at www.media. uwe.ac.uk/exchange_online/exch2_article2.php3.

9 Research Assessment Exercise submissions may be seen on www.hero. ac.uk/rae.

10 Painter, "Fine Art Practice, Research and Doctoral Awards: Part 1," in *Proceedings of the National Research Conference Art and Design in Education* (Brighton: Fribble Information Systems Inc. Ltd., with the National Society for Education in Art and Design, 1991). See also Painter and Stroud Cornock, "Fine Art Practice, Research and Doctoral Awards: Part 2," *ibid.*

11 Frayling, "Searching and Researching in Art and Design," in *Proceedings of the National Research Conference Art and Design in Education*. See also UK Council for Graduate Education, *Practice-Based Doctorates in The Creative and Performing Arts and Design*, prepared by a working group convened by Frayling. UK Council for Graduate Education, 1997.

12 Ryle, *The Concept of Mind* (London: Hutchinson, 1949; Chicago: University of Chicago Press, 1984).

13 Paul Hirst, *Knowledge and the Curriculum* (London: Routledge and Kegan Paul, 1974).

14 *The Research Into Practice Conference 2002*, University of Hertfordshire and that planned for 2004 consider epistemology and knowledge in art and design. For the 2002 papers see www.herts.ac.uk/artdes/simsim/rtos/. The 2003 AICAD Deans' Meeting held in the Disney Hall, Los Angeles initiated this debate in the US.

15 Richard Wollheim, *Art and Its Objects* (New York: Harper and Row, 1968).

16 The Arts and Humanities Research Board, www.ahrb.ac.uk. [For more on this, see Chapter 10. —J.E.]

17 See David Durling and Ken Friedman, *Foundations for the Future, Doctoral Education in Design*, conference proceedings, La Clusaz, France (Staffordshire University Press, 2000), and the email discussion list of the Design Research Society led by Ken Friedman at www.jiscmail.ac.uk/archives/phd-design. html. Also of interest in this respect is www.jiscmail.ac.uk/lists/RTI.html.

18 See Peter Medawar, *The Limits of Science* (New York: Harpercollins, 1984), and his earlier *The Art of The Soluble*.

19 CAA Board of Directors, *MFA Standards* (1977), revised 1991. [This document is available online at www.transartinstitute.org/Downloads/MFA_standards.pdf. — J.E.]

20 The recent American debate of the development of doctoral programs in studio art has focused largely on the effect such a doctorate might have on the status of the MFA as the "terminal degree," and the effect of any such change on the terms of employment of art teachers. This debate was re-opened in 2003 by the Symposium of the Association of Independent Colleges of Art and Design and in the CAA Professional Practices Committee debate "Credentializing in the Arts', in CAA Conference Seattle. 2004, chaired by Kristi Nelson, University of Cincinnati (not included in the published conference abstracts).

21 "Re-envisioning the Arts," at www.grad.washington.edu/envision/ project_resources/national_recommend.html

22 Regulations for Awards at the Glasgow School of Art, in the *Calendar* of University of Glasgow, 2001 and subsequent issues.

23 Andrew Harrison, "Shared Judgements [2002]" in *Research Into Practice* Conference proceedings, University of Hertfordshire, on http://www.herts.ac.uk/artdes/simsim/rtos/.

3

Art and Method
Henk Slager

The curricula of many institutes for art education are largely domi-
nated by an art historical model. As a consequence, one gratuitously
deploys a clear-cut duality: on the one hand, artists produce artistic
work, while on the other hand, professionals (mostly art historians)
supply frameworks for the interpretation of those works. Standard
works such as Ernst Gombrich's *Art and Illusion* and Hans-Georg
Gadamer's *Truth and Method* have provided a methodological foundation for a nearly dogmatic art historical hermeneutics.[1]
    Gadamer compares the encounter with visual art with intently
reading a letter; both entail a certain expectation. He notes that every interpretation has a horizon: that is, it is rooted in a temporality,
which also counts for human knowledge. However, in spite of such
a sense of perspective, Gadamer still believes that, in encountering
a work of art, it must be possible to locate a determinate meaning.
    Gombrich's work demonstrates a similar inclination; he spends
many words on the conventional character of representation and
the important role of the spectator in arriving at the intended meaning of the image — "the eye of the beholder." At the same time,
Gombrich believes that it is indeed possible for adequate art historical research to arrive at an iconographically exact (if not systematic
or unambiguous) meaning of a certain image. In light of such art
historical hermeneutics, the artistic image is, in fact, a repository for
determinate meanings.
    However, today's practice of visual art makes clear that it is time
to declare monolithic thought framed in binary models of truth (the
hermeneutic method) and illusion (the visual creative) as obsolete.
Moreover, the practice of art shows that art and method can connect in a novel and constructive way. In such a connection, the emphasis will shift from an art practice focused on final products to a
practice directed towards an experimental, laboratory-style environment, exploring novel forms of knowledge and experience. In

other words, artistic practice has become a dynamic point of departure for interdisciplinary experiments governed by a reflexive point of view. Critical reflection deals with questions such as what makes art art, what art should be, and what the context of art is. Such a conception of artistic activity challenges many present-day artists to view their artistic projects as forms of research.

Obviously, conceiving art in terms of artistic research has considerable, institutional consequences, since the focus on research requires an adequate curriculum in advanced art education. Ute Meta Bauer's publication *Education, Information, Entertainment* gave a first impetus to critical reflection on such a curriculum.[2] Bauer argues that the curriculum of art academies should radically break with the art historical paradigm of autonomous art in order to address current artistic developments. Furthermore, art academies and their curricula should particularly focus on the cultural preconditions of visual art, that is, on the circumstances and conditions which enable artistic activities. This means that a reflexive attention to art education should begin by researching what she calls "the political, social and media-related conditions which decisively determine the artistic concepts and practice."

In Europe, the concept of research also plays a decisive role in advanced art education in the context of the introduction of a Bachelor-Master structure; ultimately, art institutions need to start thinking in terms of PhD degrees. The three-year PhD program in Fine Art at the Utrecht Graduate School of Visual Art and Design is embedded in the structure of the MA research program.[3] In the first year, the PhD student is expected to participate in two MA seminars: "Methodology" and "Transmedial Research," during which the progress of research is discussed. At the end of the first year, the PhD student must be prepared to present a concrete plan for a research trajectory. During the next two years, the student stays in close contact with his or her supervisor; to that end, students are offered poses as teaching assistants. In addition, peer review seminars are held at least six times a year. These seminars are given by experts in the field of transmedial research; PhD students are screened critically in the course of the seminars. The research seminars also engage curatorial studies, because the experimental process of transmedial research has a direct impact on the reflection of models of presentation. A final exhibition, in a professional environment, or a series of sub-exhibitions, are also part of the research trajectory. The PhD student is expected to contextualize his or her research trajectory in an essay of approximately 30,000 words that coherently reports on the project's contribution to topical methodological discussions.

We concentrate on the status and position of the artistic image in our present visual culture. How does an artistic image relate to other forms of visual production? Our position evokes critical questions about presentation and representation. Students in the Utrecht research program first learn how to methodologically reflect on their art. Next, they are trained in developing research hypotheses and models. In addition, they are asked to think about the specificity of research subjects. Questions arise such as: What are the boundaries of the artistic domain? Where could constructive cross-overs with other fields of knowledge and visual domains be envisioned? Could those connections lead to novel concepts? In short, how can a topical artistic concept be formulated and how can an adequate visual grammar or language be developed? Is a visual language differently constituted by various media perspectives or can it ultimately be considered as transmedial or intermedial? What is, for instance, the factual input of the photographic paradigm in the field of topical visual art? Is reflection from the painterly paradigm still relevant for understanding a topical artistic production? Do the visual language of cinema and the reality of the screen influence the imagination of current visual art? And last but not least, students investigate the the contextualization of the artistic image in light of an exploration of the preconditions of artistic communication process as such. What is the optimal context for a specific, artistic image; what curatorial and communicative preconditions does such an image require; and under what circumstances should it ultimately be presented?

These research questions make clear that it is urgent to reflect on the specificity of artistic research, whether it is institutionalized or not; in such contexts the differences and similarities with other forms of research should also be explored. After all, artistic research seems to continuously thwart academically defined disciplines. In fact, art knows the hermeneutic questions of the humanities; art is engaged in an empirically scientific method; and art is aware of the commitment and social involvement of the social sciences. It seems, therefore, that the most intrinsic characteristic of artistic research is based on the continuous transgression of boundaries in order to generate novel, reflexive zones.

What then are the criteria determining the object of knowledge, when artistic research is conceived as an exploration of different academic or research zones? The concept of research unmistakably invokes certain expectations. After all, research implies an organized manner of approach, a systematic treatment of information, and a significant contribution to the information and knowledge economy. Furthermore, research could imply ethical responsibilities such as a better understanding or improvement of the world. Does that help define a characteristic element of such research? One could say that each form of research seems to be focused on how to formulate a methodology. Research might not be inspired by a great cause or an accidental discovery (it might happen serendipitously), yet it may ultimately lead to a novel, methodologically formulated form of knowledge. The force of the method seems to determine the value of the results. Continuos control should clarify to what extent methodological conditions have been applied. Moreover, although research methods obviously differ according to their fields and subjects, they share a fundamental basic principle: methodological research is primarily directed towards formulating questions and providing answers. Thus, it seems that research as such could be described most adequately as the methodological connection of questions and answers.

Attention to the concept of research can also be observed in today's practice of visual art, outside of advanced art education. However, the mostly trans- or interdisciplinary research of visuality conducted by artists is not really characterized by an objective, empirical approach. After all art does not strive for generalization, repeatability, and quantification. Rather, art is directed towards unique, qualitative, particular, and local knowledge. In that respect, artistic activities still seem to perfectly match Baumgarten's classic definition of the aesthetic domain, where knowledge is described as a knowledge of the singular.[4] Even though artistic knowledge understood as a *mathesis singularis* — because of its focus on the singular and the unique — cannot be comprehended in laws, it deals with a form of knowledge, says Baumgarten. Hence the emphasis on the singular and the unique in the aesthetic domain does not imply that artistic research is impossible, as for example the philosopher of science Karl Popper claimed. After all, an operational form of research seems to satisfy the most basic research criteria: it focuses on the importance of communication; it foments a critical attitude; and it leads to autonomous research.

In contrast to academic-scientific research emphasizing the generation of "expert knowledge," the domain of art seems rather to express a form of experience-based knowledge. Whereas pure scientific research often seems to be characterized by academic goal (and perhaps even on purposeful uselessness), artistic research focuses on involvement, on social and non-academic goals. That does not preclude the fact that artistic research as a form of idiosyncratic research still should be able to answer two well-defined questions. First, how can autonomous research take place in visual art? Second, how can the chosen methodology (as compared with research projects of other artists) best be described?

The epistemological perspective of uniqueness and divergence requires a further methodological deliberation. After all, in contrast to other forms of research, the methodological trajectory of artistic research and its related production of knowledge cannot be easily defined. However, in my view, this trajectory could be designated as a *differential iconography*, because it reveals a worldview no longer conceived as a transparent unity. Fundamental aspects such as indefinability, heterogeneity, contingency, and relativity color the trajectory of artistic research. Therefore, artistic research should explicitly request tolerance, an open attitude, and the deployment of multiple models of interpretation. Only then will it be able to manifest itself as a critical reflection on the status and position of the artistic image in current visual culture. Conceiving artistic research as a differential iconography gives it the capacity to avoid anchoring the image in a one-dimensional hermeneutic.

Thus, the most important methodological paradigm of artistic research could be described as an awareness of divergence without a hierarchy of discourses, as, for example, was the case with the prevalence of hermeneutics in art history in Modernism. Awareness of divergence implies the capacity to mobilize an open attitude and an intrinsic tolerance for a multitude of interpretations that, if necessary, could be transformed into a revolt against the danger of any one-dimensional contextualization.

One might conclude that artistic researchers continuously need to deploy a meta-perspective in order to enable critical reflection on the temporary, operational parameters of their research. Such a methodology could be considered a form of two-plane analysis based on a dual research perspective, wich I will call knowledge economy and ethical responsibility.

The perspective of the first plane is expressed in Jean-Francois Lyotard's postmodern maxim that, in their research of visuality, artists should pose the epistemological question of what art is. Or better put, in their transcendental research, artists should investigate whether the institutional or territorial foundations of the concept of art should be deconstructed. It is necessary to continuously question the concept of art. As Lyotard says, "a work of art is a kind of proposition presented within the context of art as a comment on art." If this perspective is implemented too radically or one-sidedly, art risks becoming the equivalent of its definition. "Art has evolved in such a way that the philosophical question of its status has almost become the very essence of art itself," Lyotard writes, "so that the philosophy of art, instead of standing outside the subject and addressing it from an alien and extended perspective, became instead the articulation of the internal energy of the subject."[5] Today it requiresa special kind of effort to distinguish art from its own philosophy.

The perspective of the second plane is clearly underscored by Merleau-Ponty's definition of the artist as a person who has the capacity to observe what fail to notice. After all, through merely visual means, the artist succeeds in making visible what ordinary vision fails to see. Everyday categories of perception can be dislocated in a flash. The artist compels us to see the world in a different way, according to different norms and habits. Images do not replace reality, but reveal novel visibilities, and art proposes polymorphic kinds of observation. The artistic image provides an open view while liberating the spectator from a frozen perspective. As Merleau-Ponty says: "essence or existence, imaginary or real, visible or invisible, art disrupts all our categories by revealing its dream universe of sensuous essences, of striking similarities and silent meanings."[6] From that perspective, artistic research is also connected with the search for a critical understanding of our existential conditions and the formulation of utopian proposals for improvement. Such a modernist view is inseparably linked with an emancipatory ideal: artistic research should be based on the ethical guideline of human freedom.

These planes of research correspond to the impetus of Kant's two Critiques: the Critique of Pure Reason, concerning the foundation of human knowledge; and the Critique of Practical Reason, addressing the preconditions of human morality. However, as a continuation, Kant also formulated a third critique, the Critique of Judgement, where he envisions art as an interstitial space, a zone, where both faculties of cognition, pure reason and practical reason, meet. The perspective of a third space as reflexive zone seems to be of immense interest in today's visual art, certainly after the two episodes of modernism and postmodernism, which have brought both of the two planes into play. Today, artistic research takes place in an operational and experimental way in a zone determined by a configuration of the two planes.[7] The methodological perspective of artistic research cannot be decided a priori, as it can in one-dimensional scientific research. After all, artistic research as an operational process is "an open-ended work-in-pre-growth."[8] Thus, in artistic practices, there is no form defined entirely beforehand. As a consequence, it is by definition impossible to research the artistic process by assuming that such a definition may already exist. In artistic research one should speak of a continuous, self-reflexive movement questioning the situation and determining the artist's position with regard to the spaces of analysis. The result is not a fixed concept or a static point, but the indication of a zone, leaving unmarked room for the continuation of artistic experiment. As a consequence, artistic research continually produces novel connections in the form of multiplicities characterized by temporary, flexible constructions. These constructions run up against problems, but rather than creating solutions, they keep on deploying novel methodological programs while producing continuous modifications.

In sum, topical research creates methodological trajectories determining how, why and where the operational research proceeds while also engaging in critical, parallel discourses. Such a model is in continuous flux: as a work in progress it always involves articulation, segmentation and reconstruction. In A Thousand Plateaus, Gilles Deleuze and Félix Guattari describe the zone as a unlocalizable relation of speed and slowness. One could argue that the non-localizable zone of artistic research is characterized by reflecting interactions, accelerating speed, and mutating flows of thought. Such a refuge of artistic research could be cut through by a relative stoppage of flows of thought and by points of accumulation that might introduce forms of rigidity in the variety of flows. In both processes, the two planes of analysis play a decisive role. Not surprisingly, artistic methodology as an operational, cartographic composition does not offer a closed system with a localizable structure of components. In line with Deleuze and Guattari, one could argue that the zone of artistic research "always has detachable, connectable, reversible, modifiable, and multiple entryways"[9] and idiosyncratic lines of flight. It is for that reason that it is only possible at the end of a program of research to determine whether the trajectory of the proposed methodological process has indeed produced interesting connections, accelerations and mutations. Artistic research can never be characterized by a well-defined, rigid methodology. Rather, its form of research could be described as a methodical: it entails a strong belief in a methodologically articulable result founded by operational strategies that cannot be legitimized beforehand. Indeed, that is the essential characteristic of artistic research.

Notes

1 H.-G. Gadamer, *Wahrheit und Methode* (Frankfurt am Main, 1960); E. H. Gombrich, *Art and Illusion* (London, 1960). See my *Archeology of Art Theory* (Amsterdam and New York, 1995), 133-41.

2 *Education, Information, Entertainment*, edited by Ute Meta Bauer (Vienna, 2001).

3 www.mahku.nl.

4 In his book *Aesthetica* (1758), Baumgarten introduced the concept of aesthetics as a philosophy of the senses. He says, "Aesthetics should investigate for accuracy analogous to logic, that is at the basis of scientific knowledge, the concepts constituting sensibility." In Camera Lucida, Roland Barthes describes similar research as a mathesis singularis, "a science of the person, which can attain a generality which does not belittle nor shatter."

5 Lyotard, [ ]

6 Maurice Merleau-Ponty, *L'Oeil et l'esprit* (Paris, 1964), 35.

7 Gilles Deleuze and Félix Guattari alternate the concept of zone with plateau: a self-vibrating region of intensities characterized by the absence of a logical point of cumulation or crescendo. A Thousand Plateaus, London, 1988. See also Sarat Maharaj's description of plateau in the Dokumenta XI Catalogue: "It is about duration, prolonged immersion, sustainable absorption — not retinal replication, but about production."

8 *Artistic Research, Survey of a Conference on the Position of Research in European Advanced Art Education*, edited by Annette W. Balkema and Henk Slager (Amsterdam and New York, 2004), 53.

9 Deleuze and Guattari, *A Thousand Plateaus* (London, 1988), 21.

4

Four Theses Attempting To Revise The Terms Of A Debate

Mick Wilson

[T]he problems of real-world practice do not present themselves to practitioners as well-formed structures. Indeed, they tend not to present themselves as problems at all but as messy, indeterminate situations.[1]

This essay seeks to provide a critical and historical re-contextualisation of the issues raised by practice-based doctoral research in the visual arts in order to overcome what may be described as the *ahistorical* tendency of much of the debate in respect of the PhD through visual arts practice. Four critical theses are proposed here in order to reframe the institutional and pragmatic approach to doctoral studies in the visual arts through practice. The essay is rooted in an analysis of the contingent nature of the research doctorate construct in general and the correlation of the critical re-thinking of this institution with the critical renewal of recurrent questions as to the nature and role of university education.

First Thesis

The research university ideal must be historicized in order to overcome a monolithic and pre-critical notion of "research" which inhibits the creative reconstruction of the term, and which obscures the potential plurality of research ideals. It is precisely in reactivating certain "paths not taken" in the construction of a research ideal that the values of the doctorate through art practice manifests.

Sometime around 1800, an educational revolution took place in the German states; it occurred much earlier there than it did in England or France, and it did so long before the industrial revolution reached Germany. One element in this transformation was the emergence of the research imperative, the expectation that university faculty will do original research and prepare their students to do the same.[2]

The conventional narrative of the research university points to its origins in von Humboldt's reforms of the Prussian education system and his specific innovations with the University of Berlin.[3] It is claimed that until the second half of the nineteenth century the German university was the only one in the world that had oriented itself around the idea of research and it was the only place where a sustained research training could be acquired.[4] The modern university system and its variously construed research ideals have been the subject of ongoing contention and debate regarding their nature, ethos and extramural relevance since at least the mid-nineteenth century. However, the controversies that regularly convulsed the university in respect of its identity and mission are subject to an institutional amnesia that serves to obscure the specific trajectory of these contests from one generation to another. The general consequence of this has been a tendency in academic disputes for the reproduction of ahistorical conceptions of research and of the university—epitomized in a formula such as "the idea of university."[5] Thus the institution of the university and the free pursuit of research have repeatedly come to be lauded as universal values epitomising specifically human propensities, for instance in these two representative claims: "the university is the guardian of the imagination that both defines and asserts our humanity"[6]; universities are "the only institutions charged with trying to keep, as fully and accurately as possible, what we might call 'the human record,' the record of civilization... universities regard knowledge as something that must be constantly probed, questioned, and explained."[7]

However, even a cursory effort to recall the debates of earlier generations about the role of the research university, allows easy recognition of the recurrent fault lines that open in these conflicts along the tension between knowledge for its "own sake" and knowledge directed toward a given end. As a former president of the University of California, Clark Kerr,[8] articulated this in a lecture given in Harvard in1963: the structure of the university, he said, reflects "competing visions of true purpose, each relating to a different layer of history, a different web of forces... The university is so many things to so many people that it must, of necessity, be partially at war with itself."[9] Gerhard Casper, President of Stanford University, notes "the quest for 'applications,' for research that is 'targeted,'" which has been "pressed on universities from the beginning," as well as "contemporary views worldwide that universities should be engines for economic progress."[10] He says that the original research university idea proposed by Humboldt "was developed to counteract pressures for immediate practicality."[11]

It may be posited then that this tension between knowledge as a means to an end and knowledge as an end in itself is integral to the construction of the research university: it is a necessary concomitant of institutionalising the quest for knowledge creation and innovation.

However, despite the occasional rhetorical nod towards the historical precedents for current contests, there is a consistent failure in contemporary debates to map the historical continuities and discontinuities in these disputes with respect to competing imperatives, in order either to ensure autonomy of research or to promote utility of research. Importantly, the narrative of Humboldt's ideal as the animating spirit of modern university renewal has served to naturalize a specific concept of research and repress historically available alternatives.

Thus James Turner in his analyses of the emergence of the American graduate school in the late nineteenth century argues that:

> our present notions of research and what it implies are not self-evident, not "natural." They have a history, from which "research," as we use the word, gets its meaning. And unless we recover that history as best we can, we will never understand very well just what it is we all are ultimately about when we do "research."[12]

For Turner one of the repressed "paths not taken" in the adoption of a research ideal was that of "common erudition." He presents this as an alternative research ideal derived from philology the "great nineteenth-century model of scholarship," which provided a counterpoint to the emergent hegemony of the "specialized-disciplinary" research ideal which later came to dominate, and today appears as the only legitimate, indeed *natural*, model of research. The key feature of the general-erudition ideal is described as follows:

> Philology spawned an ideal of research quite different from that in physics or astronomy. Rather than subdividing the map of knowledge into specialized territories, it encouraged efforts to situate information within the broad boundaries of entire civilizations or cultures. Rather than erecting methodological barriers that made it hard for non-specialists to pursue learning, it tended to push all sorts of diverse knowledge together into a common arena, accessible to any curious inquirer.[13]

The value of remembering such *paths not taken* as a consequence of the construction of a disciplinary ecology of specialised research cultures is clear. It is imperative that research through practice in the visual arts, in keeping with the expansive remit of contemporary art, should seek to reconnect with such alternate visions of research. The expansive purview of contemporary art might be described as a rampant desire—in the wake of conceptualism, minimalism and pop—to thematize everything and anything that offers itself in experience. But whether or not one accepts this description of contemporary art, it is apparent that a narrow discipline-specific conception of visual art is at odds with the breadth of practice and the multiplicity of engagement evident in current art.

Second Thesis

The PhD is a contingent, multiply determined construct which has historically been applied—through the action of metaphorical transfer—across divergent knowledge domains. In those transfers the construct has been modified. The PhD has been used variously as a means of establishing an institutional identity for disciplinary distinctness and as a means of policing disciplinary boundaries. Recognition of these salient operational features of doctoral research practices can be used to re-frame our understanding of the task of developing, implementing and evaluating cogent PhD processes for visual arts practices.

The Doctorate has been awarded by universities since the thirteenth century; however, as most commentators acknowledge, it has profoundly changed in character in the modern era. For most of its history the practice was to award Doctorates in specific subject areas—Doctor of Law, Doctor of Theology—but in the early nineteenth century a new award, the Doctorate of Philosophy (PhD) emerged as an award for achievement in research as opposed to distinction in scholarship. From its origins in Germany, the PhD spread slowly, and was particularly resisted, for eaxample, in some British universities. A recent British report on professional doctorate awards notes that "[i]t is salutary to recognize that in the early years of the last century, there were many voices raised in favor of the view that research obstructed the core university activities of scholarship and teaching."[14]

In the transfer of the Doctorate across national systems and subject areas, the PhD construct evolved, changed and diversified. Noting the adoption of the PhD within the American system from 1860 onwards[15] Cowen observes that "the doctorate was an extra layer on a system with very varied standards."[16] He goes on to note that in "ways that reverberate with the 1990s" the system of the PhD as the award marking a kind of "completion" of studies and certification of the professional teacher was consolidated "under pressure of working out international equivalences" between the US, and Britain and Germany. This contingent pattern of development has later been presented as a teleological process implying an inevitability to the emergence of the PhD. Intriguingly, Cowen points to the First World War—and the attempt by Britain to establish its universities as alternate destinations for American émigré students—as a formative moment in the emergence of a cohesive British PhD system: "the Foreign Office itself building on a movement within the universities, assisted in encouraging the creation of a PhD structure."[17]

In the process of narrating the professionalization of American university historians in the late 19th century, Novick disabuses the hoary myth of the German PhD system: "American students in Germany generally received the doctorate within two years of their arrival, usually for a very brief dissertation based on printed sources—hardly more than what would later count as a seminar paper."[18] He goes on to note that while universities providing the PhD may have conceived of themselves as "centers from which scholarly missionaries poured forth," they often were little more than "service stations for legitimation."

Within the German system the subject areas of chemistry and history were pivotal domains for working out the PhD system: chemistry established the relationship between the PhD and advanced research training in the service of technological and economic development while history established the institution of the seminar (as exemplified in Ranke's famous research seminar and the training of his students in the rigours of source criticism) and the priority of the *Doktorvater* relationship. In the migration of the PhD construct across subject areas the diverse aspects of this genealogy have been activated in different ways at different times. For example the PhD has been used as an instrument in constructing disciplinary legitimacy and distinction. Thus the accession of disciplines such as English literary studies or Area Studies to the status of discrete departments within university structures was bound up with the construction of a PhD process specific to these domains and the reciprocal construction of these disciplines as areas of appropriate application for the PhD award.[19]

Robert Scholes, describing the disciplinary constitution of English in his account of *The Rise and Fall of English*, observes that:

The English department as we know it was in place in the first decade of [the 20th] century... All that happened in the ensuing decades was growth... Along with growth came increasing specialization and professionalisation, as the doctorate and Germanic methods began to dominate instruction.[20]

The consequence of the attempt to achieve equivalence with the professional standing of established disciplines—to implement the doctoral system of study—was "to add intellectual stiffening" to the curriculum. This "intellectual stiffening"—the requisite rigor for realization of the PhD—is presented by Scholes as the engine of the theoretical oscillations of literary study from rhetoric to philology, New Criticism, structuralism, and poststructuralism, and from there back to rhetoric. More recently, this early twentieth-century strategy for achieving disciplinary legitimacy through adoption of the PhD and related disciplinary trappings has prompted a critical reaction. Sosnoski asserts: "In my view, disciplinarity—a condition wherein control over the production of knowledge is gained by training in methods... has shown itself to be a dubious rationale for literary studies."[21] The problem Sosnoski proposes—echoing Turner's formulation of the countervailing tendency of the philological research ideal—is that these disciplinary formulae are indebted to an inappropriate model of science, a model at odds with the subject area, but inherent in the disciplinary constitution of any subject domain.

Even as the PhD has become the accepted apprenticeship into research within the academy, and has become a prerequisite for academic jobs in most fields, it has continued to be transformed by larger change-processes such as developments in research-funding targets,the systematic implementation of research-audit processes, the emergence of various "fourth level" paradigms of PhD research training, the emergence of "taught" doctoral programs, and the proliferation of internationally coordinated sub-disciplinary specialisms. Thus, as one example of change, within the sciences doctoral studies have often been incorporated into broad team-based research initiatives whereby the individual doctoral candidate pursues a sub-strand of inquiry completely dependent upon an ongoing multi-institutional and international research project. A system of post-doctoral stages has also been elaborated within this framework, so that along with the proliferation of doctoral awards, there has also been a tendency to construct higher credentials by means of these "post-doctoral" categories. This has also been adopted in certain areas of the humanities and social sciences.

Evidently the PhD is a contingent construct: it has a certain malleability, it is clearly a historically dynamic and multiply determined construct, but it is also the bearer of a genealogy that tends to prioritize a potentially narrow conception of intellectual system and method. It is clear that the development of the PhD in visual arts practice may serve simply to consolidate disciplinary-territory construction. On the other hand, the metaphorical transfer of the concept may be taken as an opportunity to creatively redeploy the diverse meanings and variable heritages of the construct. Tuomas Nevanlinna of the Helsinki School of Art, speaking at a conference on this issue in the Netherlands, made a similar observation: "Transplanting the terminology of a science policy rife with 'doctoral theses,' 'dissertations' and 'research' is not and cannot be an innocent, value-free process."[22] However, he went on to point out that: "Nevertheless, and this is the most important point, the idea of artistic research also opens up opportunities and possibilities." Thus the potential of a radical rethinking of both the PhD and the research ideal in concert—in the context of a critical genealogical analysis—is the opening up of creative possibilities as yet undisclosed by audit-driven and policy-mandated research programs. In this respect the Northern European example of practice-based doctoral programs developed by institutions such as the Helsinki Academy recommend themselves as exemplars in a way that is different from many of the models that have emerged in the UK system in the 1990s, which was driven by the state-led audit processes of the Research Assessment Exercise, an uninterrogated acceptance of the disciplinary system of knowledges, and the concomitant economy of domain expertise.

Third Thesis

It is through overcoming institutionalized amnesia in respect to prior historical debates in respect of university practices that we may re-contextualize and broaden contemporary debate on artistic research and the PhD.

This is simply a general consequence of the first and second theses. The important issue here is the recommendation that the visual arts do not simply enact a moment of disciplinary mimicry in an attempt to purchase greater institutional standing, enhanced legitimacy, or expanded access to resources. (All these benefits accrue to an enhanced "research" profile in the subject area, as evidenced by the last decade of research investment in the UK.)

It has been noted that the university evolved through key phases of renewal and expansion in the course of the late 19th and 20th centuries. A notable phase of development took place from the 1880s through to the 1920s when the proliferation of departmental and disciplinary distinctions generated the conventional organizational structure and subject-matter divisions that characterise the modern university. As identified above, a key instrument in forging disciplinary divisions was the extension of the PhD construct and its deployment against specific domains. It is notable that once these organizational novelties were established they took on an aspect of inevitability and an appearance of being immutable. A characteristic feature of this process is the institutional amnesia manifest in the subsequent construal of the newly established organizational processes as natural, self-evident and *ahistorically* given.

This naturalized ecology of the disciplines operated throughout the twentieth century so that by the post-WWII period disciplines such as economics, history, English, sociology and so forth appeared as normative and as it were "native" to the university while such disciplinary innovations as "area studies" and "comparative literature" were required to justify themselves with reference to the normative standards and operational practices of these established disciplines in order to achieve legitimacy within the formal organization of knowledge. With the advent of "mission science" — such as the Manhattan Project and the Apollo programs — the disciplinary ecologies of the sciences began to be challenged, and the need for interdisciplinarity became a recurrent theme in university debates and policy discussions. Thus in the latter third of the 20th century the order of university departments and disciplines was subject to critique, renewal and rationalization in the service of often conflicting agendas.

The disciplinary ecology of the contemporary university is thus unstable and, historically speaking, of very recent origin. While this system, as it yields to pressures for interdisciplinary, transdisciplinary and multidisciplinary initiatives, may be a creative resource for contemporary art, it should not be taken as a fixed horizon within which to construct a discrete disciplinary identity: this would be both to ignore history and to renege on the intellectual and critical promise of contemporary art practices.

The institutional imperative — to reproduce and conserve the institution — must not be overlooked. Educators, especially educators in self-proclaimed creative practices, are attracted to a vision of themselves as agents of dynamic change and critical renewal, as bearers of cultural values which are variously above the exchange system of the market place or connected to some essential human and humanising propensity. However, it is important to register the essentially conservative force of institutionalized education: education is a key apparatus in social reproduction. While the socially reproductive aspect of education does not exhaustively specify educational processes, it is very important that we do not underestimate the consequence of the institutionalized self-regard that tenured professional intellectuals (with control of the accreditation of domain expertise) may be prone to adopt in any new disciplinary dispensation.

There is a profound lesson to be learned from the 19th Century German model of the research university, which has so captured the imagination of the contemporary research university when it comes to positing its own identity and history. That lesson is extolled in Fritz Ringer's remarkable work on *The Decline of the German Mandarins* (1969) which maps the terrible failure of these cadres of professional intellectuals to critically interrogate their own assumptions, practices and positions when faced by a broader reorientation of social and political realities outside the university. The mandarin intellectuals who claimed a morally formative role for their espoused research ideal found themselves "transported into a social and cultural environment which challenged all their values."[23] In not properly addressing themselves to the credentializing and socially reproductive role of the education they provided, these mandarins elected to cultivate an escapist vision of their role as bearers of essential values beyond the taint of the common market place. In so doing they ironically "prepared the grounds for the anti-intellectualism that finally overwhelmed them."

In expanding the reach of the PhD system into contemporary art practice, we must not be blind to the attempt to arrogate a degree of control of an extramural system of value to the university. On the other hand, we must be alert to the inherent conservatism of educational practices and the tendency of educational institutions to direct, contain and even dissipate the creative impulses of its student cohorts.

Fourth Thesis

Criticism cuts both ways. The PhD provides an opportunity for— and indeed makes necessary—a critically reflexive pedagogy. The ongoing interrogation of the supervisor's role is the precondition— or at the very least the corollary condition—of developing the reflexive doctoral practitioner.

A key theme in the development of doctoral programs in art practice is that of critical reflection—the enigmatic figure of the reflexive practitioner may be said to stalk the doctoral art studio in search of the equally enigmatic trophy of methodological rigor. Amid the calls for critically reflexive practice as the constitutive moment of the practice-based doctoral research process, there may well be a failure to enact a critically reflexive moment and interrogate the disciplinary ambitions of academically ensconced practitioners and commentators. The PhD process—if pursued by a critically re-flexive institution, one that practices what it teaches—should work to transform and even at times to delegitimize aspects of current pedagogical and organizational practices within the academy. In this regard there is much to be learned from the tradition of in-stitutional critique within contemporary art practices which have examined the dilemma of critically interrogating the conditions of possibility of their own engagement. Artists such as Hans Haacke, Fred Wilson, Barbara Kruger (to take only one narrow strand of practice)—with their interrogation of the interrelationships of cul-tural capital and *actual* capital—have necessarily encountered per-formative contradictions in their own enactment of the paradoxes of cultural patronage. The work of the reflexive pedagogue will have to engage this kind of performative contradiction in a creative manner. Again, it is a question of acknowledging the precedents from multiple domains, not so as to duplicate strategies, but in or-der to invent alternative ones.

James Sosnoski, making a similar argument about the tension between institution and avowed critical intentions, describes a sce-nario where a PhD candidate in literary studies is confronted by a line of questioning as to the definition of "deconstruction." She responds by indicating the instability of the term, and she notes Derrida's strategy of refusing fixity in the play of meanings. The ex-aminer counters by asking how it is then that a definition has been provided in a standard literary studies textbook. The candidate fac-es a dilemma. On the one hand to suggest that the cited author is in error is to open up the problem of the proprieties of the discipline, and lead ultimately to questions of the legitimacy of the institution into which legitimated access is sought through the exam. On the other hand to suggest that while definitions in textbooks are all very well, but for all that, words in practice continue to shift and remain unfixed, would seem to suggest that the deconstructive criticism that the student advocated would undermine the discipline of liter-ary study, and thus open up a further trail of desolation. In reciting this anecdote, Sosnoski remarks on the way in which the research supervisor intervenes and removes the question by noting that the candidate cannot be held responsible for the emergent potential contradictions between the contents of criticism and established in-stitutional arrangements. Sosnoski reads the situation as one where there is the possibility of operating in bad faith:

On the one hand, he [the supervisor] was acknowledging that there were incompatibilities between the postmodern theories he advised his candidate to study and the modern institution of criti-cism his colleague was bent on upholding; but, on the other hand, he was conducting an exam presupposing meanings stable enough to be construed as adequate, reliable, or correct answers. He seemed complicitous in the routine identification of stable meaning, despite his adherence to a theory of language that made such identifications dubious.[24]

The coping strategies adopted here in the face of the performative contradictions of critical practice within the institutional setting are such as to leave everything intact: the critical process has no traction as such with the institutional practice. Given the extraordinary richness and complexity of the critical practice genealogies of contemporary art—everything from Marcel Duchamp to Olafur Eliasson, from Adrian Piper to Fiona Tan—it should be a goal of the PhD supervision process to find alternate strategies to engage, if not overcome, this impasse between criticism and its institution. The potential failure to take hold of this opportunity is apparent in one of the characteristic *topos* of the practice-based PhD debate: the protracted rehearsal of the relationships between the artifactual and textual components in the practice-based research PhD outcome. The following itemizing of questions may be taken as indicative of this general discourse:

> [H]ow do you produce or examine a PhD?... Should the artwork be assessed in relation to contemporary art practice or should it be viewed as a thesis in images? Does the theoretical or intellectual investigation take place in relation to practice, or through the accompanying text? Does the artwork, like academic research, put forward a hypothesis and demonstrate a mastery of a canon or should the emphasis be placed upon technical ability and if so, how is technical ability judged? Should practice-based doctoral students be expected to write [a dissertation] of the same proficiency as conventional PhD students?[25]

On the one hand this kind of discourse that worries at the textual proprieties of the "dissertation" seems so remote from critical practice—so alienated from the texture, density and challenge of contemporary art practice—and on the other hand this debate on the role of the text has consistently failed to opportune the fertile possibilities opened by the textual turn manifest across the humanities in recent decades. It is arguable that the most vital intellectual ferment in the university in recent decades has been the multiply played-out "textual turn" whereby the familiar models of writing, reading, meaning and communication have been subject to a range of critical revisions, rejections and renewals: everything from Austin's *performatives* to Foucault's *discourse;* from Gadamer's *hermeneutics* to Derrida's *deconstruction;* from Rom Harre's *discursive mind* to Wayne C. Booth's *rhetoric.* The text in the imagination of this earnest discourse on "the role of the text in the practice PhD" is most often the pre-theoretical univocal expressive utterance of the self-present subject. It is to be expected of course that the intellectual credentials of such PhD submissions is often to be purchased on the back of endless citations of these very same author-names: Foucault, Derrida, Gadamer, Deleuze, and so forth.

A contingent twist on this discourse is provided by the extramural turn to discursivity manifest across a range of contemporary art practices and evident in both mainstream and marginal artworld contexts. Thus in 2005, London's *Frieze* Art Fair announced as one of the fair's events: "Ian Wilson: A Discussion."

In 1968 Ian Wilson made his final Sculpture. Since then he has used the unseen abstractions of language as his art form. Today Wilson's ideas are expressed as a series of philosophical discussions with the audience. These "Discussions" are an extended work in progress about the possibilities of knowledge and allow the audience the opportunity to present their own views, and to question, propose, interject and debate.[26]

This is typical of the discursive turn that characterizes an entire swathe of recent art practice. After conceptualism's embrace of the discursive, there was in the nineteen eighties and nineties a further inflection of the discursive with the question of social inclusivity. This is evident in such initiatives as the *Hirsch Farm Project.* Described by Bruce Barber as "probably the purist example of communicative action *in actio,*" the project describes itself as "an arts based think tank concerned with public art, the environment and community."[27] The project brings together individuals from a "wide range of disciplines to meet in camera for a period of a week to discuss specific topics." Indicative of the momentum of this discursive turn is the adoption of "the dynamics of how artists and other professionals communicate with a specified audience or community, and how these intentions are received" as the topic of the 1992 gathering at a farm in Northbrook, Illinois. In the last decade, there has been a further inflection of the discursive turn in the curious interpenetration of critiques of authorship, the ascendancy of the curatorial gesture as locus of debate and the multiple orchestrations of conferences, dialogues, interviews, debates and conversations all various construed as art works. (It is in part with reference to this discursive turn that it seemed appropriate earlier to speak of contemporary art's rampant desire to thematize everything inexperience.)

Given this contingent circumstance outside the university—
and it may well be that this image of the outside-and-inside of the
university is a much more permeable affair—it is remarkable to
find that the familiar "role of the text in the practice PhD" has so
consistently avoided treating the question of the textual, of the utterance, as immanent to contemporary art practice. On the other
hand it is important to caution against a simple embrace or celebration of this discursive turn. There is an equally important recourse
to the "thingly" manifest in contemporary practice also. But this
simply reinforces the point, that the questions of word-world relationships—the multifarious rhetoric of practices and of things—
are pervasively immanent within contemporary art practice: we
should seek our answers and questions—our stuff of thinking and
doing—there, and not in uncritical bureaucratic operational discourses: Not: "How can we grade this?" but "Wow, what the hell is
this thing happening here, now?" and finally "How can we change
to meet this?"

Notes

1 Donald Schön, *Educating The Reflective Practitioner* (San Francisco: Jossey-
Baas Publishers, 1987), 4.
2 Fritz Ringer, *The Decline of the German Mandarins: The German Academic
Community, 1890-1933* (Hanover and London: Weslyan University Press, 1997
[1969]), 7.
3 This conventional narrative has been challenged in certain respects
in recent years see for instance Sylvia Paletschek (2001) "The Invention of
Humboldt and the Impact of National Socialism: The German University Idea
in the First half of the Twentieth Century."
4 J. Ben David, *Centers of Learning: Britain, France, Germany, United States*
(New York: McGraw Hill, 1977), 22; R. Cowen, "Comparative Perspectives
on the British PhD" in *Working for a Doctorate*, edited by Graves and Varma
(London: Routedge, 1997), 188.
5 There is a long tradition of essays on the "idea of the University" including most famously Cardinal Newman's contribution. In Germany, where this
has been most prominent, the tradition includes contributions from figures
such as Karl Jaspers who produced three different texts under this heading
during his long publishing career. Heidegger's infamous rectoral address at
Freiburg has also been identified with this genre also.
6 A. B. Giamatti, *A Free and Ordered Space: The Real World of the University*
(New York: W. W. Norton & Company, 1988), 48-49.
7 Neil L. Rudenstine, "The Future of the Research University," in "The
Future of the Research University: a Harvard Magazine Roundtable," edited
by Ethan Bronner, *Harvard Magazine* September-Octpber 2000, pp. 46-57, 102-
05; especially 47-48.
8 Kerr originated the terms "multiversity" and "knowledge factory" in respect of the university. Kerr, as President of UC Berkley and theorist of the

new university for industry was one of the targets of the polemical critique developed by the Berkley Free Speech Movement in the mid-1960s. (Johnson, 2000; Douglass, 2000)

9 M. B. Katz, *Reconstructing American Education* (Cambridge MA: Harvard University Press, 1987), 161-2.

10 Gerhard Casper, "Come the Millennium, Where the University?" 1995, at www.stanford.edu/dept/pres-provost/president/speeches/.

11 Traditionally von Humboldt's innovations at Berlin are seen as standing in contrast with the tradition of the University of Halle, and that institution's commitments to training for the professions and to "advance the wordly practical purposes of men and the benefit of society." See Ringer, *The Decline of the German Mandarins*.

12 J. Turner, *Language, Religion, Knowledge* (Notre Dame IN: Notre Dame University Press, 2003), 106.

13 Turner, *Language, Religion, Knowledge*, 100.

14 UK Council for Graduate Education (2002), *Professonal Doctorates*.

15 The first PhD was awarded in 1861 by Yale.

16 Cowen, "Comparative Perspectives on the British PhD."

17 Cowen, "Comparative Perspectives on the British PhD," 190.

18 P. Novick, "That Noble Dream: The "Objectivity Question" and the American Historical Profession, Cambridge and New York: Cambridge University Press, 1988), 48.

19 In an interesting treatment of comparative literature, titled *Death of A Discipline* (2003), Gayatri Chakravorty Spivak summarily notes the contingent processes shaping the formation of disciplines such as area studies and comparative literature: "these two institutional enterprises can perhaps be recounted as follows. Area Studies were established to secure U.S. power in the Cold War. Comparative Literature was a result of European intellectuals fleeing 'totalitarian' regimes." (p. 3).

20 R. Scholes, *The Rise and Fall of English* (New Haven CT and London: Yale University Press, 1998), 11.

21 J. Sosnoski, *Modern Skeletons in Postmodern Closets* ([   ], 1995), 35.

22 was *Artistic Research*, edited by Annette Balkema and Henk Slager, in the series *Lier en Bloog* [Dutch Society for Aesthetics], vol. 18 (Amsterdam: Rodopi, 2004), 81.

23 Ringer, *The Decline of the German Mandarins*, 448.

24 Sosnoski, *Modern Skeletons in Postmodern Closets*, 8.

25 Fiona Candlin (2000) "A Proper Anxiety? Practice-based PhDs and Academic Unease", *Working Papers in Art and Design*, volume 1; www.herts.ac.uk/artdes1/research/papers/wpades/vol1/candlin2full.html

26 See *Frieze Art Fair Yearbook 2005-6*, London.

27 See www.imageandtext.org.nz/bruce_work_squat_essays.html.

5

Thoughts On "Research" Degrees in Visual Arts Departments

Victor Burgin

I first had to think about PhD degrees in Visual Arts departments in 2001, on my return to the UK after thirteen years teaching in a Humanities department at the University of California. I responded to such prevailing language as "research-led practice," "practice-led research," "theory-led practice," practice-as-research," "research-artist," and so on, in a position paper for a 2002 meeting of a Goldsmiths College research committee.[1] What follows is drawn mainly from this paper, and perhaps retains something of the surprise of my first encounter with the now familiar phenomenon of doctoral research degrees in art practice. Starting from dictionary definitions that underpin common-sense notions of "research" as "scientific or scholarly investigation" I go on to consider how scientific and scholarly investigation has been pursued in visual arts departments. I then describe the type of research activity that I encounter most often in such departments—one that conforms to neither dictionary definitions nor common-sense. I conclude with a brief consideration of the relation of writing to practice in the particular case of research degrees in audiovisual arts—and with a practical recommendation.

Dictionaries and Common Sense

The word "art" does not appear in dictionary definitions of the word "research." Typically, research is defined as "scientific or scholarly investigation, especially study or experiment aimed at discovery, interpretation or application of facts, theories or laws." Such a definition agrees with common-sense understanding, in which the word "research" may conjure images of white-coated scientists, electron microscopes and particle accelerators. This same common sense would probably allow that the term also apply to the image of a tweed-clad historian, among piles of documents in a dusty archive. In both cases, the outcome of research is assumed to be knowledge—of the cause of the common cold, of the behaviour of electrons, of the causes of the First World War, and so on.[2] Neither dictionaries nor common-sense associate the term "research" with the image of the artist. Picasso declared: "I do not seek, I find." The assertion succinctly confirms common-sense understanding: scientists and scholars "research"; the artist "creates." An informative research project would be to trace the introduction and dissemination of the word "research" in the self-publicity of art departments, and to correlate this discursive history with changes in government policies for Higher Education. I would suppose that the waning of the language of "creativity" and the waxing of the language of "research" has a political, rather than intellectual, cause—to be the consequence of external dictates, rather than of self-searching and self-redefinition within the art schools. Today, typically, one department describes itself as a center for "practice-based research activity," another claims to be "one of the leading centers of studio research practice." It may be that such expressions represent little more than the substitution of the word "research" for the word "creative," while the practices they describe remain largely unchanged. Such terminological evolution—necessary to survival in a potentially hostile political environment—is eccentric to ordinary language use. There is however a history of research initiatives in art departments that do conform to the popular understanding of "research"—a history of initiatives aligned along the axes of "scientific or scholarly investigation."

Scientific Investigation

The association of art and science has a long history. Bernard Berenson complained that the art of the Italian Renaissance suffered from a "fatal tendency to become science." John Constable wished that painting might become a "branch of the natural sciences." The self-styled "laboratory artists" in the Soviet Union of the immediate post-revolutionary period claimed that their work was the equivalent of pure scientific research. The late 1960s saw such initiatives as "Experiments in Art and Technology" (EAT) in the US; and the "Cybernetic Serendipity" exhibition at the ICA, London, presaging current computer-based convergences between art and technology. This history, however, is not cumulative but rather a concatenation of unrelated events. Berenson's remarks apply to contributions by painters to the development of geometrical systems of perspectival representation. Constable was speaking, in the context of the aesthetic ideology of Realism, in favour of an "objective" representation of atmospheric effects. The "laboratory artists" found political and artistic asylum in the Western market for non-representational art. EAT prospered only so long as corporate sponsors could be led to hope for a return on their investment. In an essay published in 1980, the art historian and critic Jack Burnham, who was closely involved in the major art and technology projects of the late 1960s, gives a retrospective account of his own experience of EAT: "While EAT and other art groups held out the boon of 'new discoveries' to corporations funding them, most companies were cynical and wise enough to realize that the research abilities of nearly all artists are nil."[3]

Scholarly Investigation

The modern art school owes its very existence to scholarship. In the Middle Ages, the arts were divided into "liberal arts" and "mechanical arts." The former were intellectual disciplines taught in universities, the latter were manual skills taught in artisanal guilds. In the Renaissance, painting began to be considered a liberal art by virtue of the superior learning then required of the painter—primarily in geometry, anatomy and literature (mainly classical mythology and biblical texts). In the Baroque era this change in status was used by painters in Paris to justify their secession from their crafts guild, the Maîtrise, to form the first art academy. The 1648 *Académie* inaugurated the modern art school by bringing theoretical and practical knowledge together in a coherent teaching. This newly intellectual status of art was confirmed and consolidated in the other discursive-institutional inventions of the seventeenth and eighteenth centuries—aesthetics, art history, art criticism, and so on—to form the foundations of the modern art institution. In effect, the teaching of the first academy was a response to the question: "What does an artist need to know to establish the basis of a literate and informed practice?" In 1973 I joined the Polytechnic of Central London, School of Communication, with the brief of designing the academic component of a three-year B.A. (Hons.) course in Film and Photography. My colleagues and I set out to answer the question: "What does a student need to know to establish the basis of a literate and informed practice in film and photography?" The course that was subsequently approved and taught was based on three components: history (knowledge of the evolution of changing forms of film and photography), sociology (knowledge of the socio-institutional context, and political economy, of film and photography), and semiotics and psychoanalysis (knowledge of the construction and derivation of meaning and affect in photographs and films). These three types of knowledge formed the basis of a history and theory curriculum that occupied fifty percent of the three-year undergraduate course. Inevitably, ideas and terminology from this curriculum entered the studio "crit session," but scholarly research in history and theory was never confused with the practices of critical debate in which it might be deployed: each area was recognised as possessing its own discursive specificity and criteria of legitimacy. Some students who completed the BA "theory-practice" course at PCL went on to write PhD dissertations in university Humanities departments. Today, they would have the option of studying for a PhD degree in a Visual Arts department.

Three Types of Candidate

It should be self-evident that those setting foot on the PhD degree track in a visual arts department should not be conspicuously less well-prepared than their counterparts in any other department of the university. They should be already trained—or self-educated— up to at least a minimally acceptable BA level of literacy and proficiency in the field (anthropology, sociology, semiotics, history, and so on) where they most clearly locate their intellectual interests and arguments. Training "from scratch" is the job of an undergraduate course, not a graduate program. Students should be supervised by appropriately qualified faculty. If such faculty are not available from within the visual arts department itself, arrangements should be made to enrol supervisors from other departments. A PhD program may provide a supportive environment for a type of candidate who is both an accomplished visual artist and who not only wants to write, but is capable of writing, a long dissertation.

Another type of candidate is one who received a thorough introduction to a specialist academic literature as an undergraduate, but has little experience of practical work in visual arts. This candidate is primarily interested in producing a written thesis, but seeks the close contact with an environment of art production that few humanities departments can provide.

A third type of student is one who makes works of art and who also reads enthusiastically. This student is interested in ideas, and turns concepts encountered in reading into practical projects. The research of this type of candidate typically has a mainly practical outcome, with academic work playing a subordinate and "instrumental" role. For example, I was once introduced to a student who, after reading Bachelard (and my own book) on the concept of space, made an installation of stuffed toys that he turned inside out—so that all their electronics, and other hidden details, became their exterior surface. There is nothing in either Bachelard or in my own work to recommend this treatment of stuffed toys, but if this person had not read the theory he might not have thought of doing this. This instrumental use of theory has a respectable history. For example, in 1624 Claudio Monteverdi composed the Combattimento di Tancredi e Clorinda and, in so doing, launched a revolutionary new musical style. In his introduction to the published version of this work, Monteverdi said that he had been prompted to invent this new style (stile concitato) by his reading of medical treatises. According to the medical theories of his day, there were three distinct "humors" produced by corresponding bodily states—love, tranquility and anger. Monteverdi was struck by the fact that there were extant madrigal forms to express the first two, but not the third. This got him thinking, and the Combattimento was the result. If Monteverdi had been embarking on a PhD, he would have been concerned with such things as the origins of the theory of humors in such classical sources as Galen and Aristotle; or he might have launched a critique of the idea by invoking the authority of such contemporary thinkers as Harvey, in England. His thesis might have affected the evolution of medical science in Italy, but it would not have given us the stile concitato. What is most appealing about the Monteverdi relation to "imported" theory is the fact that the result (here, a musical work) is independent of the provoking idea. Medical science today probably takes a dim view of the doctrine of humors, but this has no consequence for the appreciation of Monteverdi's music. The student eviscerating stuffed toys reads cultural theory the way Monteverdi read medical treatises. He was unable to tell me the title of the book he had read by Bachelard, nor was he able (greater cruelty) to remember the title of my own book. It had clearly not occurred to him to wonder whether there was agreement or contradiction between my own arguments and those of Bachelard, or what (if anything) Bachelard's use of the word "psychoanalysis" has to do with the Freudianism of my own work. But these are precisely the kinds of issues he would have had to deal with—given his declared point of departure in the two texts—if he had been writing a PhD. This "third type" of student is in my experience the most commonly encountered kind on a visual arts PhD degree course. The question in respect of such students is not "Are they engaged in research?"—clearly they are—the question is rather: "How are they to be assessed?" But visual arts departments confidently assessed such students before the coming of the PhD. Throughout the history of art the finished "work of art" has represented the culmination of a process of research; a large part of the routine work of artists is a work of research. Although the shift from a language of "creativity" to a language of "research" may confuse that part of common-sense inherited from nineteenth-century Romanticism it is otherwise easily justified historically. The question of whether visual art production constitutes research is not a significant issue. The substantive issue for visual arts departments now is the widespread inability or disinclination to clearly distinguish between an art work and a written thesis, a tendency to obfuscate or ignore the differing specifics of two distinct forms of practice.

Audiovisual Art Practice: An Exceptional Case?

It might be objected that the audiovisual arts are an exceptional case, one that cannot be considered within the same terms as such static objects as paintings and photographs. Audiovisual works, it may be argued—films, videos or some other form—are already discursively articulated; they not only incorporate language (as dialogue, voice-over, intertitle, and so on) but are quasi-linguistic in their very form. The analogy between language and cinema, for example, has been explored with particular rigour in structuralist film theory, not least in the work of Christian Metz. It might be argued that if audiovisual forms are inherently discursive, then an intellectual argument can equally well be presented in the form of a film or video as in a more conventional written form. Let us suppose that students in a philosophy class are set the task of writing a critical essay in response to a passage of their choice from Plato. In place of an essay, one of the students submits a DVD containing a film she has made. The film shows two women talking together in a domestic interior: one is ironing, the other is smoking a cigarette. Later, the woman who was ironing is seen putting on her makeup while still conversing with her friend. The women talk of the relationship between morality and self-interest, and between the dominant and the subordinate classes. The instructor in the philosophy class recognises the conversation as an adaptation of the dialogue between Socrates and Callicles in Plato's *Gorgias*. The instructor is both engaged and entertained by the video, but refuses to accept it in place of an essay. The student protests that her mise-en-scène of the Socratic dialogue in a space of domestic labour constitutes a feminist critique of Plato's text. She says that by conflating the space of the agora with that of the *gynaecaeum* she has exposed the fact that the discourse of Plato's male protagonists— ostensibly concerned with absolute universal truths—is in fact historically contingent. The instructor replies that to expose this fact is not to *argue* it; although the film provocatively and successfully suggests the basis of an argument, it does not *make* the argument. The example I have just given is not entirely hypothetical. The film exists, as the first of the three parts that comprise Anne-Marie Miéville's *Nous sommes tous encore ici* (1997). Miéville's film was variously received, but none of the reviews I read treated it as a philosophical commentary on Plato.

In a series of conversations between Derrida and Bernard Stiegler, first published in 1996, Stiegler raises the question of evolving supports of knowledge from the book to such multi-media supports as the DVD. Modern historians, for example, may draw upon such archival materials as documentary films—why should they not incorporate audio-visual materials in the final form of presentation of their research? The discussion of this issue leads Derrida to the question of the relation of writing to multi-media in the educational context. He recalls that in the course of his teaching in California he invited the students in his seminar "to propose a text upon a corpus of their choosing, in the usual form of a paper," Two of the students submitted videocassettes they had made in place of a paper:

Derrida: "My inclination was to accept this innovation... I did not accept [it], however, because I had the impression, in reading or in watching their production, that what I expected from a discourse, from a theoretical elaboration, had suffered from this passage to the image. I did not refuse the image because it was the image, but because it had come to substitute itself in a somewhat crude way for what I think one could have and should have elaborated more precisely with discourse or with writing. A difficult negotiation. I did not want to seem reactionary and backward-looking by saying to them: 'No, you have to send me that on paper,' but at the same time, I did not want to give way on requirements, apparently more traditional, to which I continue to hold. So I wrote them a letter to tell them, in substance, this: 'OK. I am not against that in principle, but there has to be as much demonstrative power, theoretical power, etc., in your videocassette, as there would be in a good paper. At that time, we can talk about it again.'"

Stiegler: "*A scholarly, if not scientific, practice of the image... broadly spread throughout the University... does not yet exist, but it will have to come.*"

Derrida: "It has to be encouraged, but provided that it does not come at too high a price, provided that rigour, differentiation, refinement do not suffer too much as a result... That is what I said to them... when I explained: 'If your film had been accompanied—or articulated with—a discourse refined according to the norms that matter to me, then I would have been more receptive, but this was not the case, what you are proposing to me is coming *in the place of* discourse but does not adequately *replace* it.'"[4]

A Practical Recommendation

There should be three distinct kinds of "terminal degree" in visual arts: a PhD with a "parenthetical notation" in history and theory, a PhD with a parenthetical notation in practice, and a Doctor of Fine Arts degree.

The "PhD (history and theory emphasis)" would require a dissertation comparable in length and scholarly depth to a PhD in a Humanities department, and might often involve the student in working between two departments, for example, between Visual Arts and Anthropology, or Visual Arts and History. For purposes of assessment, emphasis would be primarily on the written text. The purpose of the practical work required for this degree would be mainly to establish a first-hand familiarity with the technical and formal aspects of the type of practice discussed in the dissertation—providing a level of intimacy with visual art production which could not be achieved in a traditional Humanities department.

To satisfy the requirements of the "PhD (practice emphasis)" the student would produce both a long written essay—albeit half the length required for the history and theory emphasis—and a substantial body of practical work. For assessment there would be equal emphasis on the writing and the visual work. Various models might be proposed for an appropriate relation between the two. The model I have called "What do I need to know?" allows for genuinely "practice led" research in that the writing contextualizes the practical work, offering critical insights into the history of the art practice in question, and critically interrogating the various theories that may inform and legitimate it. The resulting thesis would be assessed on its independent merits, and should advance arguments that may be applied beyond the confines of the author's own practical work. An "artist's statement," no matter how lengthy, would not be acceptable.

The "Doctor of Fine Arts" degree (DFA) would meet the requirements of those students who wish to do further work beyond the MFA, who are interested in ideas and draw upon historical and theoretical writings, but have little aptitude for, or interest in, constructing lengthy written arguments. For purposes of assessment, emphasis would be on the practical work. For the final examination, these students would submit short essays, notes and bibliographies, rather than a structured thesis.

A "Bottom Line"

Students enrolled on PhD degree courses in visual arts departments are required to submit both the visual and the written results of their research for examination. However, there is almost universal confusion in respect of the status of the written component of the degree. Most damagingly, there are widely differing conceptions of the quality of intellectual argument and written expression that is acceptable at PhD level—not only between different departments, but between different faculty within the same department. If this current state of affairs continues that can only undermine student morale and public confidence in the value not only of research degrees in visual arts but of PhD degrees in general. The university is charged with the training and institutional legitimation of those who will transmit knowledge and critical and analytical skills to the succeeding generation. To adopt the tripartite structure I have suggested would be a minimal concession to the gravity of this responsibility.

Notes

1 My paper was not discussed on that, or any subsequent, occasion.

2 A distinction would be made between the types of knowledge produced—science offering, in this popular view, sure and certain knowledge; the findings of the humanities seen as perpetually subject to debate.

3 Jack Burnham, "Art and Technology: The Panacea That Failed," in *Video Culture: A Critical Investigation*, edited by John Hanhardt (Rochester: Visual Studies Workshop, 1986), 243.

4 Derrida and Stiegler, *Échographies de la télévision* (Paris: Galilée-INA, 1996), 158-60. Translated as *Echographies of television* (Polity, 2000), 141-43.

6

The Studio Art Doctorate In America

Timothy Emlyn Jones

In the last few years the debate of studio art doctorates in the US has progressed by a step change, largely due to the interventions of AICAD, CAA, and NASAD.[1] When I first spoke in the US about doctorates in studio art at the 2003 AICAD Symposium, I encountered the widely held negative response, *why do this thing for which there is no place and no demand?*[2] My response was to suggest that the introduction of studio art doctorates in many countries in Europe, as well as in Australia, New Zealand, and China had brought fine art education to its coming of age, on a par with and different from other university level disciplines. Indeed, at that time the US was the only part of the English-speaking world not to have studio art doctorates. Against this, I was told that, as the acknowledged "terminal degree," the MFA does for art everything that the PhD does for other disciplines in higher education. However, it was apparent that the status of the MFA as a terminal degree was already in doubt in many US universities, where it was well understood that the different academic levels of these two degrees sets them distinctively apart. Conventionally, a Masters represents new perceptions of the current state of knowledge in the subject while a Doctorate represents new knowledge or significant contributions to understanding in the subject: not the same thing at all.

The case against PhDs in studio art in America has rested more on the anxiety of academics worrying that they might need to go back to art school to regain their credentials as teachers than on any academic grounds. Indeed, this was the premise of the session "The MFA and the PhD: Torque in the Workplace" at the 2006 CAA Conference in Boston, where I was invited to act as discussant. (This short essay is based on my comments then.[3]) When speaking on this topic in Boston—only three years after my Los Angeles talk [mentioned in the Introduction to this book]—I found a markedly different response. Some universities had already accredited

PhDs in studio art and media and many more, including some of America's most prestigious independent art schools were deeply engaged in their development. The question *how?* had become the operative one in place of the question *why?* Attitudes seemed to have changed big time in only three years, as has the availability of published literature on the subject.[4] However, despite this obvious progress, the American debate of art doctorates still has one foot in the defensive realm of anxiety and the other in the imaginative realm of progress. As a European it is fascinating to see these two dimensions of American culture in tension with each other and I will be interested to see which prevails.

Rather than dwelling on any negative dimension of the culture of the art world, I would look for the American quality of an art doctorate—for it is on that front that education in American art schools and university art departments may be advanced. How the American doctorate might differ from and surpass its UK counterpart that is strongly influenced by the Research Assessment Exercise, a set formula used to inform state funding of research of a kind that does not apply in the US, is also of considerable interest. The following ten points are offered here as a form of constructive advice, based on twenty years of experience in developing art doctorates in the UK and Ireland, addressed to those contemplating the establishment of an art doctorate in a US art school or university. I hope these comments may assist those who are leading the development of the American art doctorate in their intrinsically worthwhile mission for the emancipation of art education in America.

1. Recognize that different contexts require different solutions to common problems. There is a distinctive American way of dealing with art research and research degrees in art; it may not be obvious yet, but the mission and the methods may differ from what is to be found in the rest of the English-speaking world where the studio art doctorate has now become commonplace.

2. Question the idea of a "terminal degree," which is unknown outside the US. Employment should normally go to the candidate best qualified overall for a position, not just to the person with the certificate. I understand the idea of a terminal illness, but not a terminal degree. It is worth asking whether it contributes any vitality to the education world.

3. Look to how process has been a distinctive concept in twentieth-century American art and art education, drawing from Bauhaus precedents as distilled by a range of artists from Albert Albers at Black Mountain College to Pollock and beyond. The idea of art as a process of inquiry is the keystone of art research. Process supposes an aesthetics of method as against an aesthetics of style, a concept

that has yet to be fully worked through, but one that places educational creativity at the center of aesthetic creativity in a way pioneered by Joseph Beuys. Look too to the place of John Dewey and Donald Schön in American educational heritage: their precedents for learning through activity are the foundations of the studio art doctorate. Art research, therefore, already has a strong provenance in US culture even if it is not yet widely celebrated.

4. Although describing what artists do as research might seem novel, it is interesting to see North American curators of contemporary art normalizing the language of research by describing artists as "inquiring," "exploring," and "investigating" in exhibition notes and catalogs. This discourse is widespread and it would be appropriate for the academy to respond to it.

5. Beware the hegemony of the humanities and the social sciences in formulating the best practice for fine art research. This has been one of the pitfalls of research development in the UK. I recommend looking to the natural sciences for comparisons; there, observation of natural phenomena and experimental strategies are normal methods. In the natural sciences inquiry into primary sources is a foundation of knowledge, as distinct from the reliance on secondary sources of the humanities and aspects of the social sciences. In the UK experience of art doctorates there has been much borrowing from the humanities and social sciences, especially when experienced doctoral supervisors have been taken from those disciplines to assist with the supervision of art doctorates, bringing with them paradigms and methods that distort the ways and means of art. Look too to what artists do methodologically, because there are parallels to be made with what natural scientists do when they are dissatisfied with research paradigms; it would be a shame to devalue art's own standards at a time when they are being increasingly appreciated elsewhere.

6. Take the rationale of the CAA standards for the MFA as the basis for thinking through the relationship of text and artifact at the doctoral level. The standards insist on intellectual rigour without a formula about the writing of text, let alone a formula for a number of words (which is common practice in the UK). This enlightened North American view might be contrary to the formulaic rationale of the English, but it may be the more fruitful.

7. Beware what I consider to be the typically English fuzziness of the concept of "practice-based" research in art, as if it related to research into the practice of medicine, nursing and law; those are distinct fields of inquiry that have nothing to do with the practical dimension of art. "Practice-based" research is all about inquiry into policies, modes, procedures and ethics of professional conduct in

formal settings, as distinct from the generation of knowledge and understanding through making and doing as represented by artefacts (in the broad sense widely known in art). In our debate we are talking about *doctorates in studio art*. I love the clarity of this American term, valid even when artists extend it beyond the four walls of a physical studio.

8. In looking to the UK for precedents, recognize that UK and Irish Masters programs do not normally align with the American MFA, except where there is a two year program such as at the Royal College of Art, the Glasgow School of Art, the Edinburgh College of Art, the University of Ulster at Belfast, or the Burren College of Art in Ireland (where I work). Normally the UK masters is a one year full-time MA, with the lower standards that implies. This means that the MA is a distinctly *pre-doctoral* program rather than one that can be integrated with the doctorate as may be the case with the MFA. I enlarge on this in the next point.

9. Don't think of the Doctorate as something an artist does after and separately from the MFA. Many UK universities and colleges require doctoral applicants in art to have completed a Masters prior to a Doctorate, without normally requiring this in other subjects. Instead, you should nest the MFA and Doctorate together in a 1+2 combination just like the conventional PhD in non-art disciplines worldwide. Art is not so special that its Doctorate has to be so much more time consuming, difficult and therefore expensive than other Doctorates. An integrated Masters and Doctorate is the only way to make Doctorates affordable outside an elaborate funding system such as that enjoyed within the UK.

10. Look at the differences of the research doctorate—the PhD— and the professional doctorate—the DFA—before committing to a program. The PhD is honorific within the UK because of the imperative of assessable research activity within the Research Assessment Exercise. Vast sums of institutional funding depend on the RAE in a way unknown outside the UK. In the US, Australia and New Zealand, a studio Doctorate of Fine Art (DFA) that operates within and as an extension to the conventions of the taught MFA might be more appropriate and valuable than the PhD, and already DFAs can be found in Australia and New Zealand. In the US this alternative to the PhD would build on distinctively American strengths, and find a place for the making of art as it is widely understood— undistorted and undiluted—within the pantheon of learning at the doctoral level.

Notes

1 [That is: Association of Independent Colleges of Art and Design, College Art Association, and National Association of Schools of Art and Design. The CAA is the principal US professional organization of art historians and artists; the NASAD is the accrediting body for art schools. – J.E.]

2 Symposium of the Association of Independent Colleges of Art and Design 2003 at the Redcat Theater, the Disney Hall in Los Angeles. [This is the conference mentioned in the Introduction. —J.E.]

3 It is curious how so many artists in Europe and the US claim status as 'professional' artists whilst depending on their status as academicians for an income (while duplicitously omitting information about this educational practice in exhibition catalogues and the like for the sake of appearances).

4 The AICAD addressed this issue at a Symposium at the Redcat Theater, Disney Hall, Los Angeles in 2003 that was addressed by James Elkins, myself and others. CAA has addressed these issues in several recent annual conferences of which the most recent was the CAA 2006 Conference in Boston where the session "The MFA and the PHD: Torque in the Workplace" included four strong papers by Hilary Robinson, Graeme Sullivan, Susan Roth and Cameron Cartiere, and I was invited to summarize these as discussant in a paper to be published in the *Art Journal*. That conference session mapped out many of the key issues now are being discussed internationally and I commend the papers to the reader. The NASAD has also addressed the studio art doctorate, notably at its 2005 annual meeting in Philadelphia.

7

The Non-Studio PhD for Visual Artists
George Smith

In all the varied, often intense and sometimes fierce U.S. polemics on studio PhDs, no one to my knowledge has raised the question of a non-studio PhD for visual artists.[1] In what follows I want to explore this oddly overlooked and in my view tremendously important opportunity. First, I want to situate my thoughts on the non-studio PhD within the context of my own experience. Then I will touch on the non-studio PhD as it might affect studio practice and the discourse of philosophy. At some greater length, I will want to consider the degree as it would likely affect the American university and the wider field of cultural production. Finally, I will outline a non-studio PhD designed especially for visual artists.

Two caveats: I do not propose the non-studio PhD in opposition to the studio PhD; rather, the question of PhDs for visual artists calls for more than one good answer. Secondly, let me stress that what I say will be largely personal and empirical, even anecdotal. Most of the published work on the question of the studio PhD, whether in the U.S. or elsewhere, has been painstakingly rigorous. This is partly in response to the fact that many who oppose the studio PhD rest their case on what they insist is an inherent lack of rigor in the very idea of a studio PhD curriculum. Be that as it may, since a non-studio PhD designed especially for the visual artist does not yet exist in practice, my thoughts as to its necessity and promise come from professional opinion, not research.

I

In situating those thoughts, I want to trace my steps backwards. Years have passed since I taught my first art school theory class. But never will I forget the lessons of that experience. I was in proud possession of a newly minted PhD and had been teaching literary criticism to Ivy League undergrads in Paris. The theory course I was about to teach was the first ever to be offered at the small New England art college where I'd landed a job, and I wondered if third year art students with little academic training could handle the by then notorious intellectual demands of THEORY. To be honest, I'd convinced myself they'd run me out on a rail. I was so wrong! These young artists plunged into theory headfirst. They dove deeper and got it faster than the super-smart literary critics I'd been teaching in Paris.

I soon found out there were two good reasons why: First, theory for art students meant something more than "theory": it was useful to their lives, to their aspirations and personal identity as creative expressive individuals. Secondly, because art students spent most of their time in the studio, where resolving abstract problems was the basic activity of a studio practice, dealing with abstraction was a way of life, and analytical thinking was the medium of thought. With the first assignment I also found out that artists were great writers of theory. They tended to write about theoretical/philosophical issues in concrete terms, for the obvious reason that a work of art is the concrete representation of a philosophical abstraction.

Before long I was urging my liberal arts school colleagues to send their students to art class if they wanted them to do better in physics or philosophy. What I had discovered for myself was nothing more than the truism that education philosophers and clinical researchers had been insisting on for years: that art making was crucial to cognitive development precisely insofar as it engaged the body, mind, and spirit in a singular form of creative human expression[2].

And very soon I also realized that my art theory students were making exciting changes in the studio. Even older studio faculty who had had no training and little interest in theory began to remark and appreciate the effect theory classes were having on the school as a whole. Theory became a requirement for all majors. Meanwhile, I got busy developing an MFA program that would recognize the importance of theory and philosophy in the graduate training of a studio artist. The new MFA was weighted roughly fifty-fifty between theory and practice. Degree candidates had to defend a written thesis from within the context of their studio thesis. The results were to me astonishing, partly because I was able to see first hand the level of art making that could be achieved through rigorous training in theory and practice, and also because I was amazed by the brilliance of the writing. Clear and pressing was the need for a PhD that would take these discoveries into account.

II

The necessity and promise of such a program would come to bear on at least three kinds of experience: studio practice, philosophical thinking, and lastly, university consciousness and what we have called (in Bourdieu's terms[3]) the wider field of cultural production.

As for studio practice, we know that rigorous training in philosophy and art theory increases an artist's range and vision. Critical thinking sharpens the hand and eye as well as the mind. The artist whose studio practice is informed by the history and philosophy of culture and aesthetics can redefine visual art in ways we otherwise would never know. Such opportunities are hardly limited to the classroom, the gallery, and the museum. They can change the way we see, the way we think, the way we feel---the way, in short, we operate in the world. It will be objected that great art has always done that. Yes, but not to the sweeping degree of radical becoming that is culturally required at present. Nor should we be fooled into thinking that a few graduate level courses in theory and philosophy will produce the kind of studio practice we are calling for.

And what about the philosophical thought of the artist as philosopher? Even though plenty of artists could be labeled as such, our proposition is not a simple matter of recognizing the artist as a philosopher. If we are going to produce the artist-philosopher through academic training, what is needed is nothing less than what has always been necessary in a PhD curriculum: a rigorous engagement with philosophy and theory that comes of sustained reading and discussion and culminates in a full-fledged dissertation. But why would this kind of philosophical training result in a different kind of philosophical thought just because the result is an artist-philosopher? Surely we don't mean to suggest that the artist is smarter than the philosopher or the art historian, and that therefore her philosophy will be somehow better?

Well, yes and no. The artist has no more claim to intelligence than anybody else. But because of her studio training, her style of thinking and seeing does tend to be different. Generally speaking, we might say that hers is not a way of thinking that is predicated on goals and objectives, on achieving outcomes through predetermined means; nor is it predicated on the principles of gain & loss. Rather, her consciousness might be described as intelligent imagination inclined toward creative productivity---or process. Vito Acconci would be a good example of the frame of mind I am trying to describe. He says that for him every studio project constitutes a continuation of the creative process insofar as it stems from the previous failure. Will this kind of thinking produce a better philosophy? I do not know. But it may well produce a different kind of philosophy, one that could pose questions we are as yet unable to formulate. This strikes me as an immense possibility.

As for the non-studio PhD's likely effect on academia and cultural production, we know that artists and studio art programs are generally relegated to the outskirts and fringes of contemporary colleges and universities. Without the PhD, professors of art are more or less restricted to the studio. They teach 'the labor' of studio practice, and rarely are they assigned the questions of philosophy and theory that are pressing on the status of art today. Consequently, undergraduates and graduate students learn how to make art from artists but they learn about what art means from scholars who generally do not make art. Here do we see in stark relief the academic line that is drawn between theory and practice. Throughout its long and wobbly history this thoroughly discursive boundary has mutated in width and pliancy and, according to the cultural mode of the moment, held.

And though the markers that define modern specialization have blurred and softened in the postmodern aftermath (as exemplified by multi-media artists, interdisciplinary studies, and the like), we should not delude ourselves into thinking that the main academic barrier between theory and practice will give way just because a PhD in studio practice has been introduced to the university curriculum. No matter how eloquent and compelling the argument that studio practice comprises academic research, no matter how much theory is included in the curriculum, odds are the studio PhD still will be pegged as a practical degree in the American academic hierarchy. As such, in all likelihood it still will be relegated to the university fringe---at least for the foreseeable future.

The foreseeable future as just predicted needs to change. And though I do not believe this change will take place any time soon, I do believe that the non-studio PhD for the visual artist would provide the training and credentials necessary to bring art practitioners to the center of the extremely important debates on the meaning and function of art in today's world. Their contributions to these debates would benefit students, philosophers, and art historians alike. In my view, they would change the way we think about art inside the academy and beyond. But here we should stop and ask---aren't we really trying to maintain and reproduce the modernist mode of specialization from a different slant? No. We are not retraining artists to become philosophers. We are training artists to become artist-philosophers.

Even so, there are those among the current studio faculty who would argue that the non-studio PhD is beside the point precisely because the discussion of philosophy and theory is a lively aspect of the BFA and MFA curricula, and that they, the studio faculty, do a good job leading these discussions and teaching theory in its myriad forms and dimensions. These latter claims I do not doubt. But the truth is that faculty discussions and teaching of this kind are relatively few and far between. And the more telling point is that they usually take place in the art school or within the closed critique rooms of the university art department, not across the university curriculum, nor in the common space that sustains the university's intellectual life. Which is to say that the studio departments that are talking theory are neither heard nor recognized in the wider academic community by which they have been marginalized.

I venture to say that most students in the American university never set foot in a studio art department. The non-art majors who do step in typically are looking for courses in ceramics or drawing, sculpture or painting, not theory and philosophy. Aside from the judgment of taste that develops out of everyday subjective experience, whatever the vast majority of American students may think of art comes mainly from art history core courses. The artist has little if any say in this matter. Of course, art history departments were established and developed for the very purpose of teaching students to look at art and to think about art from the art historian's point of view. The art history curriculum, or rather, its philosophy of education, explains the prevailing American attitude toward art and toward artists. And that attitude is wrong. Which is to say that the art historian's essential story is precisely the one we are trying to get rid of; it is the story that tells American students that the artist works and the historian thinks. I hasten to plead that we do not want to get rid of the art historian (or for that matter the theory professor or the philosophy of art professor); what we want is to create another historical point of view, one that shows that theory and practice were never separate in the first place---that shows, in other words, that the artist thinks.

Such was Christopher Frayling's intent, no doubt, when he coined the increasingly famous phrase, "thinking through art" (RCA Research Papers 1993/4); and such, too, were Katy McLeod's and Lin Holdridge's intentions when they appropriated the phrase as the title of their recent collection of essays on the studio PhD. But we have already touched on the unlikely prospect of a studio PhD making much of a difference in the art historical representation of the theory/practice divide between the artist as worker and the scholar as thinker.

Certainly we are a long way from Kant's definition of the genius as none other than the artist who forges new laws of aesthetics.

The change can be traced back to William James's The Principles of Psychology (1880), the first extensive American venture into the field of psychology. It is here that the Harvard philosopher's new American cognitive science would debunk Kant's long-held definition of genius. According to James, the analytic mind of the scientist and philosopher attains to authentic genius, while the intuitive mind of the artist is capable of complex but lesser modes of intelligence[5]. James's assertion did not land on deaf ears. Soon after publication, *The Principles of Psychology* was internationally recognized as the most important study ever produced on the subject of cognitive science; and while the two-volume, fourteen hundred page original edition did not find its way into the American undergraduate curriculum, the shorter version, known as the Brief Course (Harvard undergrads called it "The Jimmie"), was widely read throughout the American undergraduate curricula, especially in the rapidly developing field of education philosophy.

I dare say that today not a few studio teachers feel like they are looked down upon from the purely academic echelons of the ivory tower. Exceptions flock to mind. But whenever I might doubt the class implications of the university's longstanding division between practice/worker and theory/thinker—whenever, for instance, somebody wants to explain it away in terms of Cartesian dualism or academia's more ancient roots in Platonic idealism—I think of a conversation I once had with a photo instructor, who scornfully remarked as a matter of course that studio faculty were the proletarians of the professoriate.

Which is to suggest that for many scholars, a non-studio PhD is always already unthinkable. Not so much because it is an unconscionable idea, but because it is an idea that would hardly occur to a consciousness that is culturally constructed to think otherwise. Nevertheless, if ever the theory/practice line is transgressed, if ever a new philosophy of graduate education in the visual arts opens the way to a long over-due and badly needed overhaul of the American university's general philosophy of education, it will happen when the artist joins the scholar in the academic space reserved for thinking. This would be the space entered upon or transgressed by the artist-philosopher.

Which brings me to one final thought: The poverty of philosophy remains a failure to act. And yet a philosophy of action seems the only hope remaining in the face of our present conditions of existence. Such a philosophy will materialize, I believe, when the philosopher has learned to engage body, mind, and spirit in the concrete representation of a philosophical abstraction. Who will this philosopher be, if not the artist-philosopher?

III

In light of this question, I have collaborated with artists and scholars from around the world to design a non-studio PhD for artists. I believe we have created the first PhD program of its kind in the United States. It combines rigorous philosophical study with on-site intensives. The latter might be described as critical interventions that bring the artist-philosopher into immediate contact with the life-world of contemporary art, whether it be participants in the Venice Biennale or the critics, curators, gallery directors and artists who populate the New York art scene.

Here in the mix of theory and practice, education and experience, one can't help but think of Dewey, who never tired of insisting that a philosophy of education had better have a concrete plan---one that spells out what is to be learned, how it will be taught, with what kind of equipment, under what kind of roof, and in what kind of social environment. Otherwise, it's "wholly in the air" (28). And so I introduce the following outline of study.

General Curriculum[6]

Designed for holders of the MFA in studio arts, the program offers a PhD in philosophy, aesthetics, and theory. It is a three-year curriculum, totaling sixty credit hours of sustained academic study. Each semester is composed of two five-credit courses.

Year One
The first semester begins with a five-week residency intensive, held in Italy at Spannocchia, a medieval Tuscan castle and organic farm that offers ideal conditions for retreat-like academic study. The first year residency begins a two-semester history of philosophy, aesthetics, and theory. At the end of the residency, the seminar transitions to ten weeks of on-line instruction. Before leaving Spannocchia students meet individually with faculty to design a second course. This course is an independent study and is directed by a leading expert in the given field of study.

In Biennale years, students will travel from Spannocchia to Venice for a week of study at the Venice Biennale. Scholars and artists participating in the Venice Biennale will in turn be invited to give lectures and lead seminars at Spannocchia.

Second semester begins with a ten-day residency intensive in New York City. Seminar sessions include studio visits to New York based artists and special lectures presented by internationally recognized scholars. As with the first semester, the seminar transitions to on-line instruction at the end of the residency. And here again, the student proposes a course of independent study, to be completed under the direction of an expert in the given field of study.

Year Two

Offering advanced courses of study, year two repeats the same general curricular schedule as year one. In addition to residencies at Spannocchia and New York, study includes assignments in Milan and Paris.

Year Three

Year three commences with a two-week summer residency intensive at Brown University. Students are introduced to the basic principles of dissertation writing, and they study sample dissertations in original and published form. Following the residency, two independent studies comprise each semester. In the first semester one independent study is given over to reading and research in areas related to the dissertation; the second independent study is pursued with a view toward formulating a dissertation proposal, preparing an exploratory outline and bibliography, and drafting an introductory chapter. The second semester continues the first semester independent studies.

At the end of year three the candidate takes a written and oral qualifying examination. On qualifying, the finalized dissertation proposal is submitted. Upon approval a dissertation committee is formed.

The degree is awarded on successful completion of the dissertation, usually within the fifth but not exceeding the seventh year of enrollment.

Notes

1 My thanks to IDSVA second year student Amy Cook, whose independent study on art practice and cognitive development contributed to the present essay. In addition to sources cited below, see John Dewey, Experience and Education (New York: Simon and Schuster, 1938); Christopher Frayling, "Research in Art and Design," London: Royal College of Art, RCA Research Papers 1 no. 1 (1993/94).

2 Rudolf Arnheim, Visual Thinking (Berkeley: University of California Press, 1969); Tim Ingold, "Tool Use, Sociality and Intelligence," in Tools, Language, and Cognition in Human Evolution, edited by K. Gibson and Ingold (New York: Cambridge University Press, 1993.); Allan Paivio, Mind and Its Evolution: A Dual Coding Theoretical Approach (Mahwah, New Jersey: Lawrence Erlbaum Associates, 2007); and Frank Wilson, The Hand: How Its Use Shapes the Brain, Language, and Human Culture (New York: Vintage Books, 1998).

3 Pierre Bourdieu, The Field of Cultural Production (New York: Columbia University Press, 1993).

4 See Chapter 9. [— J.E.]

5 James, Principles of Psychology, edited by Frederick Burckhardt (Cambridge, MA: Harvard University Press, 1981), vol. 2, p. 361.

6 In December 2006, LD 462, an Act authorizing the Institute for Doctoral Studies in the Visual Arts to confer the Degree of Doctor of Visual Arts, was given a unanimous Ought to Pass recommendation by the Maine State Legislature Education and Cultural Affairs Committee and was subsequently enacted by a vote of 134 - 1 in the Maine House and unanimously in the Senate. In a State House ceremony on March 1, 2007 Governor John Baldacci signed LD 462 into law. In May 2007 IDSVA commenced instruction at Spannocchia Castle, Tuscany.

8

The Future of the Doctorate in the Arts[1]
Hilde Van Gelder and Jan Baetens

A Doctor's Degree for Artists!

In 2004 *Boekman*, a Dutch journal of cultural policy, devoted a special issue to the relationship between art and science. One of the contributors, Paul Dikker, signed a short but highly provocative pamphlet entitled: "No Doctor's Degree for Artists!"[2] A creative artist himself, Dikker emphasizes that the gap between art and science is unbridgeable. Scientists, he argues, are concerned with the description and explanation of "reality." By this concept of the real Dikker means "an empirical object that exists independently of human observation and is literally disclosed and discovered via careful research." Artists, on the contrary, express not "the" but "a" reality, namely their own reality, which functions as an "expressive tool," not as an object of perception or observation. The artist, Dikker continues, "produces a new reality." In other words, he or she uses his or her thoughts and feelings in order to create new realities and to offer them with utmost generosity to the public, adding their reality to reality tout court.

Dikker's argument does not stop there. Scientists, he insists, while relying on the crucial role they accord to the explanation of their research theme, claim to discover the "truth." The views and insights they defend shift ceaselessly and are therefore by definition "time-bounded." Thanks to their formal characteristics, works of art are the personal expression of a theme and thus lay claim to "beauty." A beautiful form can be enjoyed eternally and is therefore "timeless." For all these reasons, Dikker says, there can be only one conclusion. Because art and science belong to two completely different paradigms, artists should not preoccupy themselves with the pressures of social reality and regulations and should above all avoid accepting a "straitjacket" in the hope to obtain one day a PhD in the arts. Allow scientists to be concerned with the enrichment of the (ugly) social debate. Allow artists to retire quietly in the green oasis of eternal beauty. And let there be peace on earth.

Art and Science: Double-Ovum Twins

That is the world according to Paul Dikker. In the last decades however, the stance he defended has become an astonishing anachronism, in the world of science as well as in the world of art. More and more, his ideas are considered a complete misconception. Art and science do not only have the same mother, they are even double-ovum twins. Let us give some examples to illustrate our position; our first example comes from the world of science. Newspapers have reported recently that collaborators of a European research project have invented a new synthetic material to produce an ultra-light bottom plate for a new small car. Simultaneously, they have also developed the technology to produce at least fifty pieces a day of this plate—a necessary condition for cost-effective production. If things go well, a new car made of fiber-reinforced carbon will be available on the market in less than twenty years. Nobody will say that the work of these scientists goes far beyond the mere explanation of reality. And what kind of reality have these researchers disclosed? Certainly not the reality that God is a car!

Following Dikker's logic, inventions like these come close to the creation of a completely new reality and hence of a work of art. Contrary to the dreamlike vehicles, boats, and star ships invented by the Belgian artist Panamarenko (whose inspiration often resembles the spirit of "pataphysics"), the "car of the future" tries to transform our dreams into reality. Yet the new reality created by the scientists is not a timeless one It is a reality deeply rooted in a given temporality and spatiality. It does not belong to any eternal sphere of ideas or forms (we shall come back on this point immediately).

Dikker's definitions on the relationship between art and beauty raise similar problems. The traditional standard of beauty in art has been questioned so fundamentally since the nineteenth century that for most critics it can no longer be used as a valid criterion in the appreciation of works of art. To put it mildly, there is no longer any consensus on the meaning of beauty in contemporary art. And many observers will rightly assert that the car of the future, with its flashy design and exciting new materials, is aesthetically much more satisfying than most specimens of contemporary art.

The Myth of Timelessness

The most problematic aspect of Dikker's argumentation has to do with the idea of art's timelessness. Debatable as it may be in many other aspects, Postmodern art theory has convincingly demonstrated that the Modernist belief in the linear progression of art and its teleological evolution toward a final goal (the "essence" of the given art form), is nothing but a myth. Modernism's ideal view of a stabilized artistic object is inextricably linked with the acceptance of art's timeless essence. In twentieth century art, however, and more specifically since the new art forms of the 1960s, the hypothesis of art's timelessness has been seriously challenged, if not violently rejected. The anti-modernist ideas that have become dominant insist on the fact that any work of art, even the most apparently immobile, static or timeless one, is the locus of an internal and inherent dynamics. The basic reason for this shift is simple: all objects—and works of art are no less objects than any other ones—are subjected to the laws of gravity and entropy, i.e. to inevitable change and deterioration through time. For that very reason, a belief was generated among artists and critics that the perception of the artwork itself, as a container of time, can never occur outside of time. The thesis of the alleged timelessness of art is nothing but a rational illusion. We never stop being aware of the inherent paradox of our ideas on aesthetic timelessness.[3]

In his book *The Inhuman*, Jean-François Lyotard offers a very clear discussion of the typically modern desire to exceed its own limits and to find a kind of ultimate closure whose worldly incarnation are Utopia and the so-called Great Narratives.[4] In the Western world at least, the latter have lost much of their credibility since several decades. For Lyotard, postmodernism is the power that undermines the emancipatory project of modernism. In his view, postmodernity is not a new era, but the capacity of acknowledging the irrational dimension present within modernity, but ignored or repressed by it. Postmodernism has questioned modernism's ideal of the enlightened cogito, freed from any sensual or emotional restraint, and the subsequent cult of rationality, stability, and timelessness. Yet, this critique was only possible thanks to the foregrounding of a pre-modern aspect: that of the body and its emotions.

In art, it was undoubtedly Marcel Duchamp who played a paramount role in this evolution. His readymades were a violent debunking (among many other things) of the canon of eternal beauty; his dramatically corporeal works such as the *Rotoreliefs* of the 1930s and *Étant donnés* (1945-1966) do not obey the modernist philosophy of stable, timeless objects, as if created by eternity itself. At a historical moment (the 1910s) when this ideal still had to triumph at an international level (in American Modernism of the 1950s and Greenbergian art criticism), Duchamp had already understood that it is not possible to separate art and emotion. The latter is the flip side of the former, and vice versa, and shifts in priority are therefore inevitable. Even Michael Fried, whom many consider the most fervent defender of Modernist rationalism, had to confess in 1967 already that timelessness can only exist within time: "presentness," he wrote, "is grace."[5]

The Battle of the "Faculties"[6]

The shift from a complex modernity to a narrower, strongly rationalized modernism also occurred in academic life. A recent British study offering a comparative *status quaestionis* of higher education in arts clearly demonstrates that the Cartesian split between reason and emotion affects also the dominating educational structures in the West.[7] Art history and theory as well as musicology are hosted by university faculties, which emphasizes the rationality of their approach. The training in the practice of concrete arts and music, however, is located in specialized schools, which are separated from the theoretical environment. This "two cultures" model within the arts has created a system in which one has to make a radical choice between two types of specializations: one has to become either an artist or a theoretician.

As always, there are historical reasons to explain this situation. The initial cohesion of artistic training has evolved towards a system in which various dimensions have become more or less independent. This evolution has not been teleological, however, and it is important not to forget the role played by local circumstances in the gradual separation of practice and theory. The Greek ideal of *arête* did not distinguish between art and science, and the nine muses inspired both arts and sciences. An initial split occurred in the Middle Ages, when a distinction was introduced between the language-based *trivium* (grammar, rhetoric, and logic) and the mathematics-based *quadrivium* (arithmetic, geometry, music, and astronomy). A further step was made from the Renaissance onwards, with the creation of the academies for art and music, which aimed at creating an advanced training in the practice of arts, independently from the corporatist environment of the studio. This advanced artistic training became institutionalized by these academies, which started to organize this type of higher education in a completely independent way, outside the universities. In the nineteenth century, the conservatism of these powerful academies was infamous. In the twentieth century, however, there has been an important *aggiornamento*. Academies became colleges of art. They have been—and still are—a breeding place for less conventional, even avant-garde art practices and pedagogy. Today, academies and universities are trying to foster new forms of collaborations within a more comprehensive approach. In Belgium, as in many other countries—as the various contributions to this book amply demonstrate—that evolution is taking place along with considerable skepticism from both sides.

The University of Leuven and the colleges that are associated to it (Sint-Lucas in Ghent, Sint-Lukas in Brussels and the Media and Design Academy in Genk) have taken up a pioneering role in this development. Their efforts have resulted in according the first Belgian doctoral degree in the arts in 2006, to Maarten Vanvolsem (for a dissertation on "The Experience of Time in Still Photographic Images"). Convinced that the impact of the historical separation of theory and practice and the subsequent specialization of higher education have had dramatic consequences, the Association KULeuven has founded an Institute for Practice based Research in the Arts, where important synergies between practicians and theoreticians are stimulated and financially supported through considerable fellowships.[8] Double talents are still quite rare today, but why, for example, should a mathematician who is also a composer be the exception rather than the rule? Why is it so difficult for us to accept that it should be possible—and not just weird—to combine high-level theoretical work and high-level practical work in a stimulating way? Why do we refuse to question the role of pedagogic specialization in the lack of exchanges between theory and practice? Luckily, things are changing, and the British example, where a PhD in the arts has existed for more than two decades now, seems to suggest how fruitful it can be to encourage young people to develop simultaneously their practical as well as their theoretical skills and interests.[9]

From this perspective, the historical split between art and science seems increasingly artificial. For what is art today, and what is science? Consider the seminal study by Sir Christopher Frayling, today's honorary rector of the Royal College of Arts and one of the founding fathers of the so-called practice-based doctorates in the creative and performing arts and design.[10] Frayling's reflection has two starting points:

·The relationships between art and science—or, more generally between practice-oriented and theoretical research—are more important than their differences.

·Not all artistic output can be defined as research output, yet in certain cases this output can be considered the result of a research

process. Hence the necessity to propose a real definition of the notion of research in an artistic context.

In this regard, Frayling proposes the following three distinctions:

First, there is research *on* the arts, which he labels as "research
into art and design." This category encompasses the traditional theoretically oriented research (art history, musicology, and so on). Its
academic output is a classic PhD.

Second, there is research *in* the arts, which Frayling labels as "research *through* art and design." This category entails all artistic research that aims at exploring a certain practice or a certain material
component of such a practice. This research is process based, and
its first ambition is not necessarily the production of a work of art,
even though such a production may be part of the process. If this
type of research takes the form of a PhD research, the assessment
of such a dissertation should require both the evaluation of a work
and a substantial written report. Frayling describes this artistic paradigm as "cognitive."

Third, there is also a type of artistic research which he labels as
"research *for* art and design." This notion refers to research that
aims at producing a particular artifact or work of art. It has a very
specific goal and its output can only take the form of a final product
(to be seen or to be heard). For Frayling, who describes this artistic
paradigm as "expressive," this type of research usually does not
lead to a PhD.[11]

The Doctorate as Readymade?

Applying Frayling's terminology to Dikker's argument against the
PhD in the arts, it is clear that his defense can be understood in
terms of foregrounding the "expressive" paradigm. In this point of
view, the artist works in order to produce a specific result, which
reflects his or her feelings in a way that is as free and unconstrained
as possible. However, current methods in art historical and art theoretical research and interpretation have debunked the idea that
the making of a work of art depends in the very first place on barely
expressible emotions, or even deeper and uncontrollable passions.
To put things clearly: the opening up of the PhD towards a PhD in
the arts does not imply that any Van Gogh may now be awarded a
doctorate (unless it were an honorary degree). Van Gogh-like artists
stick to other ideals and working methods; their main goal is not
to do cognitive research, but to express themselves. Their artistic
philosophy may very well make them suspicious of any academic
environment.

Nevertheless, not all artists believe in the ideal of free and personal expression, Frayling argues. Certainly since World War II, increasing numbers of artists identify more easily with the "cognitive" model. It is not an exaggeration to say that conceptual art in the late '60s may have been the first collective outing of this phenomenon. Process art, for instance, is a notion that has been well received in Postminimalism and whose importance can still be felt today. In process art final products matter less than artistic procedures. The ethereal presentations of intellectually highly gifted artists such as Robert Barry or Douglas Huebler, to quote just the most famous representatives, or the early Fluxus creations of George Brecht or La Monte Young, laid the foundation of what we call today practice-based research in the arts. Given the reduced visibility and the relative unimportance of the material result of their art, these artists were obliged to document and contextualize as much as possible their research and working methods. In order to build such a research archive, they combined texts, video, and photography, and this mix has become quite commonplace today.

It should not come as a surprise that such evolutions within the artistic production itself have had a serious impact on the academic circuit since the late 1970s. The debates on the PhD in the arts have been made possible by the work of these artists, for it seemed quite logical to transform the documentation of artistic procedures—which was now accepted as a real work of art—into the format of a dissertation, albeit a shorter, abridged or altered one. Various contemporary artists identify with this research model and feel quite comfortable with it. They are glad to find a stronger support for their kind of art, which they are strongly committed to discuss with their peers, following the criteria generally accepted within their field.[12]

The universities should not worry too much. Even though it was Duchamp, the founding father of conceptual tendencies in art, who launched the whole process of innovation, there will be no ready-made doctorate. The criteria that are currently used in the countries that have introduced a PhD in the arts offer all the necessary guarantees to counter such a scenario (or such a nightmare, in the view of certain administrators). For the doctorates in architecture, creative writing, design, drama, audiovisual production, or painting and sculpture, the following norms are generally accepted:[13]
• The research has to be part of a registered research program.
• At the submission of the PhD, the creative part of the dissertation should be available in a permanently accessible form. If parts of the work no longer exist, the author should provide a photo reportage, video or CD-ROM that documents the work. In this

respect, we especially would like to mention the fact that the Leuven example so far has demonstrated a strong emphasis on the presentation/exhibition of the creative part at the moment of the *viva voce* [the dissertation defense]. The jury first examines the creative part, and afterwards is there an oral defense of the dissertation.
- The creative part of the work has to be accompanied by a theoretical, historical, critical or visual framework that is relevant to the meaning of the work.
- The research output must entail a written part — a dissertation — whose average length should be 30,000 to 40,000 words (for the special case of music, see below).
- The whole work should contribute in an independent and original way to the knowledge in the field and demonstrate a correct understanding of the usually accepted research methods.
- There must be a public and oral defense of the dissertation. In most cases, both parts of the dissertation — the written thesis as well as the creative part — are considered to have equal or almost equal importance (except in the case of music).

For a PhD in music, special rules apply:
- The research has to be part of a registered research program.
- At the submission of the PhD, the creative part of the dissertation should be available in a permanently accessible form.
- The size of the portfolio with musical compositions has to be "substantial," and at least one of the compositions should be written for a "great ensemble" (for instance a complete orchestra).
- The artist should provide a short written comment (3,000 to 5,000 words) that offers a commentary on the creative process.
- The compositions should both demonstrate "technical skills" and deserve public interpretation
- The portfolio is paramount in the assessment of the dissertation.

Arts and Humanities

One of the strangest aspects of this whole story is the gap between research *in* the arts (practice-led research) and research *on* the arts (theoretical and historical research). Researchers in the arts are often following experimental procedures which do not always allow them to know where will be heading. In the worst case, their research doesn't lead them to anything — except to the conclusion that the road they had chosen was not the right one.

Whereas ending up in this situation amounts to disaster in the context of research on the arts, such an apparently disappointing conclusion may signify a real breakthrough for certain artists. Researchers on the arts have developed many methodologies that tend to exclude all kinds of experimental procedures. From the very beginning of the research, one relies upon a certain number of previously assimilated criteria that enables one to calculate a priori the way to follow. If the final result is not satisfying, the assessment of the research will by definition be negative as well. The jury will then conclude that the researcher has proven unable to assimilate and use the generally accepted research methods of the humanities. If this is the way one distinguishes between art and science, then it is clear that there still is a real gap between them.

Arts and (Hard) Sciences

On further consideration, it appears that the research methods and models of the hard sciences are closer to those of research in the arts than the methods and models of the humanities. Let us take once again a concrete example. A PhD candidate in pharmaceutical sciences is asked to solve a problem related to an absorption difficulty of a certain drug. All the necessary steps in the production process of the drug have been carefully followed, yet the final tests reveal that the gastric wall seems unable to dispatch the chemical to the rest of the body. Without a solution of this crucial problem, it will not be possible to introduce the new drug on the market. After some preliminary tests, the ambitious young researcher concludes that strawberry extracts may be reliable to facilitate the absorption of the drug by the patient's body. Unfortunately, after a year and numerous experiments on laboratory animals, the results turn out to be unsatisfying. The strawberries neither do offer the expected result. A woman of character, our young researcher starts over from scratch and eventually discovers, after two years of new experiments, a successful alternative. This time, serendipity has worked.

It is self-evident that in the pharmaceutical PhD, the researcher will document also the unsuccessful part of the work, which took a whole year of apparently useless efforts. At the time of the PhD defense, the assessment of the final result will take this first part of the work into account, and the members of the jury will judge it as well, following the scientifically accepted criteria in the field. Why did the first experiment fail? Why did the researcher only notice the failure after one year? Was the approach sufficiently independent and innovative, and did it offer enough guarantees to the production of new knowledge and enlargement of the research context? Were the research questions transparent enough, first at the level of the structure and the process of the research, second from the perspective of the expected outcome? Are the definitive results relevant enough for other researchers? Were there good reasons for choosing this research topic rather than that one? And last but not least, does the final result make a real contribution to global innovation in the field?

What is at stake here is a paradigmatic vision of scientific research. Certain researchers adhere to a method that has been developed by the logical positivism of the Vienna Circle at the beginning of the twentieth century. Logical positivism employs the so-called verification principle: it reduces theories to elementary data and checks their correspondence with empirical data. This method has been used extensively in historical research, for instance, but even there its limits have become apparent, for the study of historical documents is just the study of documents describing historical events, not of the events themselves. Logical positivism solved this problem by toning down the "verification" claim, which was reinterpreted in terms of "confirmation." In this new model, the overall model was no longer strictly empirical but hypothetico-deductive. Logical empiricists tried to infer as many conclusions as possible from a given theory, and these conclusions were then tested for their empirical reliability. The more a theory is able to pass this empirical test, the more its scientific character will be reinforced.

Quite different research models are also possible, such as the one based on the falsification principle introduced in Karl Popper's critical rationalism. This approach takes as its starting point that all propositions and theories are nothing but hypotheses, which have been questioned as critically as possible. Hence scientific research is not an approach that starts from a given theory, but an approach that gradually builds one. It is a permanent process of trial and error, in which a theory becomes more scientific through the systematic exclusion of falsified facts. Critical rationalism, the research model that is closest to the methods of research in the arts, has had a strong response in biomedical sciences. But increasingly, elements of it are being introduced also in the humanities, for instance in pedagogy where practice-based teaching and the critical analysis of learning outcomes are now wide-spread.[14]

Towards a Revision of Scientific Criteria?

It should be possible to apply analogous criteria to the field of research in the arts. In certain counties such as the UK or Finland, there already exists a strong policy concerning this line of inquiry, and a number of experienced have relied on the strong symmetry between the experimental method in artistic research and the laboratory research in other fields to propose a concrete interpretation of the criteria for the assessment of the so-called practice-led PhD in the arts. At the same time, and here the consensus is not as complete, some institutions such as the University of Art and Design in Helsinki or the Royal College of Art in London, go much further and have proceeded to a general reform of their research criteria in the humanities themselves. More and more, these institutions accept the idea that a doctorate in the arts is no longer necessarily "practice-based" in this sense that it should be aiming at and ultimately amount to the production of a work of art.

In this more advanced scenario, a PhD in the arts still has to include a creative portion, but the interpretation of such a creation becomes much broader. Curating a major exhibition (or a series of exhibitions) and editing its catalogue can be sufficient for such a PhD. What is meant by the "creative output" of the artistic research is interpreted on an ad hoc basis, which opens for instance the possibility of presenting the results on CD-ROM or on the internet. It goes without saying that these developments are opening many doors to new research possibilities in the humanities in general. Certainly for researchers in the field of museum studies, whose demanding agendas often prevent them from writing a traditional PhD, this new type of doctorate may prove a tailor-made solution. Most recently, following the logic of a PhD in Creative Writing (which we discuss below), new have appeared for art critics to obtain doctoral degrees on the basis of their art critical writing.

Many other examples can be imagined. In the current framework, a specialist in the restoration of medieval manuscripts can only get a PhD if he or she follows the classic methodologies of art history. He or she will first be obliged to take a traditional MA degree in art history (quite different from the existing MA's in restoration) and then to accept the straitjacket of a PhD in art history (with no place whatsoever for restoration practice). Following practice-led training in restoration by the doctoral degree is not only profitable to the candidate, but to society in general.

Creative Writing

And what applies to research in the arts, may apply to other fields in the humanities as well. The example of literary studies, and more specifically creative writing—a subject that is hardly acknowledged in continental European universities, to put it mildly—may be a good case in point. Semiotically speaking, it is of course a great advantage that a writer can reflect on his or her own work through the same medium as is used by the creative work. It is also good to know that, as an academic discipline, literary theory is much younger than art history. Until the nineteenth century, the only people who reflected on the art of writing were the authors themselves (contemporary readers with a strong interest in theory are still reading Poe's "The Philosophy of Composition" and Flaubert's correspondence, because these are the places where to find the best reflections on writing). Even in the twentieth century, where literary theory has boomed, real knowledge on what writing really means continues to be produced by the authors themselves. A major example is Francis Ponge's *Pour un Malherbe*.[15] This "book" on the founder of French classicism in literature is not only interesting because it blurs all known boundaries between genres—is it an essay? is it theory? is it poetry?—but also because it gives an insight view on the relevance of rule-bound writing (or to translate it in the terminology of this article: of "cognitive" artistic research). It is not possible here, unfortunately, to discuss the depth of Ponge's practice-led knowledge,[16] yet it is clear that Ponge's writing articulates a specific kind of knowledge that is different from the theoretical knowledge on writing produced by critics and theoreticians who do not write themselves.[17] The combination of these two elements—on the one hand the semiotic family resemblance between theory and practice in creative writing, on the other hand the uncountable historical examples of theoretical research provided by literary practitioners, should be more than sufficient to make a strong plea for a PhD in creative writing in European universities. An impressive example is Jean Ricardou's self-defense "Fiction step by step."[18] In this work, which was awarded a PhD degree by the University of Toulouse, the author gives a detailed account of how he wrote one of his novels, *La prise/prose de Constantinople*,[19] and, most importantly, explains and motivates why he did it the way he did it.

Conclusion

The evolution towards a practice-led PhD is a major transformation of the research landscape, inside and outside of universities. In the UK, companies such as Philips, Ikea and Habitat have provided a strong financial impulse for young PhD doctorates in product design. All available figures indicate that those graduates have found jobs that enable them to valorize their practice-led knowledge.[20] We can only recommend other countries to follow the UK example, and to embrace the new doctorate without any reluctance.

Notes

1 This text is an expanded version of an essay previously published in the Belgian journal *Context K #2* as Van Gelder and Baetens, "De toekomst van het doctoraat in de kunsten" (2005).

2 P. Dikker, "Geen doctorsgraad voor kunstenaars," *Boekman* 58/59 (Spring 2004): 189–90.

3 For a more extensive discussion of these issues, see Van Gelder, "The Fall from Grace: Late Minimalism's Conception of the Intrinsic Time of the Artwork-as-Matter," *Interval(le)s—I*, 1 (Fall 2004): 83-97, available online at http://www.ulg.ac.be/cipa/pdf/van%20gelder.pdf, accessed August 2008.

4 Lyotard, *The Inhuman: Reflections on Time*, translated by Geoffey Bennington (Stanford : Stanford University Press, 1992).

5 M. Fried, "Art and Objecthood." *Artforum* 5 (June 1967): 23. Republished in Fried, *Art and Objecthood: Essays and Reviews* (Chicago, London: University of Chicago Press, 1998), 172.

6 In his 1798 essay "Der Streit der Fakultäten," Kant already made a strong plea for the upgrading of the "lower" Faculties (Natural Sciences, Arts, and Philosophy) that, contrary to the "higher" ones (Theology, Law, and Medicine), were not entitled to award a PhD degree.

7 See Michael Jubb, "Categories and Definitions of Research in the Arts and Humanities," in *Practice-based PhD in the Creative and Performing Arts and Design*, edited by Hilde Van Gelder, e-publication (CD ROM), proceedings of an international conference on the subject at STUK, Leuven (10 September 2004).

8 See http://associatie.kuleuven.be/ivok/ivokeng/index.htm.

9 See for instance F. Laevers, "Understanding the world of objects and of people: Intuition as the core element of deep level learning," *International Journal of Educational Research* 29 no. 1 (1998): 69-85.

10 Frayling, "Research in Art and Design," *Royal College of Art Research Papers Series*, vol. 1, no. 1 (1993). [This paper is available online, for example at www.constellations.co.nz/index.php?sec=3&ssec=7&r=687#687, accessed September 2008. —J.E.]

11 An exception is here the (British) PhD in music, whose written counterpart is allowed to be very short (5,000 words).

12 See for example the *Journal of Visual Art Practice* (www.intellectbooks.com/journals/jvap.htm).

13 For this information, we are greatly indebted to our colleague Javier Gimeno Martínez, who made an extensive report on this subject for the IvOK (Institute for Practice based Research in the Arts): J. Gimeno Martínez, "Eindrapport Inventarisatie Internationaal Onderzoek in de Kunsten," supervised by F. Baert and Van Gelder (Leuven, 2004).

14 We are indebted for this example to Jan De Vuyst (IvOK, Leuven).

15 Paris: Gallimard, 1965.

16 It would involve for example an analysis of his refusal of Paul Valéry's stances on the role of constraints in literature.

17 We hope to come back on this crucial example in another article.

18 This text has been included in *Nouveaux Problèmes du Roman* (Paris: Éditions du Seuil, 1978).

19 Paris: éditions de Minuit, 1965.

20 These and other figures were presented by Sandra Kemp, Director of Research at the Royal College of Art in London, during her lecture at the aforementioned symposium in Leuven (2004): see S. Kemp, 'Critical Practice: The Development of Studio-based Research at the Royal College of Art,' in H. Van Gelder (ed.), Practise-based PhD in the creative and performing arts and design, e-publication (cd-rom), proceedings of an international conference on the subject at STUK, Leuven (10 September 2004).

9

On Beyond Research and New Knowledge

James Elkins

There are three arguments in this chapter: first, that the paradigms of *research* and *new knowledge* are artificial imports from UK administrative terminology and should be abandoned or rethought from the ground up; second, that it is necessary that the new PhD degrees, whatever shape they take, be fully at the level of PhDs in the fields to which they make reference; and third, that the studio-art PhD degree is an opportunity to rethink not only the place of visual arts in the university, and not only the place of creative arts, but the coherence of the university as a whole.

My principal example will be the book *Thinking Through Art*, the second book on the subject of studio-art phds.[1] *Thinking Through Art* can be read—although this wasn't the editors' intention—as a barometer of thinking about the university in general. I wonder if there is an academic relation more vexed, less satisfactorily theorized, and more seldom solved than the relation between studio art departments and other departments in the university. The kind of abstract talk about theory, discipline, knowledge, research, and method that is used to articulate the parts of the university feels stretched and distorted when it is applied to studio art. Those distortions have a lot to say about the coherence of the university in general, because they reveal the kind of work that words like *theory* are normally intended to do. Hence the studio-art PhD degree is an ideal place to begin to reconceptualize the unity of the university.

Why Research *and* New Knowledge?

To a reader outside the UK, New Zealand, Australia, and the countries influenced by them such as Ireland, Sweden, Norway, Denmark, Singapore, and Malaysia, it may seem strange that in order to validate studio art within the university it is necessary to speak about the production of visual art as a kind of *research* that results in *new knowledge*. In the Introduction I mentioned that Timothy Emlyn Jones gave a paper—a version of Chapter 2—to an audience of the deans and presidents of North American art schools in Los Angeles in fall 2003. When it came to the concepts of research and new knowledge, some in the audience were incredulous: Why, one asked, do we want to start thinking about visual art as if it were a science? And what, another wondered, is the new knowledge produced by an artist like Picasso? Jones's paper (Chapter 2) reviews the curious literature that has sprung up to justify, adapt, and amplify the concepts of research and new knowledge. And Jones is right, as he says in Chapter 6, that in the years following that 2003 conference art schools and art departments have become more sanguine about the studio-art PhD. He doesn't mention what I consider to the the insidious consequence of that sanguinity: talk about *art as research* and art as the *production of new knowledge* are now commonplace in committees in the US and Canada. We are adopting the UK administrative terminology.

It needs to be said that the initial impetus behind the terms *research* and *new knowledge* is purely economic—a point well made by Charles Harrison in Chapter 10. In the UK, Australian, and Irish systems (and I assume in others as well) university departments receive money and allowances to hire more teachers based on the levels of their students. Undergraduate students count relatively little, MPhil students more,[2] MA students still more, and PhD students most of all. It therefore makes good fiscal sense to implement PhD programs in every department of the university. Studio art departments have been able to do this by subscribing to the standardized language that governs the addition of new disciplines: any new discipline in a university has to be conceptually independent, and must endeavor to add to knowledge through new research.[3] That last term, *research*, also has an institutional meaning: budgets and hiring are quantified not only by student numbers, but by the number of conference papers, books, and essays each faculty member produces. (It will surprise readers outside the UK system that departments actually keep track of the total number of pages each faculty member has generated. New hires are even considered partly on the basis of the page count of their publications. The bookkeeping involved is monumental, and so is the periodic Research Assessment Exercise, RAE, that compiles the results—see Harrison's chapter in this book for the grisly details.) So research itself carries the specific denotation of a quantified volume of production in refereed journals, academic presses, and conferences. In the UK the RAE and the Arts and Humanities Research Board

(AHRB) have formally adopted *research* and *new knowledge,* making them unavoidable in the working of the university.

As Jones documents in Chapter 2, a cottage industry of theorizing has sprung up with the intention of adapting *research* and *new knowledge* to fit the studio context. This literature has been around for some time—it first appeared in the 1970s—and so it has come to seem natural, as if research and new knowledge were as necessary to the consideration of studio art as terms like *technē, eidos,* and *mimesis* are to theories of representation.[4] Writers like Graeme Sullivan and Donald Schön provide examples of the apparently natural uses of words like *research*—uses that are actually driven by institutionally-motivated uses of those words in art education, administrative documentation, grant applications, and university self-descriptions. For example, although it seems unobjectionable when Schön says "intuition" makes practice into "creative practice," surely it stretches the meaning of the word *research* to conclude that intuition also makes "creative practice (but not all practice) research, that is to say, the programmatic generation of new knowledge in a defined field." I think it would be a good idea to try to avoid torturing existing uses of words like "creative" and "intuition," just so they can fit better with the bureaucratically-motivated senses of words like "research" and "defined field." The naturalization of *research* concerns me—it has become ubiquitous, and can be found in most chapters of this book.

Several years ago, I was invited to a university in North America to help advise on the creation of a new studio-art PhD program. The words *knowledge* and *research* were used frequently, and without comment. At one point I asked a faculty member if she thought her own artwork produced knowledge. She said, "Yes, and in general I think artwork brings new knowledge into the world." I asked her what knowledge is produced by a Mondrian painting. She said, more or less, "That isn't a fair question, because Mondrian did not have a rigorous research program."

To me that epitomizes just how deeply ingrained the UK administrative jargon has become. I assume that instructor finds work less interesting if it is made without a "rigorous research program." I don't think so, but I didn't ask her, and I can imagine that in time, work done without palpable research might well come to seem less interesting.

The Relation Between Research As It is Used in Studio Art, and Research As It is Used in Other Departments of the University

There are several consequences to the naturalization of *research* and *new knowledge*. First, their naturalization prompts authors to distort their own arguments to fit *research* and *new knowledge*, even when those concepts are incommensurate with the authors' own ideas. Second, among authors who set out to avoid the model of art as research, there is still a tendency to identify research with science—an unhelpful proclivity that is nicely epitomized in a book called *The New Production of Knowledge: The Dynamics of Science and Research in Contemporary Societies.*[5] (This conflation of research with science is also unhelpful because it crushes the sciences, social sciences, law, medicine, and engineering into a methodological monolith, perpetuating the idea that research is itself a well-defined term.)

In the question-and-answer session at the 2003 conference, it was pointed out that *research* usually means work that is verifiable (or falsifiable) and repeatable. Frayling makes the same point, starting in a common-sense fashion with the dictionary definitions of research. The identification of research with falsifiability, hypothesis, and experiment is made, I think, mainly by scientists and people in the "harder" social sciences such as economics. In literary studies and other humanities, it would be difficult to find people who would describe their research in those terms. Someone else in the audience at the 2003 session pointed out that in the history of modern art, *research* is a debated term. Picasso disputed the claim that his work was research; he presumably hoped to escape from the early twentieth-century scientific paradigm for modern art.[6]

I agree with Jones when he stresses, in Chapter 2, just how much work needs to be done if *research* in the ordinary, scientific sense is to be adopted in the new degrees:

In this early stage of development we need to clarify what is not yet known but necessary to the further development of art and design research. Such an agenda for the development of art and design research, in my view, could usefully include the following: a full literature review; a review of examples of inquiry through artistic endeavor in modern history; a sociology of artists; a theoretical basis for intuition; an advanced theorization of how knowledge may be embodied in or represented by a work of art; an aesthetics of artistic method as distinct from one of artistic style; a comparative methodology of artistic production across cultures; and an international consensus in the definitions and boundaries of those subjects loosely bunched as art and design, so that debate of specialization and interdisciplinarity might be better facilitated.

I wouldn't produce the same list, but I couldn't agree more that work needs to be done: without concerted effort of a kind that has not yet begun, *research* in fine art will not be respected by people elsewhere in the university.[7]

In Chapter 6, Jones advocates looking to the sciences as a model for research in the humanities. I don't agree with that, first because I don't think the majority of artists would find such a model useful (Jones's artistic practice is unusually methodic and experimental, very much like research), and second because I don't think the arts can come up with an understanding of research that will be plausible to scientists—and if the ultimate purpose of thinking about research isn't to foster conversations across university departments, and to promote the new degree as a PhD, then there is little reason to retain the concept of *research* at all. As Victor Burgin says in Chapter 5, "the word 'art' does not appear in dictionary definitions of the word 'research.'"

The Concept of *New Knowledge*

The idea that studio work produces *new knowledge* is equally problematic. One way to defend the idea that the studio produces knowledge is to invest the materials of art with an intellectual or conceptual status. Donald Schön's interest in "research in action" (described in Chapter 2) is a way of acknowledging that intellectual work is involved in materials. Fair enough, but that also has its vexed history in modern art. It comes, first, from phenomenology as in Husserl (and later, Merleau-Ponty and Bachelard) and from anthropology as in Claude Lévi-Strauss, and it was imported into art history by Hubert Damisch and *October* contributors such as Yve-Alain Bois who have been interested in materiality. The idea is being revived, in an "animist" form, by W. J. T. Mitchell.[8] Younger scholars in art history, such as Hanneke Grootenboer, have explored the idea that painting, or paint, is a kind of thought. Jones looks elsewhere for criteria—he mentions Gilbert Ryle and Paul Hirst, and it would also be possible to cite Mark Johnson and his phenomenological approach.

There are many possibilities, some from fine art, others from anthropology and phenomenology. But all of them stretch the meaning of *knowledge*, and they are therefore all special pleading. In order for "the production of new knowledge" to make sense as a justification for PhDs in art, it would be necessary to have a university-wide consensus about the expression *new knowledge*. And that, I propose, would be impossible, both because the potential sources within the humanities are so diverse and so poorly correlated, and because when artists do say their work produces knowledge, they they don't often use that word in a sense analogous to the way scientists and other use it.

Legitimate Uses of *Research* and *New Knowledge*

My purpose in this chapter is not to stop all talk about research and new knowledge. For some artists, those terms fit very well. Frayling's examples of artists who conduct research includes Leonardo, Stubbs, and Constable (and Victor Burgin also enlists Constable in Chapter 5) but the idea of research also fits a number of contemporary artists. There are some artists, like the Yes Men or the Critical Art Ensemble, whose work creates knowledge, but even there the purpose is more empowerment and social action than knowledge per se. I have met some studio instructors who think of their work as research in a number of very interesting ways, and I have met a smaller number of studio instructors who think the purpose of their work is to produce new knowledge. (There are other artists—I have met a number in meetings on the new degree—who believe their work produces knowledge but do not want to put that knowledge into words. I will discuss them below.)

In theory there would be places for such art practices in studio-art PhDs. But for the majority of artists, *knowledge* isn't what art produces. Expression, yes. Emotion, passion, aesthetic pleasure, meaning. But not usually knowledge... so do we want to write that concept into the official statements of purpose of the new programs, when it may fit only a tiny minority of students?

No one outside the arts is likely to be persuaded by *any* of the formulations of *research* and *new knowledge* that have appeared in the art literature. No long-term dialogue between the arts and the sciences is likely to be built on the foundation of a shared method of research or a shared purpose of the creation of new knowledge. Second is the fact that for *most studio artists,* the operative words *research* and *new knowledge* are an awkward fit. These new programs deserve better: they deserve a language that is at once full, capacious, accurate, and not borrowed from other disciplines.

In the following sections I briefly survey a half-dozen strategies for avoiding *research* and *new knowledge.* I have numbered them; they are the beginning of an open-ended list. Afterward, I will make some observations about the opportunity this confusion affords for reconsidering the unity of the university.

1. Using *Understanding* Instead of *Knowledge*

Jones mentions *understanding* briefly in Chapter 2, as a synonym for *knowledge*; but the concept was distinguished from knowledge and rejected by Frayling in 1993, as Judith Mottram notes in Chapter 1. As far as I know, there has been no discussion on the differences between knowledge and understanding. The concept of *understanding* is promising because it has a much deeper and broader intellectual history than the current administrative uses of *research*, going back to nineteenth-century German discussions of *Verstehen* in Wilhelm Dilthey and others. Even so, the words *understanding* or *Verstehen* have their own problems: what does not add to our understanding of the world? Even if I repeat what someone else has said verbatim, I am still adding to our cumulative understanding of the world.

It would be good to have a concerted discussion of understanding, beginning with Dilthey's definition, and continuing on to critiques of Dilthey by Heidegger and Gadamer. One issue that would be helpful to raise in this context is Dilthey's use of *Erlebnis* (significant lived experience) alongside *Verstehen*. *Erlebnis* has resonance with current interests in phenomenology and performativity, and might conceivably provide a bridge back to Dilthey's humanism. Perhaps then it would be possible to arrive at a revised sense of *Verstehen* that could underwrite contemporary studio-art programs: but without serious inquiry, it would not be a good idea to adopt *understanding* because it would be likely to become an ill-defined stand-in for *knowledge*.

2. Using *Interpretation* Instead of *Knowledge*

In *Thinking Through Art*, Iain Biggs offers another way to redefine *new knowledge*, citing Paul Ricoeur's idea that "metaphoric language… provides new knowledge, but in a way that makes us arrive at it through the work of interpretation." Interpretation has been widely theorized in hermeneutics, and also in legal theory, so it is a plausible alternate to knowledge.[9]

A problem here might be that the genealogy of Ricoeur's hermeneutics, which includes Gadamer and Dilthey,[10] is used in the humanities but is not an uncontested way of thinking about interpretation; a model based on Ricoeur would therefore be in need of further argument.[11] But *interpretation* is significantly broader than *understanding*, and has a much more wide-ranging literature to accompany it. If I were asked to make a choice, it would be interpretation, because it would keep dialogue with other fields open.

3. Using *Writing* Instead of *Research*

Kerstin May's excellent essay in *Thinking Through Art,* called "The Gesture of Writing," tries to rethink other basic terms of art education, especially writing (using a little-read book by Vilém Flusser[12]) and the nature of the essay. This, it seems to me, is very promising: aside from asides to Hélène Cixous and Mark C. Taylor, her essay reads like the first two entries in a glossary of studio art instruction. It is conceivable that a sense of studio-art instruction as performed narrative could substitute for the uses of *research.*

The drawbacks here are clear, however, because narrative theory is only a part of literary criticism, and it is not widely used outside of literature. Narratology per se has not been a current concern in literary criticism since the 1980s.[13] It is not surprising that May has to cite Flusser and Taylor, because most of the writing on essay-writing was done before the poststructuralist critique that is mainly associated with Barthes and Derrida. After poststructuralism, it has seemed impossible to write in a non-fiction way about the essay as a non-fiction genre, because the foundational claim of poststructuralism in this regard is the indissolubility of "creative writing" and "expository writing," or "writing" and "philosophy."[14] Cixous is a central choice, and I could imagine using Gregory Ulmer as a source for a more performative (he would say "heuretic") sense of writing and its involvement in the making of sense.[15] My colleague in Chicago, the artist and theorist Joseph Grigely, puts ideas of Ulmer's to very good effect. Carol Mavor and Joanna Frueh are other writers who are deeply involved in making sense through narrative.[16] Mavor and Frueh are especially pertinent because they write about visual art: Mavor is an historian, and Frueh is an artist. But aside from work like theirs, most theorization of writing is not about visuality.

4. Finding a New Theory to Replace *New Knowledge*

Another possibility is to reject the forced choice between *research* and any single term, and try instead to build a theoretical position for studio-based academic work that could be comparable to theories used in other fields. This happens throughout the book *Thinking Through Art.*

Naren Barfield's essay "Spatial Ontology in Fine Art Practice" is an example; her purpose is to demonstrate that a wide range of concepts of space are relevant to creative practice research. Another is Ken Neil's résumé of some concepts of the Real in Slavoj Žižek and Hal Foster; another is Jim Mooney's meditation on Lacanian and

Levinasian concepts, titled "Painting: Poignancy and Ethics." One purpose of each of these essays is to find a voice for studio art in the university, and to that extent they share a problem, because the concepts they utilize tend to apply to several disciplines but not specifically to visual art. The Real, as Neil exposits it in his essay "Entity and Ground: Visual Arts Practice as Critical Differentiation," is to some degree native to the criticism of visual arts, but psychoanalytic theories of the Real have been deployed in many fields. Mooney's vocabulary is very adventurous, but it has also been used in literary criticism and theology.[17] It is not that these essays aren't tailored to visual art, but that the theories they exposit cannot be used to define studio art specifically.

It has been a trope in art history from the 1970s to the present that the discipline borrows theories from other fields, and that it borrows them after other fields have abandoned them.[18] There is truth to that, and any collection of theories from other fields, brought into studio art instruction, is likely to suffer the same fate: it may be widely useful, but it will not provide the indigenous accounting that is required, according to the logic of the university, of every field.

5. Avoiding *New Knowledge* by Talking about the Nonconceptual

One difference between what happens in studio art and in, say, physics, is that it appears that more of the content of the studio is outside conceptualization: it is nonverbal, uncognized, tacit, extra-linguistic, nonconceptual. Perhaps, then, a theory of advanced degrees in studio art should try to incorporate some sense of what happens outside language and logic. At its least successful, this strategy for avoiding *new knowledge* is the principal example of what Harrison calls "defensive and poorly argued assertions of the difference of artistic concerns and priorities"; but at its best, this strategy can engage one of the foundational properties of art—its visual, non-linguistic nature.

(I am talking here about theories of the *outcome* of artistic work, of the artwork itself, and how it is understood. It is a different matter to ask how artists think about their work, which often involves the idea of uncognized or nonconceptual action. My colleague in Chicago, Frances Whitehead, theorizes artist's knowledge as *tacit knowledge*. That project is different in kind from the claim that the *product* of artistic work is tacit knowledge.[19])

If the nonconceptual experience of visual art is taken as aesthetic, then the problem of the place of studio art can be posed as a version of Kantian aesthetics, and so distinguished from conceptual judgment. This form of the conceptual / nonconceptual divide is played out in various ways in *Thinking Through Art*. Kenneth Hay's well-researched essay "Concrete Abstractions" describes the Italian philosopher Galvano Della Volpe, who argued for the unity of aesthetic and conceptual by means of a hybrid concept, the "determinate" or "concrete abstraction."[20] The relation between Kantian aesthetics and conceptual judgment can be relevant in discussions of studio instruction, but perhaps mainly in contexts where the aesthetic has a central role in the conceptualization of art instruction—and that is not often the case.

A second approach to the nonconceptual is to emphasize its complementary relation to ordinary logical or instrumentalized discourse. The interest may then be in showing the compatibility, interpenetration, interdependence, or fundamental unity of what Jean-François Lyotard called *discours* and *figure*, discourse and the figurative element that accompanies and disrupts it.[21] Texts that argue this way tend to begin from Derrida's sense of *écriture*, as in Jeff Collins's essay "Derrida's Two Paintings In Painting: A Note On Art, Discourse and the Trace" in *Thinking Through Art*, which summarizes the main arguments.

A third approach might be to draw on theories of nonsense, insanity, and madness as they have been elaborated by Foucault. Perhaps the best author here is the under-utilized Jean-Jacques Lecercle.[22] By borrowing from Foucault's analysis of madness, the discourse of art could be positioned as an outsider in relation to norms of society. That would not entail tarnishing art with the old stereotypes of the mad or Saturnine artist: it would be an analysis of what is taken as sense and nonsense. Art instruction could be repositioned in those terms, with interesting results.[23]

Those are three possibilities. Authors who work in one way or another across the conceptual / nonconceptual divide cite a very wide range of authors to support their proposals. Hay shows the relation between Della Volpe and Marx, Gramsci, Lucàcs, and Croce. Also in *Thinking Through Art*, Clive Cazeau cites Kant, Nietzsche, Schopenhauer, and Sartre in his essay "Categories in Action: Sartre and the Theory-Practice Debate," although it could be argued that again his principal source is really Heidegger. In his essay "Hybrid Texts And Academic Authority-The Wager in Creative Practice Research," Iain Biggs concentrates on "material" versus "meaning" or "thought." Cazeau mentions several pairs of opposites he means to critique: conceptual versus aesthetic, theory versus practice, verbal versus visual, mental versus physical, and objective versus subjective.[24]

Certainly one challenge for adjudicating the conceptual and the nonconceptual is reining in the synonyms to which they give rise. A more difficult obstacle, I think, is answering accounts of the visual that decline to posit *any* dialectical pairs such as sense / nonsense, for example W.J.T. Mitchell or, in a different way, Gottfried Boehm.[25]

6. Redefining *Research* So It Is Not Dependent on the Sciences

Some writers have tried to rework the concept of research specifically so that it responds to the concerns of the humanities, and avoids the empirical, epistemologically limited protocols of its normal usage in the sciences. In this book, the most extensive attempt along these lines is Chapter 3, written by Henk Slager. He argues that artistic research transgresses scientific, humanistic, and social-science kinds of research, taking elements from each and reworking them into a new, unpredictable whole. That is true, but it does not help a university-wide dialogue on research because it will sound incomplete or evasive to people in the sciences and social sciences. It is definitely true that "artistic research seems to continuously thwart academically defined disciplines," and also true that "art knows the hermeneutic questions of the humanities; art is engaged in an empirically scientific method; and art is aware of the commitment and social involvement of the social sciences." (Although I would have said art "sometimes knows," is "sometimes engaged," and "sometimes aware.") But I do not think it is helpful, on the public stage of the university, to propose that "the most intrinsic characteristic of artistic research is based on the continuous transgression of boundaries in order to generate novel, reflexive zones."

This is a problem that is external to the concerns of a self-determining, intellectually independent art department, or an independent art academy or art school. In those terms, configurations like Slager's can be immensely helpful. But it is a serious issue when it comes to the university. I am afraid I agree with Charles Harrison's formulation in Chapter 10: "As a consequence of the fact that science generally provides the most rigorous paradigms of research, claims for rigor in research in the arts tend to be couched in one of two manners: either they are weak imitations of scientific proposals, or they are defensive and poorly argued assertions of the difference of artistic concerns and priorities." I don't find Slager's account "defensive" in the least: it is buoyant and inventive. But it would be seen by people in the sciences as inadequately argued. If studio-art PhDs are to be integrated into university life in North America, and if the road to that integration includes a redefinition of *research*, then it will be necessary to be very careful about what is meant by "continuous transgression of boundaries." Not because academic values exclude transgression! —but because it is not clear what a *continuous* transgression might be. What kind of enterprise defines itself as being in continuous, unpredictable motion against other discourses? The closest I know is a kind of simplified reading of Deleuze, in which one hopes for more-or-less continuous vectorial deterritorialization and nomadism, to borrow Deleuze's terms. In practice, even the most determinedly fluid and transgressive agendas settle down, and it's an account of that settling that is missing from the hopes of some writers in the arts.

Slager ends with an admirable claim: he says visual art research foes not have a fixed methodology, but "entails a strong belief in a methodologically articulable result founded by operational strategies that cannot be legitimized beforehand." Perhaps the most promising kinds of redefinitions are those that can achieve a persuasive articulation of their unpredictable results, together with a solid theory demonstrating that their results will, in fact, be unpredictable.

7. Avoiding *New Knowledge* and *Research* by Emphasizing Practice

Some of the authors in *Thinking Through Art* are untheoretical in the specific sense that they are interested in providing examples of practice rather than reconceptualizations. Tim O'Riley's essay called "Representing Illusions" is an example: he mixes descriptions of artworks (Marcel Duchamp's neglected *Stéréoscopie à la main*, Alfred Hitchcock's *Rear Window*, Ilya Kabakov's *The Man Who Flew into His Picture*) literary criticism (Mikhail Mikhailovich Bakhtin), analytic philosophy (G.E. Moore), Russian formalism (I.S. Shklovskiĭ) and film criticism (David Bordwell) to justify the proposition that "a work's meaning is found neither in the work itself, nor in the hands, eyes or minds of the artist or viewer... it is apparent only in the space between them." This thesis has been argued, using different points of reference, by Heidegger, Benjamin, Adorno, Arendt, Lacan, and most recently Kaja Silverman. O'Riley's paper is thus an example of the problems of idiosyncratic citation that concern me in some of the literature defending the studio-art PhD; I will have more to say on that in a moment. But because it is an artist's statement and not a contribution to visual theory, it would not make sense to describe his mixture of sources as a fault.[26]

Writing that proceeds by examples, building old arguments using new materials, is an interesting way forward: provided, I think, that it does not present itself as a contribution to theory—because then the eccentric range of references, and the absence of crucial sources, the interest in performativity and practice over the construction of durable theories, would again put such writing at the margins of academic interest.

I was very glad to see Elizabeth Price's essay "sidekick" in *Thinking Through Art*, because it is a brilliant example of a particular kind of artist's writing.[27] It is a pure research report. She describes herself building a "boulder" of tape; when she says "sometimes I am not sure myself if the boulder has been made in the way I claim," she is writing just as a scientist would in a lab notebook: that kind of doubt rarely has a place in publication, but it is definitely in the spirit of scientific research. There are times and places when studio art instruction really does become research-based practice, as opposed to practice-based research. Timothy Emlyn Jones's own artistic practice works along these lines, because he sets himself carefully framed problems (for example, making sprayed-ink drawings of certain dimensions, in a certain amount of time) and there are other examples, of which Bridget Riley is perhaps the clearest and best known. That particular kind of art practice—I think it derives ultimately from the Bauhaus—is an example of of work in which the research and new knowledge models fit nearly perfectly... except that they don't fit at all, because the result is a *practice*, not a *knowledge*. Writing like Price's is conceptually clear and rhetorically persuasive even though it does not aim to be a new or reworked theory of any sort. Anyone who has heard Riley talk about her paintings knows the strange feeling her accounts produce: she says things like, "What would happen if I painted in four colors, using barber-pole patterns, in stripes two cntimeters in width, and placed the barber poles four centimeters apart?" —and then she answers those apparently scientific questions by simply showing the resulting painting. Riley has a *practice* that mimics research, not a research program that produces knowledge. Her accounts of her work are compelling, but they will not wash on the other side of the university, except as an entertainment, because her use of concepts like *research* is nonsensical from a scientific standpoint. Her *practice*, on the other hand, is fascinating, and so is Price's.

Practice is a tricky word, because in the US it can signal performative, creative, material-based activity, but in the UK it resonates with the common name for the new degree, "practice-based research." In that sense I am also in agreement with Jones when he suggests, in Chapter 6, point number seven, that we avoid *practice*, as in the UK expression "practice-based research," because it seems to echo practice in medicine, law, and nursing. Like any other word that's going to be made to do a lot of work, *practice* would have to be examined to see if it can bear the meanings we want to assign to it. If *practice* is to make sense as a substitute for research or new knowledge, it will have to be developed as a series of acts. Otherwise practice is susceptible of being reduced to the artwork itself, which will then appear *as* the practice, as in my next entry.

8. Avoiding *New Knowledge* and *Research* by Proposing The Art Object Itself as Knowledge and the Product of Research

In this case, *research* doesn't mean the procedures and methodologies of inquiry, hypothesis, and testing, but the result itself—and that result is, by its nature, non-verbal. The artwork or art event *shows*, as Wittgenstein said, instead of *saying*.

Here it is helpful to use Christopher Frayling's categories of research *into* art and design, research *through* art and design, and research *for* art and design. I will discuss these more fully in Chapter 11, because Frayling's schema assumes the word *research* from the beginning—exactly what I am trying to avoid here. But his schema applies well in this case. His first category, research *into* art and design, is the typical business of art history. The second, research *through* art and design, is the usual configuration of studio-art PhDs, and it involves working with visual art in order to achieve a communicable result. The paradigm of research *through* art requires that the result be articulated *as* research: hence the requirement of a PhD dissertation to accompany the artwork.[28] The third category, research *for* art and design, is the one that troubles Frayling. As he puts it, "thinking is, so to speak, *embodied in the artifact.*" The goal is no longer knowledge in the way that the university recognizes it but "visual or iconic or imagistic communication."[29] As Judith Mottram notes in Chapter 1, this third category had still not appeared in the mid 1990s, and it remains both problematic and rare.

Although Frayling does not cite it, there is a large literature on the idea that thinking can take place *in* and *through* works of visual art. Paintings, in particular, have been said to embody thought, or to have a kind of thinking proper to themselves. Writers as different as Gaston Bachelard, Hubert Damisch, David Freedberg, Louis Marin, Jean-Louis Schefer, and W.J.T. Mitchell have proposed ideas along these lines.[30] It wouldn't quite be right to say this field is contested, because I do not think anyone has attempted to correlate the different theories. There is some talk in visual studies about Mitchell's notion of *picture theory* (that pictures produce theory, that they are theory), and some talk in art history about Marin's ways of reading images (that they elicit thoughts about reading, even though they are not legible). There is also talk about the agency of visual art, but so far those conversations are disconnected. If the art object itself is to be the *new knowledge*, instead of the dissertation, a great deal more work will have to be done to define what kind of thought inheres in the object itself, and what might be said about it.

Notice a distinction here: in this theory, it should not be possible to articulate the pertinent thoughts or arguments that are embodied in the artwork. If that were possible, then the claim would not be that the artwork embodies thought, but that it enables thought—and then the discussion could return to Frayling's second strategy, research *through* art and design, and there would be no need to insist on the artwork itself as the end point of research. Here the claim is that whatever counts as knowledge or research (or any other source of sense or meaning) simply *is* the artwork. No instructor can come along with a clipboard and extract that information.

In my experience, many artists want to believe a version of this claim, because it means that what they produce cannot be reduced to words: but at the same time they are willing to write dissertations about their work, and read what others may write about it. That misunderstands the radical nature of the claim itself.

The Importance of Talking to Everyone in the University
These last few pages suggest some of the ways of working around *research* and *new knowledge*. Before I return to the list, I want to expand a little on the third theme of this essay, the idea that these kinds of questions might help re-ignite discussions about the unity of the university as a whole. One purpose of the contributors to *Thinking Through Art* is to find a force, an imprimatur or status or intellectual weight for the theory of visual art instruction that will be analogous to the operation of theory in neighboring disciplines such as literary studies, philosophy, European sociology, and anthropology. For that reason it is important that each new theory connects to existing theories in other fields. It will matter a great deal that the new theory appears well-researched to specialists in that theory, and that it be shown to be connected at pertinent points to existing writing. To put it in practical terms: the authors in *Thinking Through Art* should expect, or want, to be cited and discussed by scholars in the relevant disciplines, not because such a response would be the best measure of the new work (the new work will form its own public, and adapt to its own purposes), but because interest on the part of the wider university is a condition for being taken to have a position—and finally, a discipline—that speaks to existing concerns.

Idiosyncratic or inadequate citations are a liability. An example of this issue is Gavin Renwick's essay, "Spatial Determinism in the

Canadian North." In suggesting that unnoticed "forms of knowledge" in among the First Nations of Canada exist as alternatives to "the dominant worldview," Renwick cites James Clifford but not the larger literature of compatibility or incompatibility of world views, which began with Nelson Goodman and Benjamin Whorf.[31] In his introductory section, Renwick quotes Clifford about the possibility of being "freed of the notion of the 'field' as a spatialized... site of research," but that may sound implausible or unhelpfully utopian to scholars in the humanities who work on disciplinarity.[32] Renwick's essay depends on a Heideggerian sense of language and meaning and a Heideggerian opposition to what Renwick calls "Technical Rationality." His source is the design theorist Clive Dilnot—not especially widely read as a philosopher—who is himself deeply dependent on Heidegger. To connect Renwick's concerns with ongoing conversations in other disciplines, it would be necessary, I think, to cite Heidegger directly and to bring in pertinent secondary sources. Otherwise Rewick's contribution risks appearing under-researched and therefore less than fully engaged. Several of the most imaginative essays share this difficulty, for example Siun Hanrahan's piece called "Poesis: Making Meaning," which discusses confusion, conversation, and incompletion, or Mooney's essay on lamella, the sting, and the caress, or Milos Rancovic's essay "Frozen Complexity," on statistical fractals, lossy compression, and algorithmic complexity: they are independent-minded and poetic, but it might be hard to find them a hearing either among academics unconvinced of the place of studio art, or among specialists in the scattered sources they both employ.[33]

These essays are, in the usual expression, artists' statements: the very genre that writes its own exclusion from "serious" academic discourse. My sense is that scholars or artists who set out to locate concepts that might be apposite for visual art instruction need to be especially careful that their contributions are specific to visual art instruction, and that they are researched at the level of the pertinent journals and disciplines. Here is how Victor Burgin puts it, and I entirely agree: "Most damagingly, there are widely differing conceptions of the quality of intellectual argument and written expression that is acceptable at PhD level—not only between different departments, but between different faculty within the same department. If this current state of affairs continues that can only undermine student morale and public confidence in the value not only of research degrees in visual arts but of PhD degrees in general."

The Difficulty of Knowing How to Judge the New Theories
    One consequence of a new field, whose writing does not yet

have the pliable constraints provided by disciplinary conventions, is that it can be hard to know how the work might be defended or justified. Naren Barfield, for example, sees concepts of space as appropriate contributions to the ontological content of fine art research, complementing its often strong epistemological content. Yet how can she know that it is "desirable" to balance the artist's traditionally high quotient of "epistemological" findings with ontological ones (contributed by spatial concepts), or that "significant and meaningful practice-as-research is contingent on successful reconciliation of the 'epistemic' and 'ontic' states of the practical research project"? Why couldn't it be equally successful to let the ontological languish, or to play off an imbalance between the two sides? I am not disagreeing with the adoption of spatial terms or ontological concerns, but I wonder where the theory comes from that justifies Barfield's interest in reconciling or balancing the two sides. That theory, the one that drives the theory explicit in her text, is elusive: as it well might be given the elusiveness of the entire project of theorizing art practice in these ways. (The project makes sense differently when it is in context of her own art practice.³⁴)

Another missing piece of the jigsaw puzzle is the theory of these theories. So far, the university hasn't had to come to terms with competing versions of self-descriptions of *research* or *new knowledge*. The studio-art PhD might well enjoin those conversations.

9. Replacing *Research* with Doubt Instead of Theory

I want to close with two ideas I find especially promising. Reading *Thinking Through Art*, one can get the impression that a critical mass of writing might help re-attach studio art practice to the university. Yet it is important to guard against the assumption that new discourses, concepts, theories, or methods can meliorate the problem. I find that universities, as they are embodied in actual faculty committees, do not resist studio art because of its lack of theory, even though university rhetoric can make it seem that is the case. In my experience university administrators resist any subject that appears to lack hierarchical instruction: an enterprise does not appear *as* a field or discipline unless it demonstrates a hierarchy of learning from primers through surveys and on to specialized, monographic texts. What keeps studio art on the margins is its apparent lack of stepwise, graduated instruction in college-level courses— knowledge that could be "assessed" (in the UK term) or "graded" (in the North American term) rather than being judged exclusively in studio-art critiques. It seems suspicious that there are relatively few prerequisites in studio art curricula. Can a field really be a legitimate academic discipline if you can jump in at sophomore or junior level, or skip entire media and techniques?

As Stanley Fish has argued, the university wants knowledge—or any reasonable substitute for that concept—that is amenable to academic values of coherence, plausibility, connectedness, fruitfulness, and that is susceptible to concerted, analytic inquiry. None of that seems to pertain to studio-art instruction. This means it may be misleading to say that universities are waiting for Theory, or resisting creativity per se, or devaluing visuality. What they want is hierarchical instruction and academic coherence.

It's true university administrators are sometimes dubious about studio art departments because they seem to lack something that could be called theory; that can be addressed not by discovering new theories but by acknowledging the issue is an open problem whose negotiation can form the very basis of a studio art department. I find it heartening when Biggs calls for "an open acknowledgment of our 'inevitable inadequacy.'" Something of that kind could be a viable starting place for a new discipline—one that would be engaged in questioning its place more systemically than in some established disciplines. Taking doubt of that kind as a founding gesture, a studio art department that grants PhDs could find a very broad consensus among the humanities and sciences—a consensus that might be dramatically reduced or eliminated if the department were founded on any number of specific theorists or theories, from Nietzsche to Della Volpe.

10. Replacing *Research* With the Disjunction between Making and Studying

Like the authors in *Thinking Through Art*, I am engaged in finding ways to argue that art production has a place in the university. The problem is immensely difficult, as the essays in that book testify. As a token of that difficulty I note that not one of the authors addresses the conceptual disjunction between making art and studying it. Most of the contributors are interested in how the making of art can be theorized, but there is another problem that is prior to any talk about art: the experience of making—its exact pedagogy, its methods, knacks, and skills, its feel. In *Thinking Through Art*, only Rancovic and Price mention anything exact about the experience of making, but that experience, rather than conceptualizing the art, is at the root of the incommensurability of studio art production and university life. The essays in *Thinking Through Art* could be taken as a description of a strange activity *that is finished* and requires conceptualization. But in studio art classes, in the university, the process is not finished—and in fact the process itself is the subject of the classes.

This is a simple point, and each of the authors in *Thinking Through Art* is well aware of it, because they are all art makers. But I think this is where the real conceptual difficulty lies: it is hard enough to find the right words for visual art, but harder still to take the making along with the talk about the making. Let us continue to think about the studio and the university, but not imagine that the problem is adequately addressed until we have found ways of addressing the relation of university life and the act of making art, as opposed to the variegated and often fascinating ways of talking about the relation between the university and finished art.

Three Conclusions

First concerning *research* and *new knowledge:* if you live in the UK or Australia, and the RAE and AHRB are inescapable, and you are interested in setting up a program that grants the DCA (Doctorate in Creative Arts) or PhD, then provide the university with the appropriate texts and then simply ignore what you've written. (If you live in a country that is influenced by the UK—such as Ireland—then do the same.) Words like *research* and *new knowledge* should be confined to administrative documents, and kept out of serious literature. The field is too large, and too full of promise, to be hobbled by narrow and inappropriate administrative jargon. I would be interested to see degrees conferred in any of the configurations named in *Thinking Through Art;* but I do not think it is promising to import the technical language of administrative quality control into the theorization of the studio.

Second, concerning the level of scholarship in the new degrees: no matter how the new degree is configured, it is essential either that the scholarship in the dissertation is at the same level as scholarship that is produced in whatever fields (anthropology, philosophy, art history) the dissertation addresses, or that the dissertation addresses its use of the scholarship of other fields, defending idiosyncratic readings and incomplete research. There is no simple way to make this choice, because it is wholly legitimate for a new field to turn an existing body of scholarship to new and unexpected uses. It can be argued that the art world has already produced its own versions of several discourses; parts of Lacanian psychoanalysis, for example, have been largely remade as film theory, so that the kinds of references to Lacan made in film classes and in studio conversations cannot usually be correlated with the primary texts as they are known to specialists in psychoanalysis. But if a creative-art PhD thesis cites existing discourses in a manner that would not seem acceptable to a PhD-granting committee in the fields in question—as many in *Thinking Through Art* do—then it is absolutely essential to build in a commentary on the writer's purposes: a commentary that would ideally also demonstrate that the author knows the discourses and chooses to ignore or distort them. Otherwise creative arts PhDs will become isolated within the university.

Third, regarding the challenge posed to the university: I think the new degrees can conceivably become the focus of university-wide debate about the unity or fragmentation of the contemporary university. It would be good to revive those debates, which have lagged slightly after a renascence in the 1990s.[35] My own uncertainty about the concepts or strategies that might replace *research* and *new knowledge* is a reflection of how tricky this subject is. Universities have not been set up to think about the confluence of making and studying, understanding and knowledge, practice-led research and research-led practice, writing and seeing. Studio art practice could be the place to carry those discussions forward. Or it could be just another extension of threadbare concepts from UK pedagogy, twisted to fit the instrumentalized academic practice of contemporary art.

Notes

1 There's a story behind this chapter. It was originally to be published in Katy Macleod and Lin Holdridge's edited volume called *Thinking Through Art: Critical Reflections on Emerging Research* (London: Routledge, 2005). The editors had asked me to write the Afterword, and I read the book in manuscript and wrote a 5,000 word essay. I sent it to them, and I was amazed to hear in response that they thought it was too critical of the contributing authors. I have to say they behaved impeccably: we exchanged several emails, in which I expressed my surprise and suggested that the field of creative-art PhDs needs criticism. Eventually they decided to publish an abbreviated version, shorn of my detailed criticism. Everyone interested in the field should read *Thinking Through Art*; it even contains a different version of Jones's essay (Chapter 2 in this book). Macleod and Holdridge then edited my Afterword as they saw fit (I had nothing to do with their editorial decisions), and printed the shortened version in their book. For the full text of the original version, with more detailed comments on the authors in MacLeod's and Holdridge's anthology, see *The New PhD in Studio Art*, no. 4 in the occasional series called *Printed Project*, edited by James Elkins (Dublin: Sculptor's Society of Ireland, 2005). That publication is hard to find outside of Ireland; I can provide copies on request.

2 For the MPhil, see "A Glossary of Terms" after the Introduction.

3 For an introduction see www.ahrb.ac.uk/research. It is pertinent that the documents that serve as the guides for studio-art PhD departments are often very brief. In 2008, I saw the document that spells out what *research* means in

the Visual Research Centre at the University of Dundee, Scotland: it is a half-page long.

4 A good example of how naturalized the concept of research has become is the collection of papers theorizing the MA and MFA degree, produced in Utrecht in 2008. The editorial introduction to that collection, by Henk Slager, mentions "research" in the third sentence—it's taken for granted that MA programs are about research. Slager uses the word "research" automatically, in sentences like this: "The question of the position of one's own artistic research leads us also to the theme of the research environment." This is despite Slager's own position, articulated in Chapter 3, which corresponds more with several of the alternates I list in this essay. See "A Certain MA-ness," edited by Henk Slager, special issue of *Makhuzine: Journal of Artistic Research* [Utrecht School of the Arts] 5 (2008), 3, 4. It is interesting that the word "research" does not occur in the North American definition of the MFA, adopted by the College Art Association, online at www.transartinstitute.org/Downloads/MFA_standards.pdf, and also discussed in Chapter 2.

5 Gibbons et al., *New Production of Knowledge* (London: Sage, 1994).

6 The interview with Picasso is discussed, in context of research in the studio-art PhDs, in Christopher Frayling's "Research in Art and Design," cited in the Introduction.

7 When Jones argues that "a research question may inquire into a problem to be solved; a creative opportunity to be explored or exploited; or an issue to be examined, whether any of these be technical, procedural, philosophical, theoretical, or historical. Whichever of these a research question may be it must also take the form of a query such as: what; what if; how; when; why; why not; for whom; by whom; or any other form of question," I do not think he has a formulation that would provoke assent among philosophers of science—but this is exactly the kind of elaboration that is necessary. (See Chapter 2.) I would say the same of Henk Slager's formulation in Chapter 3: "research as such could be described most adequately as the methodological connection of questions and answers... indefinability, heterogeneity, contingency, and relativity color the trajectory of artistic research. Therefore, artistic research should explicitly request tolerance, an open attitude, and the deployment of multiple models of interpretation." This kind of exploration makes good sense in the humanities, but it does not bring practice-based research closer to research as that concept is understood elsewhere in the university.

8 This is developed, for example, in *What is an Image?*, edited by James Elkins and Maja Naef, in the series Stone Theory Institute, vol. 2 (University Park, PA: Penn State Press, forthcoming).

9 For interpretation in law see for example J. C. Coleman and B. Leiter, "Determinacy, Objectivity and Authority," in *Law and Interpretation*, edited by A. Marmor (Oxford: Clarendon Press, 1995), and T.A.O. Endicott, "Putting Interpretation In Its Place," *Law and Philosophy* 13 (1994): 451-79. There is a good introductory article on hermeneutics online, on the Stanford Encyclopedia of Philosophy, plato.stanford.edu/entries/hermeneutics/, accessed September 2008.

10 For Dilthey see *Hermeneutics and the Study of History*, edited by Rudolf A. Makkreel and Frithjof Rodi (Princeton, NJ: Princeton University Press, 1996); for Gadamer, see *Philosophical Hermeneutics*, translated by David E. Linge (Berkeley: University of California Press, 1976); for Ricoeur, *The Conflict*

of Interpretations: Essays in Hermeneutics, translated by Willis Domingo et al. (Evanston, IL: Northwestern University Press, 1974).

11 In addition, Biggs ties Ricoeur's formulation to a pseudo-Nietzschean version of the Apollonian-Dionysian duality and to an allegorical reading of Greek modalities—Zeus as "legislative and executive power," and so forth—which would be hard to square with Ricoeur's hermeneutics.

12 Flusser, *Gesten: Versuch einer Phänomenologie* (Frankfurt: Fischer Taschenbuchverlag, 1994).

13 Mieke Bal's *Narratology: Introduction to the Theory of Narrative*, translated by Christine van Boheemen (Toronto: University of Toronto Press, 1985) is, as far as I can tell, no longer read, and neither are books like Ihab Hassan's *Paracriticisms: Seven Speculations of the Times* (Ubrana, IL: University of Illinois Press, 1975).

14 A good source here is *The Art of the Personal Essay: An Anthology from the Classical Era to the Present*, edited by Philip Lopate (New York:Anchor, 1995 [1994]).

15 For Cixous a good starting place is *"Coming to Writing" and Other Essays*, edited by Deborah Jenson (Cambridge, MA: Harvard University Press, 1991); for Ulmer see *Heuretics: The Logic of Invention* (Baltimore, MD: Johns Hopkins University Press, 1994).

16 For Mavor see *Reading Boyishly: Roland Barthes, J.M. Barrie, Jacques Henri Lartigue, Marcel Proust*, and D.W. Winnicott (Durham, NC: Duke University Press, 2007); for Frueh see for example *Erotic Faculties* (Berkeley, CA: University of California Press, 1996).

17 See further Mooney, "Praxis-Ethics-Erotics," PhD dissertation, Royal College of Art, 1999, unpublished.

18 The references are in my "The Unease in Art History," *Qui parle* 6 no. 1 (fall/winter 1992): 113–33.

19 Whitehead and I are co-organizing the third annual Stone Summer Theory Institute, in 2009, on the subject "What do Artists Know?"—we will produce a book with the same title, vol. 3 of the *Stone Theory Institute* (University Park, PA: Penn State Press, forthcoming c. 2010). The contributors will include theorists of extra-linguistic, tacit, and otherwise unarticulated knowledge, such as Philip Johnson-Laird and Roy Sorensen. See www.stone-summertheoryinstitute.org, accessed September 2008; Johnson-Laird, *How we Reason* (Oxford: Oxford University Press, 2006); Sorensen, *Thought Experiments* (New York: Oxford University Press, 1992).

20 Della Volpe, *Critica del Gusto* (1960). Questions might be raised both within and outside this project. In the project's own terms, it is unclear how successful Della Volpe is in distinguishing among media or in finding a concept that might have direct effects on existing ways of talking about studio practice, art theory, and art history. (Form and content remain problematically distinct in many parts of art history: but can the concept of concrete abstraction mend their difference?) In larger terms, it might be asked whether a reconciliation of form and content, or aesthetic response and cognition, is sufficient for understanding the current forms of studio art instruction.

21 Lyotard, *Discours, figure* (Paris: Klincksieck, 1971). (The book is famously, notoriously, untranslated.)

22 Lecercle, *Philosophy Through the Looking-Glass: Language, Nonsense, Desire* (LaSalle, IL: Open Court Press, 1985).

23 As far as I know, no one has pursued this possibility. I argue for the nearly complete lack of sense in studio art instruction in my *Why Art Cannot be Taught: A Handbook for Art Students* (Urbana, IL: University of Illinois Press, 2001).

24 He cites Schopenhauer on the universal and particular, but interprets the passage as a matter of objectivity and subjectivity, and soon after as an instance of the conceptual and the aesthetic.

25 This is developed in *What is an Image?*, co-edited with Maja Naef, vol. 2 of the *Stone Theory Institute* (University Park, PA: Penn State Press, forthcoming), with contributions by Boehm, Mitchell, and others.

26 See O'Riley, "Representing Illusion's Space: Narrative and the Spectator in Fine Art Practice," PhD dissertation, Chelsea College of Art and Design, The London Institute, 1998, unpublished.

27 See the full report in Price, "sidekick," PhD dissertation, University of Leeds, 2000, unpublished.

28 The other theoretical source here, aside from Frayling, is Donald Schön, whose notion of *thinking through art* corresponds with Frayling's *research through art* in that both entail written communication of results. See the section "Art and Design Practice Considered as Research" in Chapter 2 for more information on Schön.

29 Frayling, "Research in Art and Design," 5. Frayling epitomizes the difference by citing something E.M. Forster's aunt said to him: "How can I tell that I think until I see what I say?" Frayling says that exemplifies research *into* art and design. He proposes this sentence to epitomize research *through* art and design: "How can I tell what I think till I see what I make and do?" And he exemplifies research *for* art and design with the sentence: "How can I tell what I am till I see what I make and do?" I am not entirely happy with these three sentences, because research *through* art and design, as well as research *into* art and design, are also about subjectivity. It is also not quite right that the first sentence is "that I think"; it should be "what I think." And most important, the third and most problematic sentence does not capture the confusion of subjectivities that is often important to claims that artworks possess thought—for example, it would not always be right to say that once an artist sees what she produces, she can then say what she thinks.

30 This is the subject of a work in progress, titled "Can Pictures Think?" (2006).

31 See Davidson, Inquiries into Truth and Interpretation (Oxford, 1984). There is also an anthropological literature on this subject beyond Clifford; see for example The Post-Development Reader, edited by Rajid Mahnema and Victoria Bawtree (New York: Zed Books, 1997).

32 For further bibliography see my "Nine Modes of Interdisciplinarity in Visual Studies," reply to Mieke Bal,"Visual Essentialism and the Object of Visual Culture," Journal of Visual Culture 2 no. 2 (2003): 232-37.

33 See Hanrahan,"A Combined Philosophic and Artistic Research Methodology," PhD diss., 2 vols., University of Ulster, 1996, unpublished.

34 Barfield,"Integrated Artworks: Theory and Practice in Relation to Printmaking and Computers, and the Influence of 'Non-Euclidean Geometry' and 'The Fourth Dimension' on Developments in Twentieth-Century Pictorial Space," PhD diss.,Camberwell College of Art, 1999, unpublished.

35 References and discussion are in my *Visual Practices Across the University,* with contributions by 35 scholars (Munich: Wilhelm Fink Verlag, 2007).

10

When Management Speaks...[1]
Charles Harrison

This is an abbreviated excerpt from an already brief essay written by Charles Harrison for a symposium at The Laboratory, the research unit of the Ruskin School of Drawing and Fine Art at Oxford in 1999. The full paper appeared in Research and the Artist: Considering the Role of the Art School, *edited by Antonia Payne. The portion reprinted here is one of the clearest rejections of the PhD in the UK.*

Part of what Harrison says here concerns the Research Assessment Exercise, a kind of measuring-stick for academic achievement in the UK. Even though the RAE is changing and is slated to be replaced, I have included these passages here because other writers in this book refer to the RAE, and because the RAE is an excellent model of the hypertrophied quantification of research—and in that sense its ghost continues to haunt discussions of the PhD. For an introduction to the RAE, the the Glossary of Terms, at the beginning of this book, following the Acknowledgments.

This excerpt is divided into two parts: the first pertains to the RAE and what counts as research in that context; the second directly addresses the nature of research in the studio-art PhD.

1

In the awkward, uncomfortable and badly theorized relationship between teaching and research, it remains the case that those who put all their energies into teaching are much less likely to be promoted than those who put their energies into research (despite the fact that the latter may be doing so at the expense of those who put their energies into teaching). I am not in a position to say how much this may be the case in art schools or within those university departments that call themselves Fine Art departments. But I am sure that the borderline between what gets called *teaching* and what gets called *research* will be fuzzy in many such institutions, and I rather suspect that consequent relations of exploitation will pertain in at least some cases. (I see some art school heads nodding in the audience.)

There is a strange, vicious circle in the relationship between so-called research productivity and research funding, and particularly under the regime of the Research Assessment Exercises (RAEs). I count myself fairly lucky that, as a consequence of my having a certain publication record, I am able to draw upon a measure of research funding. But let me be explicit about what that involves. I draw between about £500 and £1,000 per annum in research expenses, and most of that pays for overseas travel to art exhibitions. These are either exhibitions of work that I might propose to write about (it being much easier to attract funding if it is associated with prospective publication) or exhibitions in which I have a slightly more practical investment, working with my friends in Art & Language (when it is also sometimes possible to claim that I will be generating some form of publication).

Let me describe briefly the slightly ironic circle that is thereby created. As most of you will know—indeed I suspect this is one of the motors driving the whole present occasion—there is a relationship between supposedly measurable research output and the status and funding of university departments. My friends and colleagues within the practice of Art & Language make art. They do so without sponsorship or funding from outside and they live almost entirely upon whatever sales the product of the studio can be made to generate. In various kinds of relationship with that artistic work I am able to generate forms of publication, or to claim a share in forms of publication which are part of our collaborative output. These can be added to my research tally within the university and therefore to my "research points." These, in turn, contribute towards a "departmental score" in RAEs. My university department or faculty is funded according to its research tally, to which I contribute in this fashion. So, research funds flow back to the University and those funds are then disbursed *within* the University. Precedent suggests that what will then happen is that monies in part secured by the relatively high score I contribute to my faculty the Faculty of Arts—will be filtered off to help support the relatively weak and unprofitable research in the sciences undertaken elsewhere in the university.

I hope that from this brief description you can see how one kind of product generated in one place—the studio—results in funds being made available to support what arc generally regarded as more politically and socially useful spheres of activity both within the universities and elsewhere. Of course, no financial benefit flows *back* to the studio.

In the announcement for this presentation, I was dignified with the title of "Professor."[2] I do indeed hold a personal Chair (that now much devalued piece of furniture). I am fortunate to have slipped under the net just before the Open University changed the criteria for promotion. What is now required is some strong evidence of administrative work in pursuit of the university's institutional ends and policies. Given that I would be unlikely to meet the criteria now prevailing, I was lucky to have passed under the barrier on the basis of a good batting score in the field of publications.

I do not mean to sound entirely cynical about the kinds of scores and measurements that are now applied. There are clearly some advantages to a system which requires academics to show some measurable research output, and I suppose that there may be similar gains if people within art schools can similarly be motivated to produce in areas which may have long been unproductive. It means that some of those people who have been able to free-wheel along in academic institutions, treating their jobs as forms of sinecure, have been pressured to work for publication. I am unsure, however, just how far the world stands to benefit from the material thus generated. I say this without complacency. I have to consider (as I often do in the late hours of the night) whether I might not myself be one such *de facto* synecurist, gaining a certain amount of spurious credibility through the sheer quantity, rather than the quality, of my publications. It seems to me that this is a criticism to which all of us should regard ourselves as potentially subject.

There is certainly more research being conducted nowadays. However, I question whether Dr. Pilsbury[3] can feel entirely confident that the climate generated by the AHRB[4] is also resulting in better research. I think that there is too much research. There are too many bad academic journals and too much bad material is being published. There is more than anyone can read, more than makes sense and more than can sustain reasonable, interesting, critical and intellectual value. What we now have is an effective system of institutional vanity publishing. I know of at least one university where anybody who publishes an article, anywhere, receives a little pat on the back and a "contribution to their expenses." It used to be £250, but it will no doubt have gone up by now. Things like this are happening all over the system.

I am quite sure that the short-term pressure of the RAE is one of the motors that is driving the system—and this despite the talk that we hear about opportunities for funding long-term research projects. One would like to think that the present system can be improved, but there are few grounds for optimism. Many of you will no doubt be able to confirm my own experience of the grounds on which academic research appointments arc currently being made. Many so-called research lectureships are being created out of RAE-generated funds (or in expectation of their receipt) and they are being awarded to individuals who arc not necessarily the most interesting candidates, not necessarily the ones you know can think on their feet in an interview. Instead, they are being offered to those who have a contract for a book—a book likely to be published within the timing of the next RAE. That the book may be redundant, boring—yet another tedious addition to some student's already overlong bibliography—is apparently irrelevant. One would like to believe that the driving forces can still be reined in. But in many cases it is already too late. Appointments have already been made in the interests of short-term research, and no doubt in some cases at the expense of better candidates.

I continue with what is perhaps best characterized as a confessional story. For some time, I worked very happily and very profitably with Paul Wood—a friend who happened to become a colleague—on a large and fairly ambitious project to produce an anthology of Art Theory. As far as possible, we worked consciously and deliberately outside the institution, in our own homes and in our own time, and we sustained a continuing conversation about the kind of material that we would include in the book. In an important sense for me and, I think, to some extent for Paul, the project was morally, intellectually and socially connected to what we remembered of the Art & Language Indexing projects of some twenty years before. The book was successful and the publishers suggested that we might produce a sequel. The sequel required us to undertake considerable reading in languages in which neither of us was competent, and particularly in German. It therefore seemed to us that we would need a research assistant who could read some foreign material for us. We consequently applied to the Open University's Arts Faculty for some ad hoc, interim funding to enable us to employ someone on a part-time basis. The application was successful and the person we recruited, though he was not paid nearly enough for the work that he was undertaking, proved to be extremely good value. Such good value was he, in fact, that the project grew. The planned second volume spawned a third. Encouraged by the apparent success of the project, the Faculty encouraged us to apply to a national body for rather more substantial funding for the book. Having spent some three weeks completing all the necessary paper work and submitting an application, we were successful in gaining a grant worth £50,000 over two years. Our former research assistant—by now our colleague—was thus funded for a two-year research fellowship. So far so good.

But of course the fellowship was administered by the university and was claimed almost as its own. Gradually and insidiously a project that had flourished under its conversational aspect became accountable and institutionalized. In the process, it changed and became harder to accomplish. It had become estranged; unresearch-like; at worst, another aspect of university administration. I am not quite sure *how* this happened. I certainly do not mean to point the finger at my co-editors, nor do I mean to suggest that there was ex-plicitly malign and malevolent influence at work. I suspect a certain weakness on my own part. Perhaps the point is that certain kinds of conversational and critical activity arc vulnerable in ways that we are unwilling to acknowledge when funding is at stake.

Let me try and put together these two aspects of my own experi-ence—the "art" aspect [Harrison's involvement in Art & Language, of which he had spoken previously] and the "univcrsity" aspect. Some while ago, the Open University—which, under its current Vice Chancellor, is an ambitious and expansive body—either rook upon itself or was persuaded to adopt the role of validating body in place of the disbanded Council for National Academic Awards, acting for those institutions that wished to become "self-certifying" in respect of their research programs. In effect, the Open university set itself up as an agency to which other academic bodies could ap-ply for validation of their research projects. This meant that propos-als for PhD research in various kinds of institutions with Fine Art departments started arriving in the University, with the task of as-sessment filtered out to appropriate academics. I only really knew about this when proposals started landing on my desk. I suppose as a consequence of my slightly anomalous history and position I received the proposals which were "art-like" rather than straight-forwardly academic—the ones that no one knew what to do with or how to assess. I was not asked if *wished* to look at them; they simply arrived as a sort of unwelcome extension to my work load. At first, I did my best critically to assess them. After a while, though, I came to feel that I was being drawn hack into some of the more unwel-comc aspects of those days—long ago now—when I used to spend a lot of my time teaching in art schools.

2

I conclude, then, with some slightly more formal thoughts. These are the products of that experience, of acting, as it were, as an asses-sor-in-bad faith. As has been suggested already, the most rigorous paradigms of research are—at least supposedly—derived from the study of science. I think it is certainly true that the most interesting work on criticism and the growth of knowledge tends to take its specific cases from the fields of scientific discovery and controversy and *not* from the arts. I suspect that there may be good reasons for this. One of the better reasons is that, in science, you can generally at least tell what is, and what is not, research. In the arts—certainly in the practice of art—you cannot. As a consequence of the fact that science generally provides the most rigorous paradigms of research, claims for rigor in research in the arts tend to be couched in one of two manners: either they are weak imitations of scientific proposals, or they are defensive and poorly argued assertions of the difference of artistic concerns and priorities. In this latter case, the notion of difference is sabotaged by the problem of distinguishing what, in the practice of art, is and is not research. This problem is aggravated in circumstances where there is no longer any accepted progression in practical and professional skills from the basic craft practices learned in the studio to the supposedly more fancy and intellectual kinds of activity discussed by Patricia Bickers.[5]

It seems to me to he very symptomatic that, under the regime of the RAEs, researchers in the humanities are required to rank their publications according to whether or not they have appeared in "refereed" or "unrefereed" journals. In the former case publications have tended to attract at least three times the score of the latter, more or less regardless of the length, interest, quality and originality of the work concerned. In science, the test of peer-group review may reasonably be applied to some new research finding or hypothesis. Applied to work in the humanities however, the demarcation is largely irrelevant and insignificant. It is indicative of nothing so much as the snobbery of those who try to apply it.

These absurdities have been compounded over the past three decades, as art colleges and departments have been drawn ever closer to the world of higher-educational bureaucratic pretension. The partial and informal sample with which I found myself presented at the Open University suggests that proposals for post-graduate work tend to follow one or other of the patterns I have already described, being either poor imitations of science-like proposals or weak assertions of the difference and unmeasurability of work in the arts. They therefore tend to dramatize the absurdities entailed. Of the proposals that I saw—and I certainly do not mean to point to any particular individuals or institutions in saying this—I think that the great majority were victims of the processes in which their authors were caught up. Of those that I sampled, some of the applications were hopelessly misguided, some simply inappropriate to the institutions concerned, some farcical, a few interesting but very inadequately formulated.

I do not mean to sound too school-masterish. 1 am simply speaking out of the experience of somebody who, under the new and, I think, properly more stringent regimes to which we are all subject, has been required to scrutinize applications. Indeed, I have to scrutinize my own post-graduate applications very carefully these days, to ensure that I do not take on people who may not complete, people who I feel I am not competent to supervise and, particularly, people who I am not interested in supervising (since if I am not interested, I should not be doing it). I think that we need to be very careful about who supervises whom and for what reasons.

Given my own cautions, I found it a sad observation that one of the few things common to all the applications I was asked to scrutinize was their being supported by statements of the absolute competence and willingness of their sponsoring supervisors—this despite the fact that no competent supervisor, it seemed to mc, could have allowed any of them to pass uncorrected. They had only to have looked at anyone of the attached bibliographies, I would have thought, to see that it had been generated entirely automatically, that it was completely arbitrary, or that it was altogether inappropriate to the project put forward.

The conclusion I draw from this is that there is clear convergence of interest between those who are eager, for political reasons, to encourage so-called research in art, and those artists employed as teachers in higher education—whether they be dedicated but deluded, or trapped and desperate—who need to defend the credibility or increase the funding of their departments. The embarrassing or sad result, I suggest, is that the only real requirement made of students is that they should be willing to present (and of course somehow to fund) themselves as "researchers," and that their gratitude for the opportunity should prevent them from complaining about the lack of any sensible direction. I am sure that you have all heard stories about departments running taught-MA courses[6] full of overseas students who cannot understand English and to whom nobody speaks. It would be no loss if that sort of thing were prevented.

There is some irony, it seems to me, in the fact that the present enlargement of opportunities for mystificatory research projects, particularly those in art theory, is in part a consequence of the demise of modernist critical protocols, of the fall of the old life-drawing-and-hand-and-eye-co-ordination model of art teaching, and of their replacement by a pedagogy wedded to art teaching as An Theory teaching. The irony of this situation is that those who argued for the critical relevance of Art Theory thirty years ago did so in explicit opposition to the mystificatory equation of artistic practice with research. Theory is, I think, of some merit in the arts as critique and as a form of insurgency—and it is best left alone by funding bodies.

In the face of all this, it is hard to know what positive suggestions one might wish to offer. It seems to be a condition of modernism that art tends to die in modern institutions. We cannot produce artists in the way that the East Germans used to produce athletes. It may just be that design can be fostered, but it has been clear for some time—since the end of the 1930s at least—that art and design are set on diverging trajectories and that this is the more true the closer design comes to that which can be institutionally fostered. It may also be true that the mushrooming of Art Theory as a quasi-academic subject will, in the end, offer some opportunities for rigorous, if generally very tedious study. However, it has to be said that most of what passes for Art Theory at present is little better than low-intensity Social History of Art or heavy-breathing Cultural Studies. This notwithstanding, nobody should be deluded that they can now reproduce as matters of institutional convenience those exotic and highly contingent circumstances under which it made sense thirty years ago for Art Theory to be pursued as a critical form of art practice.

So, a conclusion—a sort of conclusion. For many years, like most people who often feel oppressed by those kinds of institutional tasks that they have to perform to earn their salaries, I have wondered what I would say if somebody from some extraordinarily and inconceivably generous funding body offered to buy me out of my employment so that I could spend more time working with my artist friends. What would I say? 1 have always thought that I would say "no," because there is a sense in which the tension between the two "halves" of my existence is productive, for me at least. We should all have to struggle a bit; we should all have to work to find our practice, and to negotiate it within some kind of real world. Also, 1 am not an artist and I have no intention of pretending to be one. In this situation of tension, I at least have to fight for such autonomy as my work will sustain; to ensure that my research—or whatever I call it—is at least in some sense my own business.

But if I ask myself—as I have been moved to do by the invitation to come and speak here—how I would answer were this same offer to be made to me now (an offer to buy me out of what remains of my time at the Open University), now I think I would say "yes." What has made the difference? What has made the difference is the Teaching Quality Assessment Exercise [TQA] and the RAE, both of which I find wasteful, arbitrary and thoroughly demeaning. I owe it to my institution, I suppose, to make clear that I do not say this out of institutional sour grapes. The department within which I work scored "excellent" on both counts, whether deserved or not. My point is not simply about the amount of preparatory work that these assessments require. It is not just a problem of their being an interruption to more productive forms of activity (it seems to me reasonable that one should have to interrupt one's terribly important personal research in order to submit to *some* kind of criteria of assessment). The real problem, I think, is that the two kinds of activity (research and involvement in TQA/RAE assessment) are *qualitatively* incommensurable: not simply quantitatively but qualitatively. The kinds of procedures that are involved in the assessment processes—the forms of self-bureaucratization required—are not, I think, compatible with the moral character of research as I understand it.

I live my life and have conducted my career to date under what I take to be the long dialectic of modernism, which incorporates two different models of how the artist may relate to the larger world and in particular, to some possible source of funding. On the one hand there is what we think of as the standard modernist model, the Greenbergian model of the avant-garde holding on to its critical autonomy while tied to the ruling class by an umbilical cord of gold. This is roughly the Capitalist model. Secondly, there is modernism's other half: the dream—at once seductive and repellent—of a culture both sponsored and to a large extent determined and defined by the state, where one loses a large measure of one's autonomy but gains a sense of security and of the value and relevance of one's activity. It is between these two possible poles that most of us here have lived out our professional lives, insofar as we have thought about these things.

But now there is a third way—and it makes my blood run cold. (I assume, of course, that this is my age speaking, but I have nothing else to speak from.) This third way is a kind of supposedly benevolent, enlightened culture resting upon an ideological base of monetarist Darwinism, in which the desirability of competition is the motor driving force. And let us make no bones about it: the pot out of which we derive our research monies is never going to be limitless; it is a cash-limited pot. Institutions are bidding competitively with each other for money and, consequently, are also bidding competitively with each other to attract staff. This is not necessarily synonymous with bidding to attract the most talented researchers; the need is rather to attract those most likely to produce research *in a form that is quantifiable and measurable.*

And then let us say that you have been successful in the competition and that your department has been well funded. As the monies flow in, you and your colleagues, in turn, have to bid in competition with each other. This is the world in which we now live. Under this regime, on what grounds are we going to represent the *value* of the projects in which we are involved? If I have a dream—it is not simply a dream, rather an experience—of research as something that is co-operative and collaborative, then it seems to me that I can now only keep that dream alive outside those institutions which offer me employment.

There is an old Art & Language adage, a slogan of some twenty-five years ago, from the days when we were last collectively and purposefully involved in trying to recruit the interest of students in art schools and in producing consciousness-raising posters. The slogan is "when management speaks, nobody learns." Since it was conceived, nothing has happened to change my opinion. Now, when management starts speaking of "talent" and "innovation" and "creativity," I am afraid that I shudder.

Of course, this is not altogether a new situation. I cannot resist finishing with a quotation: "If, finally, the conquerors succeed in molding the world according to their laws, it will not prove that quality is king but that this world is hell. In this hell, the place of art will coincide with that of vanquished rebellion, a blind and empty hope in the pit of despair." That was Albert Camus in 1951. If I had any advice to offer to the aspiring young researcher in pursuit of funds it would be this: if you have a good project and some company, work on it, talk to people, get on with it, exploit whatever available resources there may be—but never apply for project funding.

Notes

1 [I thank Paul Bonaventura for bringing this publication to my attention, and Charles Harrison for permission to reprint this excerpt.—J.E.]

2 [This is "Professor" in the UK system, which is different from the American one. Departments seldom have more than one Professor. J.E.]

3 [David Pilsbury, then Head of Research Policy at the Higher Education Funding Council in England.—J.E.]

4 [Arts and Humanities Research Board, www.ahrb.ac.uk, also discussed in Chapter 2.—J.E.]

5 [Bickers also contributed to the symposium volume; at the time she was editor of *Art Monthly* and senior lecturer in Art History and Theory at the University of Westminster.—J.E.]

6 [Graduate programs in which students take seminars, in the North American manner, rather than attending tutorials with their instructors, as in the usual configuration of the MPhil and the PhD in the UK.—J.E.]

11

The Three Configurations of Studio-Art Phds

James Elkins

This is a revised and expanded version of a talk I gave in fall 2003. My notion was to describe the studio-art PhD degree in a neutral fashion, as a philosophic problem. I left aside all the pressing problems of the job market. I did not mention the fact that the new degrees have spread quickly in the UK in part because departments get funding based on how many advanced students they have, and that PhD students generate more money than MA students. (That, I think, is the elephant in the room in all UK discussions of the degree: people may sound disinterested, or motivated by ideas alone; but the raw fact is that institutions get money for PhD students, so it pays to set up these programs.) I didn't raise the question of whether or not graduates with the new degrees would have an unfair advantage over those with MFAs—and even that they might compete for two jobs at once, one in their chosen artistic medium, and the other in their academic field. And I didn't say anything about whether most student artists at the MFA or MA level are capable of writing 50,000 word dissertations or doing PhD-level scholarship.

In short, I gave the talk pretending that the new degree has no economic, practical, or political dimensions. I did that because it seemed very important—and it still does—to consider what the degree might mean for intellectual and creative life in the university. I was interested in the abstract, ideal configurations of the new degree. Can it contribute new ways of thinking about interdisciplinarity? Can it help reconfigure the conventional ways of conceptualizing the difference between making something and studying it? Can it help justify the presence of studio art departments in universities? Can it provide models for bridging history, theory, criticism, and practice—models that might have meaning even beyond the humanities?

None of this is to say that the philosophic issues raised by the PhD in studio art can help solve the economic, practical, or political problems; or that those problems are less important than questions of conceptualization.

But it would be a pity, I think, to see the new creative-art PhD spread through the US and Europe, and not be theorized as cleanly as possible.

Each of the philosophic models I propose here could be implemented in a number of ways: the student's research, for example, could be weighted as two-thirds of the degree, and the visual art as one-third. Several such configurations are already in place, and they are discussed elsewhere in this book, especially Chapters 1, 2, 5, and 8. What is missing is a theorization of the possibilities in the abstract, before the exigencies of actual departments and resources come into play.

It seems to me that the PhD in visual arts is inescapable: it is on the horizon. What is needed is an investigation into the conceptual shapes that the new degrees might take. The US is well positioned to do this, and to become the place where such programs are rethought from the ground up. At least there's a chance of doing that in the US, because it does not have the administrative structures and jargon (mainly "research" and "new knowledge") that have shaped the development and implementation of doctoral programs in the UK. The studio-based PhD might begin again, differently, in the United States and elsewhere.

(After I wrote this chapter, I searched the text for the words *research* and *knowledge*. They are only used here to describe *other disciplines* such as art history, philosophy, and anthropology. I hope this shows that it is possible to go a long way without depending on such words.)

I will propose three configurations that the new PhD degree might take. This chapter was originally a supervisor's report for a creative-arts PhD dissertation called "Beyond the Surface: The Contemporary Experience of the Italian Renaissance," written by Jo-Anne Duggan for the University of Technology, Sydney. (You can get an idea of her dissertation by reading the excerpts in Chapter 12.) Duggan was a candidate for the DCA, Doctorate of Creative Arts.[1] She is a photographer, and her special interest is photographing art inside museums; her dissertation explores the history and theory of that practice. The report I wrote for her was the basis of this paper, because I found that her thesis is a mixture of what I think are the three principal possibilities for combining PhD-level scholarship and creative work.

The first model is relatively common, and the second and third are rare but, I think, preferable.

First Model: The Dissertation is Research that Informs the Art Practice

I think the most obvious relation between the PhD candidate's scholarship—the written dissertation or thesis—and her creative work is that the dissertation informs the artwork. The artist positions her scholarship so that it variously supports, modifies, guides, or enables her art practice. Alternately—and this is the logical inverse of the first option and also its inevitable correlate—the artist positions her practice so that it variously supports, modifies, or enables her scholarship. In the first case, the student is an artist first and foremost, and she intends her doctorate to help her make more compelling artwork. In the second case, the student's strength is her scholarship, and she wants to improve her doctorate by engaging with the production of art. An example of the first would be a student who researches the history of anthropological theories of the gift in order to make more informed artworks whose theme is giving and receiving. An example of the second would be a student who researches the history of Renaissance altarpieces, and wants her writing to be informed by a hands-on understanding of how altarpieces were made.

In Chapter 5, Victor Burgin calls the second of these options "PhD (history and theory emphasis)." In what follows I am mainly thinking of the first option, because it is by far the most common. It would be wonderful if more people in history of art were inclined to make paintings in order to study their history, or if more people in visual studies were interested in producing videos in order to write about advertising and film. That is a longstanding interest of mine, and it might conceivably become common if studio-art PhD programs grow up in collaboration with history of art, visual studies, and anthropology.[2] But what actually happens in studio-art PhD programs is usually the first option, in which the students are principally interested in how their doctoral-level scholarship might inform their art practice.

Within this first large grouping I distinguish five kinds of written dissertations. They depend on which department in the university supervises the written dissertation.

1. *The dissertation is art history.* Perhaps the most common option is to write an art historical dissertation, covering the history of practices that lead up to the writer's own practice. The student would normally have a supervisor in history of art, and one in studio art. In some Australian theses (see Part Two of this book) the dissertation is written in anthropology, archaeology, sociology, or

geography, but art history is the most common choice. Among the advantages to this model is that, in theory, the candidate would be able to go on to teach in a department of art history (or anthropology, or sociology) as well as in a studio art department.

A guiding assumption of this configuration is that art history can strengthen, or at least productively inform, art practice. I think the point is often true, but it is debatable as an assumption, if only because so many artists have done so well by misinterpreting, travestying, simplifying, or otherwise distorting works and ideas that an art historian might say are most pertinent to their own practice. It's also the case that moments in art history were made possible by the artists' carelessness or ignorance of the relevant art history. It can be argued that German Expressionism depended, around 1910, on an insouciant disregard of academic criteria. If Kirchner or Nolde had acquired PhDs, with the history of German art as their field of research, it is possible that they might never have been able to break the grip of academic work as effectively as they did. It matters that there have been times and places in art history where it would have been inappropriate to educate artists using a theory-intensive regimen of research and writing. In some cases such an education might even have hurt the resulting practice. In the question-and-answer session after the talk in 2003, I mentioned Sol LeWitt's minimalism: if he had a studio-art PhD, and if he had chosen mathematics as his research area, he might never have undertaken some of his own projects, because—as Rosalind Krauss has argued—they rely on a low-level understanding of geometry and math.

It is not difficult to raise this kind of question within art history as it is presently constituted, because "reception history" (*Rezeptionsgeschichte*), especially in the paradoxical and critical forms that it has been given by Michael Holly and Mieke Bal, is well suited to consider problems of indirect, inaccurate, repressed, or illogical influence. Georges Didi-Huberman's revisionary critique of art history, which follows Warburg and Freud, offers another model. These authors haven't considered the question of reception from an artist's point of view, but the theory is in place to allow that kind of exploration.

What is more difficult for both art history and studio art is the thought that art history might not always be beneficial for students. I would say it is generally supposed that knowledge of art history is in itself not a bad thing: but for a working artist, it may also be that too much art historical knowledge might hamper or even ruin ongoing art projects. An enormous amount of research needs to be done on this *historical* question: what kinds of art might be served by PhDs? What kinds are, potentially at least, inimical to it? As the new degree proliferates it may be easy to lose track of this question, because presumably the students and faculty who are attracted to the programs will already believe they might benefit from PhD-level instruction. I don't doubt that some strains of contemporary art require high-level conceptual work: Thomas Crow has claimed that some advanced work in the visual arts proposes philosophic problems whose difficulty matches or surpasses what is studied in academic philosophy. But it is important to consider that there is no general account of what kinds of art are not well matched to PhD-level research. That may sound like an inappropriate demand, but consider that other academic fields have sturdy criteria for evaluating which college graduates might be suitable for further study. The fact that relatively few art students in the UK out of the total of those with college degrees are attracted to the PhD does not constitute a solution to the problem of determining which kinds of art practice are suited.

In Canberra I met Ruth Waller, whose MA thesis was on fifteenth-century painting. (Her work is excerpted in Chapter 15.) Her own painting, she said, was enriched by her detailed historical knowledge. But in the history of art, artists' assessments of their influences are notoriously unreliable: artists commonly claim to be influenced by other artists even when those influences turn out to be inscrutable, idiosyncratic, or otherwise unavailable to historians and other viewers. One of the many fascinating questions raised by the new PhD degrees is whether advisors should get involved at that level: should an advisor point out that an increase in historical knowledge might *not* be good for a given practice? St. Andrews is an example of a program where it is assumed that historical knowledge (in their case, of photography) will be relevant to current practice, and in my experience the official self-descriptions of PhD-granting programs claim or assume as much. It would seem more prudent, and more historically responsible, to raise the question in each individual case. It may be a good idea to offer special seminars in studio-art PhD programs, in order to continuously explore the relation between the intellectual scope of the PhD-level research and various historical practices of art. Such a seminar might explore, as an ongoing issue, whether or not the art history that the PhD candidate is learning is helping or hindering their art practice.

Another issue with a dissertation supervised in history of art is when it might be appropriate for the student to break out of the art historical way of writing—meaning, roughly, the guiding intention of elucidating some past practice—and speak in her own voice—meaning, here, the desire to *use* the historical material to effect an ongoing and separate art practice.

For example Duggan mentions "the Renaissance artist's quest to truthfully imitate nature—or as I see it, represent vision" (p. 10 of her thesis). The first phrase belongs in art history; the second in criticism or in an artist's statement. A pure history of art PhD thesis would likely omit the second phrase or justify it in the name of some larger argument, if only because it is anachronistic in a way that the first phrase isn't. (A Renaissance humanist wouldn't say they are "representing vision.") Duggan could have made her assertion into a moment of reflection by inserting a comment about transitions between art history and artist's interpretations. She could have written something like this: "I'll just note in passing that I am aware that these two interpretations are potentially on either side of a gulf. One one side is a commonly received description of Renaissance practice, and on the other a formula that points to current interests in vision and visuality. That paradox will be an ongoing theme." That way Duggan could have made a theme of her small break with art historical practice. Yet even an explicit acknowledgment wouldn't solve the problem of the disjunction between two disparate ways of conceiving the purpose of art history, or ensure that her dissertation would work more effectively as a support for her art practice—but each acknowledgment of the problem would let readers and supervisors have a greater share in the project.

2. *The dissertation is philosophy or art theory.* An artist's scholarship can also support her practice if the scholarly component is philosophy rather than art history. The dissertation might be a philosophic investigation of, say, the phenomenology of video practice instead of the history of video. A philosophic thesis, in this context, can be thought of as an organic development of the artist's statement. It could be supervised in a philosophy department, or in an art department, or in the history of art: but the supervisor would, in this case, be treating the dissertation *as philosophy or theory* rather than history.

The same questions of relevance apply here: even though the PhD student might believe her practice is supported by her philosophic inquiry, the relation might appear very differently to her viewers, critics, and (eventually) her historians. Often artists' theories turn out to be irrelevant to what comes to be taken as most important about the work. And as art instructors know, students who construct elaborate theories about their work sometimes use theory not for its content as much as its rhetorical force: the philosophy or theory of art serve as a smokescreen, hiding what is actually of interest in the work. (Or, in the studio, hiding problems the artists suspects her work may harbor.)

Parts of Duggan's second chapter are philosophy, for instance her focus on "the physicality and auratic presence of the Italian museums" (p. 40), and art theory is threaded through her dissertation. When an art historical dissertation is intermittently philosophic (by which I mean, in this context, that it pauses to seriously consider issues of art theory outside of the historical circumstances in which they were originally developed) it might tend to appear that the philosophy helps support the art history. If the purpose is to write a new theory of a period or practice, then it will probably be necessary to bring the philosophy out of its matrix in art history—out of its role as conceptual support for empirical inquiry—in order to have it stand together with the creative work. If Italian museums are to be said to have an "auratic presence," and if—for example—Walter Benjamin or Rudolf Otto were to be the authors that support the concepts of presence or aura, then the claim is critical and philosophical, and not art historical. In an art historical text, one that is not part of a creative-art PhD, such an interpretation of Italian museums could be justified as part of a wider examination of the history of ideas about Italian museums, and "auratic presence" could occupy a place in twentieth-century theories about museums. In Duggan's thesis the passage I have just quoted is a temporary departure from art historical writing, because it works as an interpolated truth about museums rather than an idea with a specifiable genealogy.

It is not immediately clear whether Duggan intends her observation about auratic presence to be read as an observation about Italian museums in general, or if she means to offer it as a historically delimited judgment. The ambiguation is not necessarily productive or meaningful. How much, a reader may ask, does Duggan believe in the auratic presence of Italian museums? Does she believe that sense of presence is also a historical phenomenon, or that it matters that the judgment itself has a history? In art history, the philosophy is assumed to be historically specific (Benjamin's sense of the aura was developed in response to a certain time and place), but in creative work the philosophy can directly support the art practice no matter how historically distant the philosophic term is from the contemporary art practice. For that reason I think that such philosophic moments are in special need of being made explicit when there is also creative work involved.

Another example occurs a few pages earlier, when Duggan writes: "Surrounded by a crowd no less than twenty people deep, [Botticelli's] paintings have a presence" (p. 17). When does she, or did she, feel that Botticelli's paintings have an intrinsic "presence"? How much of that sense of presence is generated by the crowd and the excitement of seeing the originals? An art historical version of Duggan's sentence would put the judgment in a historical frame. She could write, for example: "Because they are surrounded by a crowd no less than twenty people deep, Botticelli's paintings seem to have a presence." Because hers is a creative-art PhD dissertation, there is no reason why she cannot equivocate between philosophy and history. Supervisors of such dissertations, however, will have to ponder the meaning such equivocations between art history and philosophy can have, given that the texts are intended not "simply" as philosophy, but as adjuncts to particular artistic practices. I would wonder under what circumstances it would *not* be useful to spell out the distinction between philosophic and historical judgment.

3. *The dissertation is art criticism.* The student's scholarship can also support her art practice if the dissertation is art criticism rather than philosophy or art history. This is, I think, the most common form of creative-arts PhD dissertation, and it can also be found outside the visual arts. I have seen an example produced in the PhD program in creative writing run by the University of Houston. The student, Mark Caughey, wrote a hundred-and-fifty-page critical examination of his own poetry, which served as an introduction to the dissertation (which was a book of his poetry).

In the UK, creative-art doctorates of various kinds have been around long enough to get an uneven reputation; some are not much more than over-extended Master's theses, with a written component that is essentially critical in nature and an admixture of art history and art theory. Such dissertations tend to be supervised in history of art or simply in the relevant art department. They are, in that sense, very similar to the theses ("dissertations" in the UK and Ireland) that are written by MA or MFA art students; those texts tend to be mainly art criticism, aimed at elucidating the student's practice. An immediate challenge to the development of the studio-art PhD in the US is to find ways of preventing it from slumping into a protracted MFA thesis. To that end, it is important to reconsider two issues that are constitutive of art criticism in the academy.

The first is self-reflexivity. The purpose of the juxtaposition of art criticism and artwork at the doctoral level would presumably be to reach a pitch of sophistication in the description and evaluation of one's own art, on the reasonable grounding assumption that improving self-reflexivity is a central purpose of graduate study.

As far as I know, self-reflexivity is not doubted as a goal in any graduate studio art program. I love Mick Wilson's way of putting this in Chapter 4. "A key theme in the development of doctoral programs in art practice is that of critical reflection," he writes: "the enigmatic figure of the reflexive practitioner may be said to stalk the doctoral art studio in search of the equally enigmatic trophy of methodological rigor." There are two problems here, which I think should be divided: Wilson's concern is partly with methodological rigor, which is not my concern at the moment. His other interest is self-reflexivity—how it might be defined, where it might be found. In 2003 the promotional text for the program at Goldsmiths, for example, said the course is for "artists who would like to explore and develop their understanding of their established art practice." The same confidence in the importance of self-reflexivity can be found in the administrative texts that support the new degree in the UK: self-reflection is mentioned, for example, by Donald Schön, who is discussed in Chapter 2.

Yet many artists have made compelling work even though they had no idea of the critical matrix to which their work belongs, and despite the fact that they were only minimally reflective about their own practice. It is also true that some artists' work thrives on self-awareness; for artists of that kind the new PhD degree might be ideal—although there is no account of what kinds of art have been best served by self-awareness. This idea that self-awareness is a desideratum for PhD-level instruction needs to be treated as a problematic assumption, not as a guiding principle. In my experience, the value accorded to self-reflexivity is never questioned. It needs to be.

A second issue with creative art dissertations that take the form of art criticism is that the subject of art criticism is virtually never taught in PhD programs in philosophy or history of art. Art criticism appears as a historical subject in history of art curricula—there are courses on Baudelaire, Diderot, and so forth—but not as a practical subject.[3] In the absence of structured sequences of courses on practical art criticism it is dubious that art-critical dissertations can be effectively read and critiqued *on a PhD level*. It would, of course, be possible to find philosophers or art historians who could assess such dissertations, but only for their logic (if they were read as philosophy) or historical veracity (if they were judged by an art historians).

4. *The dissertation is natural history, or economics, or any number of fields outside the humanities.* In this option, the candidate looks further afield than stdio art, history of art, or philosophy. At the 2003 conference David Williams, Chair of Art at the Australian National University in Canberra, said that it's very popular option among his students to write a "subthesis," as they are called, in the sciences. The student has an art practice, in any medium, and chooses to obtain a PhD in Biology, say, or in Genetics: whatever field they are qualified to enter.

I think a science or non-art dissertation, set to the purpose of furthering an art practice, is an entrancing prospect. Let me mention three questions, two abstract and the third practical.

(a) If the dissertation is to be assessed according to the protocols of the discipline in question then it will have to *be* science, economics, medicine, law, or engineering: it will have to exemplify its field as if the candidate were not also an artist. If that criterion is abandoned then the dissertation can be *about* science, economics, medicine, law, or engineering. Such a dissertation would be the equivalent of a PhD in the history, philosophy, or sociology of science: that is, it would be an interpretation of the particular branch of science. (For a history of science doctorate, for example, the candidate may have to obtain a PhD in the relevant science.)

Presumably the option of writing *about* the science or other discipline would not be open to students whose dissertations are supervised, at least partly, in the different departments in question: but I mention it to underscore that a creative-arts PhD might not be modeled on existing interdisciplinary or dual degrees. If the function of the dissertation is to further the art practice, then the dissertation will necessarily be at least partly a matter of observing, adapting, appropriating, and critiquing the non-art discipline. That relation between art and science, in which the artist borrows whatever she wants from science, is a historically normative one, but it means that the new degree will not be a *combination* of science and art in the way that a dual degree in biochemistry and genetics would combine those two disciplines.

(b) If this kind of dissertation (either the dissertation *as* science, or the dissertation *about* the science) becomes popular in the US or the UK, it will need to be asked when combinations of art and science (or any non-art discipline) are a sensible direction for visual art. Historically speaking only a tiny fraction of Western art has been centrally informed by science and other non-art subjects despite a vocal minority of scholars who study the subject. Only a few contemporary artists, such as Dorothea Rockburne, Eduardo Kac, and Vija Celmins, effectively bridge the sciences and art.[4] Is it cogent to promote cross-pollination if there is no broad call for contemporary art that addresses science? I find this fourth option one of the most interesting because it makes good use of the university, mixing sciences and humanities in new ways. But there is a danger of producing more marginal practices that do not participate in the principal conversations about contemporary art.

(c) The practical point I want to mention, and the only purely pragmatic subject I want to raise in this chapter, is that if this fourth option becomes widespread, then art schools will be left behind. Universities, in the US, will be the best positioned to offer combinations of sciences and visual arts, and art schools will play marginal roles.

5. *The dissertation is a technical report.* There are media and kinds of artmaking that are not fully mastered by students at the MFA level. At Alfred, New York, a school well known for its ceramics program, there is a laboratory that specializes in high-tech, non-art ceramics; they have in the past made the tiles that protected the Space Shuttle. When I visited the laboratory was not utilized by the MFA students as much as it could have been because the students lacked the education in inorganic chemistry. A PhD program in ceramics could remedy that. Printmaking techniques like metal engraving are commonly omitted from the MFA; they could be taught given a few more years' worth of courses. At the 2003 conference at which I first gave this paper, Christina DePaul, Dean of the Corcoran College of Art, told me about advanced fabric techniques; she noted that an MFA is not usually sufficient to teach them. A PhD in fabric or fiber arts could accommodate the missing techniques. Frayling's 1993 paper also mentions materials science inquiries as an example of "research through art and design."

There are many advanced industrial materials that are not taught in art schools, and a PhD would be a way to institute a kind of catch-up in the relevant contemporary materials science. Such a degree would also help meliorate the disjunction between current engineering, with its many sophisticated materials, and art practice, which still keeps mostly to oil, clay, metals, paper, and wood.[5]

It would be possible to institute a PhD-granting program of the kind I am exploring here, provided that the advanced techniques are documented in doctoral-level written dissertations. Such a program would have a strong historical precedent in the Bauhaus, which made extensive use of contemporaneous industrial manufacturing. In the US, university studio art degrees in the first half of the century often combined research dissertations with art practice. In the early twentieth century, Midway Studios at the University of Chicago (where I got my MFA in the 1980s) turned out theses on the manufacture of public fountains and public sculptures with water features; the students made fountains, and also learned the plumbing and engineering. In that sense, the PhD in "advanced techniques" would be, effectively, a creative-arts PhD with a dissertation in engineering.

Second Model: The Dissertation is Equal to The Artwork

In the first model, the dissertation is a repository of research that informs or otherwise aids the art practice, or, in the opposite model I did not explore, the art practice is a repository of new experiences that informs or otherwise aids the scholarship, represented by the written dissertation. The remaining models don't work in either of those eways: in them, the dissertation is implicated in the artwork, or even considered *as* the artwork. That has the advantage of freeing the scholarship from its ultimately informational or supportive role (or, conversely, freeing the practice from *its* supportive role), and potentially making the research equal to the artwork—or even making it *into* the artwork. In this second model, the dissertation is considered as conceptually or experientially equal to the art. The research doesn't support or inform the art, but complements it, with each one illuminating the other. I will divide this second model into two possibilities.

1. *Research and artwork comprise a new interdisciplinary field.* In this case the studio-art PhD might be considered as an example of the confluence of disciplines that is currently congealing into the field called visual studies or visual culture. As in some visual studies programs, the studio-art PhD becomes an opportunity for a student to collect an idiosyncratic collection of disciplines, with art just one equal among others in a collection of disciplines. Some visual studies programs, like the one I am involved in at the School of the Art Institute of Chicago, permit MA—and eventually, PhD—students to submit combinations of writing and multimedia work including performances. This model differs from the fourth example of the first model (*"The dissertation is natural history, or economics, or any number of fields outside the humanities"*) because there, the non-art field is used to inform the art project; here, the non-art field or fields are all taken to be equal contributors to a new constellation of interests.

In visual studies, the sky is the limit, and in US universities it is effectively possible to arrange any configuration of disciplines. I have strong reservations about this option, because historically art practice has been excluded or marginalized in university curricula, so that combining it with academic fields as if it were just one among many equal but different options might obscure the very deeply rooted differences between studio art and other university departments and faculties. The conceptual disparity between a dissertation comprised of elements of anthropology, film, and art history (to take an example I encountered recently), and a dissertation comprised of anthropology, film, and studio art, is large. Victor Burgin's essay, Chapter 5, quotes an illuminating interview in which Derrida tells how he declined to accept visual work in lieu of written work, because the visual work was incompletely conceptualized. Even aside from this issue of conceptualization—even if the visual components of a mixed-media dissertation were themselves highly conceptually articulated—the place of studio art in the university is problematic. Visual art juxtaposed with written material should not be regarded as an option that is no more problematic than a written text in anthropology juxtaposed with a written text in sociology. A written dissertation that includes studio art is a different kind of creature, requiring a justification different from the theorizing that currently addresses the convergence of academic disciplines into the field of visual studies. (The same observation about the difference between studio practice and other disciplines applies, in reverse, to art schools, where academic disciplines exist in abbreviated forms, tailored for visual concerns. In those cases, what counts as theorizing is sometimes not equal to its equivalents in university departments, and at other times is not well integrated into the predominantly studio-based curriculum.)

It is superficial, I think, to imagine that art practice can just be added to an eclectic selection of disciplines composed by the candidate. There are academic pursuits that result from combinations such as anthropology + sociology + linguistics, or art history + archaeology + semiotics, but there is no academic practice that combines creative work with any other discipline.

The concatenation of new fields, centers, courses, and concentrations can also lead to the breakdown of boundaries between disciplines, and in that respect I am in sympathy with Mieke Bal's comments in the *Journal of Visual Culture*.[6] She argues that there is no payoff in policing disciplines, and that new configurations should question each of the participating disciplines. In many ways the new field of visual studies works by not worrying the boundaries and ostensive purities of disciplines, and in that respect it can be a model for the creative-art PhDs of this type: they need not keep disciplinary fences intact.

It seems likely to me that studio practice may be the strongest component in these collaged PhDs, whether or not they break down disciplinary borders. The PhD candidate's studio art practice will often turn the other disciplines to its purposes, in effect making the dissertation into an expanded artist's statement. It will be difficult, I think, to argue convincingly that the collection of non-art disciplines has equal standing to the artwork. In Duggan's thesis each one of the chapters is ultimately *fully* the work of an artist and not of an historian of photography, an historian of museology, or a theorist of the gaze, because all of her examples are aimed at a personal rethinking of her own desires.

2. *Research and artwork are understood as wholly separate projects.* This possibility is like the previous one, in that the student's art practice and the associated non-art disciplines are imagined to be equal participants in the overall project of the PhD. The difference is that the new configuration of fields is not understood as a potentially coherent project, but as a juxtaposition, whose rationale does not need to be analyzed. Even the candidate herself might not be sure of the pertinence of her scholarly interests; she might just have a strong interest in both video art, for example, and scholarship in some other field. In this case the function of the faculty is to help advise the scholarly portion of the dissertation and the art practice at an appropriate level, leaving it up to the student to work through the possible connections between them. This is in some measure the model adopted by the Canberra School of art, and it is represented in several of the examples in Part Two.

I find this option the second-most intriguing. It is interesting to contemplate what an artist might accomplish by keeping two sets of activities separate from one another for the duration of a PhD program, without being asked to formally theorize their connection. It also seems wholly in keeping with the way art is often produced, in the company of many disparate interests that do not, at least for some time, seem to be directly linked to one another. It avoids the usual academic demands of coherence and intellectual synthesis—which again is appropriate for much of visual art. And it acknowledges that art is a lifetime occupation. If I think that I need a professional-level understanding of tort law, even though my practice is abstract oil painting, then it should be my right to pursue both those apparently unconnected interests through the PhD. Eventually, I may come to understand the connection, but it isn't the university's responsibility.

This model would be directly opposed to a universal criterion of MFA programs, that they help nourish the artist's single voice or style: and that would be an interesting assumption to question. (That assumption is one of the few unbroken threads in the tattered fabric of the MFA, which has never been well theorized.⁷) This model would also circumvent the common assumption that self-reflexivity is an unexceptionable good. It would make fascinating use of the resources of the university, by finding new configurations of fields without proposing that they have underlying similarities or points of convergence. And it would remove the difficulty of deciding how advisors in different fields can collaboratively supervise a combined creative-art PhD. (More on that below.) In short, the radicalism of this option is intriguing.

The models I have named up to this point have serious, if also potentially productive, conceptual flaws. The third and last model is the most interesting to me—and raises even more difficult philosophic and practical problems.

Third Model: The Dissertation *Is* the Artwork, And Vice Versa

The final option that occurs to me is to imagine the scholarly portion of the thesis inextricably fused with the creative portion, so that the artwork is scholarly and the scholarship is creative. (This could be entailed in Christopher Frayling's third and most problematic option, which he calls "research as art and design," except that in his example the outcome is only art, and the art is presented as research. What looms on Frayling's horizon is a studio-art PhD that consists only of an art work or exhibition, with the implication that it is itself a product of research. What I am considering here is that, but with the symmetrical addition of a written dissertation that asks to be understood as fiction.⁸)

I have seen attempts at this solution, including a multimedia dissertation done at the University of Chicago that includes a CD, photo exhibit, 16mm films, and a written dissertation that was only ancillary, and not fully explanatory. But I haven't seen examples in which the scholarship melts into creative work, or asks to be read as creative work instead of research. In the University of Chicago thesis, for example, the writing was clearly situated in art history, anthropology, and film studies, and it remained distinct from the student's films, CDs, and photographs. As I mentioned in Chapter 9, under the heading "Avoiding *New Knowledge* and *Research* by Proposing The Art Object Itself as Knowledge and the Product of Research," it is common in the art world—not just in MFA or PhD programs—to find artworks that imply they are themselves the repositories of new knowledge and the results of research, even though the new knowledge cannot be adequately translated into words, and even though the research will remain partly or wholly private. Because that kind of implication is commonplace, I am not concerned about its appearance in PhDs programs such as the one in Plymouth, England, which has pioneered in the reduction or elimination of the written dissertation. It is undoubtedly true that it is deeply problematic, if not aggressively obscurantist, to claim that a work of visual art should be understood as research and as producing new knowledge while *at the same time* insisting that the research and knowledge inhere in the paint, clay, or pixels of the art itself and not in language.

But I think that in considering this, it is indispensable to also consider the possibility—which follows immediately and inevitably—that conventional, discipline-specific, written PhD dissertations in other subjects (any subjects, from art history to engineering) might be considered the same way, *as if* they were art. This would seem to undermine the very possibility of having the studio-art PhD be considered as an doctoral degree at all. And yet, why not? Why not try to write a PhD dissertation in history of art *as if it were fiction?* Why not present a visual studies dissertation as an artwork, and ask that it be judged that way, instead of as a work of logical argumentation and empirical evidence?

Again I divide this into two possibilities.

1. *The dissertation is intended to be read* as art, *and the visual practice* as research. The models for this radical fusion of non-fiction or expository text into creative work would be writing by scholars such as Michel Serres (who mixes history of science, philosophy, and fiction) or John Berger (who mingles poems and art history)—but there are very few such examples. If such a dissertation existed, it would be extremely difficult to evaluate in an academic setting because the entire apparatus of scholarship, from the argument to the footnotes, would have to be legible *as creative writing.* (The result would be like Nabokov's *Pale Fire,* or, more provocatively, like his supposedly impeccable philological scholarship—which ends up being both fictional and unreadable—in his edition of *Eugene Onegin.*) I have come across this problem in a class I teach on art criticism, because some critics (including Peter Schjeldahl, Joanna Frueh, Dave Hickey) think of themselves primarily as poets—which has to mean, among other things, that content is secondary to voice and style. That kind of art criticism is only about art by chance, as it were: it might just as easily be about television repair, or TV news, provided the voice and quality of writing meet the writer's and the reader's expectations.[9] I think it would be difficult to imagine this kind of writing as a dissertation that is to be evaluated by faculty in scholarly disciplines. Logically speaking, such a thesis would be in no need of fact-checking anyway. (Could a chemistry professor evaluate a chemistry PhD *as poetry?* Wouldn't she have to limit herself to checking the student's research—and wouldn't that be, by definition, beside the point?)

2. *There is no research component: the visual art practice, together with its exhibition and supporting materials, simply is the PhD.* The argument here is basically that visual art practice should not borrow from other academic fields, but remain true to its own media and purposes. It has also been said that the studio-art PhD, in any of the forms I have been listing, is inherently unfair because it requires a student to complete doctoral level work in an academic field *and also* create doctorate-level visual art. (Both these arguments have been proposed by the Plymouth College of Art and Design, the first to radically reduce the written component of the PhD.)

I think this last and most radical possibility is also the most interesting. It is a logical endpoint for the new degree, because each of the foregoing models presupposes that visual art practice can be taken to the level of the doctorate. This last option is simply more consistent than the previous models, because it permits the visual art practice to carry the burden of competence that will allow it to be taken as a doctoral-level accomplishment *aside from* whatever writing might support or augment it.

It goes without saying that this final possibility presents severe problems when it comes to assessment. How is a studio-art instructor to determine if the studio practice is at PhD level? I think this question is, in its very form, unanswerable, and it is not a productive approach to the general problem of assessing the new degrees. It may be more sensible to ask first how how supervisors might read and respond to the dissertations that are produced in all the possibilities I have discussed *except* this final one. When guidelines for assessing those models are in place, it might make more sense to try to say what PhD-level assessment creative art might look like.

The Problem of Assessing the New Degree

Consider, in this regard, the fundamental philosophic problem underlying all assessments of the new degree. I think Mick Wilson is exactly right when he says, in Chapter 4, that "ongoing interrogation of the supervisor's role is the precondition of developing the reflexive doctoral practitioner," and I would add that some understanding of the supervisor's role is a precondition of and studio-art PhD whether or not it associates itself with the value of reflexivity.

In my experience, combined studio and scholarly PhDs are supervised by scholars and creative artists in the disciplines nearest to the candidate's interests. That is appropriate and inevitable. But when the thesis is ultimately bent on supporting ongoing artistic practice, as opposed to understanding and interpreting that practice, it is not logical to have the text checked by experts in different academic disciplines, even when the dissertation is not to be considered as artwork, as it is in the model I have just described. Why? Because the purpose of the candidate's forays into different disciplines is to mine them in order to further her artwork. Hence normal scholarly criteria of truth, the production of new knowledge, thoroughness, clarity, and scholarly protocol just do not apply. The dissertations can still be checked, and the candidates can be advised as if they were students of art history, anthropology, and other disciplines: but in fact they aren't, and the normal protocols of readings by specialists is not logically appropriate. In Duggan's case, why try to be accurate or thorough about the history of museums in Italy? Why consider previous photographers of museums? Why not write a personal, or partial, or partly fictional account of the history of photographers of museums? What logic assures the reader, or the candidate, that such approaches wouldn't be better? When I was advising Duggan, I wasn't sure whether it made sense for me to be thorough, and ask Duggan to acknowledge and read every source on a given subject, as I would have asked a history of art student to do. I wasn't sure because I had a sense of Duggan's own interests as a photographer, and I could guess, roughly, which sources she might find interesting. But *what discipline was supporting me* when I made those decisions? It *could not* have been art history, because that discipline enjoins completeness. It does not include training in the selection of sources for creative purposes. I chose based on my own experiences in my MFA program, my sense of Duggan as an artist, and my years of teaching in an art school. And what discipline was that, exactly?

Because this point has been elusive in the literature, let me put it another way. A PhD dissertation on, say, seventeenth-century Dutch group portraits might be impeccable by art historical standards—it might include all the relevant literature, primary texts, restoration reports, and the latest interpretive theories—and yet fail as the support for an ongoing art practice. The art historian who supervises such a thesis *must* read with an eye to rigor, argument, research, and all the normal criteria of excellent in art history, because as an art historian she has no choice—there is no possibility of improvising different criteria for art historical excellence other than ones determined by the current state of interpretation in the field. And yet such an art historical reading *can never* be sufficient or even demonstrably appropriate for a practicing artist. What matters for the student, presumably, is something about the historical material that can be *used* in their own art practice. If the studio-art PhD candidate tells the supervisor, "I am interested in the awkwardness of the poses," then the supervisor might send the student to sources that help address that particular interest. But at that point the art historian stops assessing the thesis as a contribution to seventeenth-century Dutch group portraiture, and begins acting as a bibliographic research assistant to the student. What is at stake is no longer how the dissertation might contribute to the understanding of the subject, but how the dissertation might illuminate an interest the student has developed in awkward-looking portraits.

It's a simple problem, and it almost seems invisible: but it is enormous, and it has no solution. If a supervisor cannot evaluate a thesis according to the current interests of the field in question, then *there is no way* to evaluate the thesis short of an improvised critique—and that, aside from bibliographic matters, is something that can be done by any number of readers in different fields. The specialist no longer acts as a specialist in her own field. And what does it mean for an art historian to read a text as if it were produced solely for the production of art? The question barely even makes sense in art historical terms, and that is not even allowing for the radical final possibility I have just presented, in which the dissertation is exhibited *as art* from the beginning.

Notice, too, that all this assumes the student has control of what she wants and needs, and that she can formulate questions well enough so that the supervisor can just lead her toward the appropriate historical resources. But often in art history that has not been the case. Artists seldom know exactly why they want to see a given image or master a given body of knowledge. And if a studio-art instructor has a hard time figuring out how to direct a student, how much less likely is it that an art historian—a specialist on some far-flung period of art—or a philosopher, or an anthropologist or chemist or engineer, will have a better idea? It seems that the problem of evaluating creative-art PhD simply cannot be solved unless disciplines give up their shapes and readers step outside their normal interpretive habits: exactly what might make the new degree so interesting, and at the same time ensure it cannot be commensurate with other degrees.

I am thinking that from now on I will agree to supervise studio-art PhDs only if the student can explain why historical accuracy is necessary or appropriate, and when the other readers have worked out the limitations of their roles. I don't think there is a solution to these problems, other than just assigning people to read *as* art historians, or *as* photographers, or *as* anthropologists... but that amounts to assigning blindnesses that may not be in accord with the readers' interests. Nor is it satisfactory to say to a supervisor: "Please just read this for accuracy, and suggest missing references," because that shrinks the function of the supervisor from the de facto representative of a discipline or field to a reference librarian. I think I will supervise dissertations if they include a kind of secondary critical commentary which reflects on this dilemma and sets out a theory of the supervisors' roles and limitations.

In the end this problem is one of reading, and it has to be addressed *as a paradox*, and not with an eye to solving it. It would make sense to put seminars on theories of reading—especially Paul De Man's—at the heart of the new programs. Translation theory, too, could play a part, and so could anthropological theories of interpretation. Perhaps the new degree should be understood a fundamental critique of disciplinarity itself—in which case it might fruitfully engage with existing debates about the nature of interdisciplinary, transdisciplinary, and subdisciplinary work in many other fields.

If courses on these conceptual problems were built into the new degree programs, then the nearly intractable difficulties posed by the new degrees could be addressed within the dissertations themselves. That might not increase the students' self-reflexivity (which might not be a good thing, even if it were possible) but it would make the new PhD degrees more interesting, and certainly more challenging, for the university as a whole.

Notes

1 For this see "A Glossary of Terms," and Chapter 6.
2 In lieu of a section in this chapter, see my "Histoire de l'art et pratiques d'atelier," translation of "Why Art Historians should Draw: The Case for Studio Experience," *Histoire de l'art* 29–30 (1995): 103–112; "Warum Kunsthistoriker malen lernen sollten—ein Plädoyer für Werkstatterfahrung," in *Subjekt und Medium in der Kunst der Moderne*, edited by Michael Lüthy and Christoph Menke (Zurich and Berlin: Diaphanes, 2006), 87-114; and an older version of the same material in *Our Beautiful, Dry, and Distant Texts: Art History as Writing* (New York: Routledge, 2000).
3 This is discussed in my *What Happened to Art Criticism?* (Chicago: Prickly Paradigm Press [distributed by University of Chicago Press], 2003), and at length in *The State of Art Criticism*, co-edited with Michael Newman, with contributions by Stephen Melville, Dave Hickey, Irit Rogoff, Ted Cohen, Guy Brett, Katy Deepwell, Joseph Masheck, Peter Plagens, Julian Stallabrass, Alex Alberro, Whitney Davis, Abigail Solomon-Godeau, and others, vol. 5 of *The Art Seminar* (New York: Routledge, 2007).
4 This is taken up in *Visual Practices Across the University*, edited by James Elkins, with contributions by 35 scholars (Munich: Wilhelm Fink Verlag, 2007).
5 In a sense this kind of PhD exists in a few North American and UK institutions, where art students can continue to pursue their studio practice for several years beyond the MFA, eventually earning the PhD (or D.Litt.). However those programs are not PhDs in the sense I am speaking of here, because they do not combine ongoing studio practice with scholarly work at the PhD level.
6 Though not in sympathy with her comments on my essay. See my "Nine Modes of Interdisciplinarity in Visual Studies," reply to Mieke Bal, "Visual Essentialism and the Object of Visual Culture," *Journal of Visual Culture* 2 no. 2 (2003): 232–37; in Spanish as "Nueve modelos de interdisciplinareidad para los estudios visuales," *Estudios visuales*, edited by José Luis Brea 2 (December 2004)
7 As Howard Singerman and others have noted, the MFA is scarcely theorized. It was hastily adopted, and rarely revisited. See my *Why Art Cannot be Taught: A Handbook for Art Students* (Urbana, IL: University of Illinois Press, 2001). One of the very few analyses of the purposes of the MA and MFA is "A Certain MA-ness," edited by Henk Slager, special issue of *Makhuzine: Journal of Artistic Research* [Utrecht School of the Arts] 5 (2008), ISSN 1882-4728.
8 Frayling's paper is background reading for several of the essays in this book; it is available for example at www.constellations.co.nz/index.php?sec= 3&ssec=7&r=687#687, accessed September 2008. See the Introduction, and the chapter by Hilde Van Gelder and Jan Baetens, for further information.
9 *The State of Art Criticism*, co-edited with Michael Newman (New York: Routledge, 2007), takes up this question.

Part Two

Examples

I asked these artist-scholars (there isn't an easy term for what they are) to choose 3,000-word excerpts from their theses. I edited their texts slightly to ensure they are readable, mainly by deleting passages that refer to other parts of their theses. My emendations are marked by bracketed ellipses […]. Each excerpt is introduced by a summary, which is adapted from the authors' abstracts and from personal correspondence (fall-winter 2004). I also asked for illustrations both of the work they studied in their theses and of their own work, when the two are different. Footnote citations have been made uniform (see the note appended to the first footnote in Jo-Anne Duggan's text).

12

Jo-Anne Duggan

Dr. Jo-Anne Duggan's thesis was the first DCA (Doctorate of Creative Arts) I was asked to read. It is called "Beyond the Surface: The Contemporary Experience of the Italian Renaissance." It is a study of the ways that Italian Renaissance art has been viewed in museums: not a common subject in art history, although it could fit well with some programmes of visual studies. Her thesis is not a conventional investigation of the history of display (a theme common in contemporary scholarship of museums); nor is it a history of representations of display (a theme that would be less common, but still normative as history). It is, in part, a study in the history of photography, because most of her evidence is photographs of the interiors of museums: but she is concerned with "art and the subjectivity of the viewer's own gaze" as well as "the intersection of cultures, histories, the past and the present." She writes that she was interested in "the personal, physical, cerebral, sensorial and temporal experiences of art."

As an artist, Duggan is a photographer, and she intended the thesis to combine her two interests. The influence was reciprocal: her photographic practice informed her interpretations of photographs of Renaissance artworks, and her scholarship of the history of viewing informed her photography. She writes:

In a peculiar act of doubling, I was making art about the experience of viewing it, and through image-making I believe that I was able both to explore and to comment more profoundly on the experience of these museums. While my research and writing at times responded to these images, it also inspired them. I integrated the past, history and art with contemporary theories that are relevant in the study of vision and today's art viewing, and relied on numerous writers across the broad fields of visual arts, art history and theory, museology, historiography and cultural tourism.

For Duggan, museums that have Italian Renaissance art "paradoxically intersect "high" art with a phenomenal popularity that appears ever-expanding through endless reproductions and representation." Ultimately, she hopes that her thesis will "argue for a slower, more considered engagement with art, that encourages the viewer to experience the sensual as well as the intellectual aspects that this opulent environment offers."

Excerpts from

"Beyond the Surface:
The Contemporary Experience of
the Italian Renaissance"

by Jo-Anne Duggan

In making images that are founded on the Renaissance, I am conscious that Renaissance art itself is centred on the eye of the beholder, perspectivally designed around the most advantageous viewing point to read the depicted space. As part of this "rationalization of sight" the structure of painting heralds the viewer as integral to the artwork.[1] I play with this idea in my own images, deliberately acknowledging the presence of the viewer within the photograph, and the viewer of the photograph. The viewer is pictured in each image of *Before the Museum* (the first key exhibition for my doctorate), and more profoundly their vision is implied through the use of obscure camera angles that mimic the museum-viewing process, recalling what Johannes Meinhardt referred to as "the physiognomic gaze'[2]. It is this very isolated human activity of viewing which underpins the *Impossible Gaze* (the final exhibition for my doctorate).

By focussing on museum viewers I am concentrating on their engagement with the visual. Susan Best suggests that "vision allows a kind of communion between subjects and objects."[3] In discussing the possibilities of vision, it must be signalled that there are different modes of engagement and activities involved in viewing. The viewer makes both conscious and subconscious decisions as to where they direct their sight, and to what capacity they wish to engage with what they see. Vision consists of distinct modes of activity; looking, directing the movement of the eyes, and seeing, which requires concentration as part of a thought and judgement process. Norman Bryson describes that "vision is portrayed under

two aspects: one vigilant, masterful, "spiritual," and the other sub-
versive, random, disorderly," and further explains their correlation
as an "intermittence of vision, a series of peaks traversed by valleys
of inattentiveness."[4] These patterns of looking and seeing are further codified as the gaze and the glance. The gaze is an intelligible
engagement and a contemplative state. It is the focus of attention,
like the focus of a camera lens on its subject. The glance however,
is the more whimsical attribute of sight, rapidly consuming the ve-
neer of a multitude of objects without engaging in analysis or reflection. The glance's continuous movement mapping objects and
architecture, is subordinated by space as the viewer moves through
it, while the gaze, consciously punctuates this movement.

   In the museum, the viewer surges through the performance of
gazing and glancing. However, Peter de Bolla also proposes a third
mode of viewing, what he terms the look. De Bolla describes this
activity "as an oscillation or pulsation between the gaze and the
glance as the eye shuttles back and forth between penetration and
reflection, depth and surface."[5] I would argue, however, that the
look is more than a transitional action that ensures the uninterrupt-
ed flow of vision, and that it is akin to "searching," consciously or
not.[6] In the museum, the viewer's sight weaves in and out of focus
and attention, superficial interest, detachment and lapses into passive distraction.[7] Jonathan Crary argues "that attention and distraction cannot be thought outside of a continuum in which the two
ceaselessly flow into one another, as part of a social field in which
the same imperatives and forces incite one and the other.'[8] It is this
notion of continuum that I suggest signifies all viewing. Beyond the
attention or distraction of the viewer, the subjectivity of intellectual
vision that I have discussed elsewhere, alongside the physical at-
tributes of sight are all in a state of continuous movement. Both
the individual and the environment govern the speed of this visual
exchange.

   As both museum viewer and photographer my physiological
vision oscillates between the gaze and the glance. As viewer, I am
rapt in a sensory encounter that not only triggers all the regimes
of sight, but also involves the aural and the olfactory, as well as
the desire for tactile experience. For the viewer *as* photographer,
my gaze becomes more intense and more deliberate, a focus of
attention that is beyond that of the casual observer, privileging
sight above all senses. Once behind the lens, like Roger Cardinal's
description of Barthes, I too "hover in the disembodied realm of
pure seeing."[9] I consciously re-orient my sight to direct the lens, the
focus of which locates my gaze for later viewers. Preoccupied with
the image in the viewfinder, I both critically and intuitively frame

the space before me, dissecting the environment into compositions, ordering the layers of time evident in the museum.

Crary evokes William James's "stream of consciousness" to illustrate the viewer's engagement in the activity of looking. He describes "the fundamentally *transitive* nature of subjective experience—[as] a perpetually changing but continuous flow of images, sensations, thought fragments, bodily awareness, memories, desires."[10] I use Crary's comment to reinforce the idea that the bodily or lived experience of the museum viewer is involved and extremely complex, based on not only vision, but also an extensive and inclusive sensorial engagement. To "make-sense," as Vivian Sobchack outlines in her paper, "What My Fingers Knew: The Cinesthetic Subject, or Vision in the Flesh,"

> the overarching mastery and comprehension by our vision of its object, and vision's hierarchical sway over our other senses all tend to occlude our awareness of our body's other ways of taking up and making meaning of the world.[11]

Sobchack declares that "we possess an embodied intelligence that both opens our eyes far beyond their discrete capacity for vision," and explains "our capacity not only to hear, but also to touch, to smell, to taste, and always to proprioceptively feel our dimension and movement in the world." Although Sobchack's paper is a discussion of the cinematic experience, I would like to extend her inclusive sense theory to further advance my own discussion of the museum viewer's experience. (Although vision is necessarily given priority as my way of communicating to an audience.) Just as we are "touched" by the Renaissance images seen in the museum, these feelings are compounded by the experience of the museum itself. The sensorial perception precedes any analytical or reflective thought. As Sobchack describes, "We see and comprehend and feel…with our entire bodily being, informed by the full history and knowledge of our sensorium," and the senses "more radically inform each other in a fundamentally non-hierarchical and reversible relationship."[12] Informed by their reflexive responses to the museum environment, the viewers make sense of what they experience in a multi-dimensional way. However, with such fleeting viewing periods (that are discussed throughout the thesis) there is little time for contemplation of the individual artworks, and it is perhaps their total sensorial experience, the *feeling* of the Renaissance that will be most remembered: the visual confusion of artworks, the hushed tones of other visitors combined with the shrill beeping of infrared sensors, the texture, substance and scent of ancient pigment mixed with oil, and the crowds and stifling heat that engender the viewing experience.

Presented amongst the Baroque decoration of the Palazzo Pitti, its Galleria Palatina and Royal Apartments, each artwork and object is afforded no separate space for contemplation, but is immersed in the interior decoration. *Impossible Gaze* depicts the palazzo's interiors, which are richly layered with textures and patterns on every surface from the elaborate wall-coverings, carpets and curtains, to the frescoed ceilings. [...]

These elaborate rooms are punctuated by contemporary lighting, museum signage indicating visitors' routes and emergency exits. The humidity and temperature monitors and laser-beam security guard against visitors, keeping their curiosity, lumbering bags and body heat at a safe distance from the artworks and furnishings. Even the velvet curtains are protected by silk netting, while the burgundy silk cords foil any desire to caress the luxurious surfaces. My sensuous images rekindle their palpability yet offer no tactile gratification. Although the viewer cannot touch the objects in my photographs they can, as Sobchack proposes, feel their "texture and weight."[13]

Impossible Gaze creates an intense visual experience. It concentrates on the sensorial act of viewing. This work constructs much more than the communion between the viewer's eye and the singular artwork by alluding to the other senses that come into play in this environment. Here I am exploring the multi-sensorial experience of visiting Renaissance museums. Ironically, Baudrillard suggests that "To make an image of an object is to strip the object of all its dimensions one by one: weight, relief, smell, depth, time, continuity and, of course, meaning.'[14] Yet in my photographs these are the very qualities that I call upon. My images are "haptic" in that, as Laura Marks explains, they "engage the viewer tactilely."[15] In *The Skin of the Film*, Marks elaborates on the difference between optical and haptic vision.

Haptic looking tends to move over the surface of its object rather than to plunge into illusionistic depth, not to distinguish form so much as to discern texture. It is more inclined to move than to focus, more inclined to graze than to gaze...

While optical perception privileges the representational power of the image, haptic perception privileges the material presence of the image.[16]

This materiality is brought to the fore in *Impossible Gaze* as my lens dwells on the delicate textures belonging to history and re-presents them in the fragile form of photographic paper. Importantly, as

Marks notes, that depending on the viewer's "own sensoria" they will experience these images, both the original interiors, and mine differently.[17] [...]

As photographer in this environment, my position changes from the distant observer evidenced in *Before the Museum*, to the active viewer in *Impossible Gaze*. Seizing on fragments of artworks and objects layered with wall, floor and ceiling decoration, this exhibition shifts the viewer's focus to the spaces in-between the historic artworks. In this body of work the in-between becomes the centrepiece. To explore more fully the experience of viewing in the museum environment *Impossible Gaze* returns to the activity of the gaze and the glance and effectively reverses their roles. By focusing on the more ephemeral and ambulatory aspects of the glance in the museum, I have immobilised it for a new viewer's gaze. The intuitive and idiosyncratic experience of museum viewing is made up of incessant ocular movement over walls and objects, through rooms and between artworks. My images express Bryson's observation that the path of the glance "is irregular, unpredictable, and intermittent."[18] Here again I intimate the notion of human vision, approximating the viewer's line of sight as they move through the corridors of the museum. I trace what lies in the path of their glance. My lens directs the attention of new viewers to the peripheral details in this environment.[19]

Impossible Gaze follows the direction and movement of the viewer's eyes as they traverse the museum, occasionally repeating imagery to represent the glance's continual mapping of space. Here the eye uses two types of vision to process information, foveal and peripheral.[20] James Elkins describes peripheral vision as what happens at "the blurriest margins of the field of vision." Objects seen "peripherally are not just blurry but also differently proportioned. They are distorted and hallucinatory, and they need motion in order to exist."[21] Whilst perceiving objects in motion, vision occurs in a stream of continuity, constantly pulled between proximity and distance, and oscillating through the gaze and the glance. This idea of motion in the museums is important as it intimates both the different activities of vision, as well as expressing the ephemerality of viewing. Bryson suggests the transient, and often sideways, mobile demands of the glance are opposed to the duration of an immobilised gaze, which generally occurs straight ahead, "prolonged" and "contemplative."[22] Ross Harley refers to the idea of visual perception while moving, or "perception-in-movement," as a "motion landscape."[23] Harley also describes this "mobilised vision" as a "multi-sensorial experience," where the effects of looking while moving involve "the body in panoramic perception."[24] This engagement of the senses enables the viewer to not only navigate the museum but to viscerally experience the space they inhabit. The viewer can feel for example, the cold smoothness of the stone floor, and sense the weight of the timber beneath the gilded frames and the softness of the velvet upholstery. They can smell and taste the mixture of scents in the age-laden air, and hear the cooing of other viewers and their shuffling feet.

Impossible Gaze plays not only with the viewer's eye but also their body movement as they wander through the corridors. Constricted by the confined spaces or guided pathways the viewer is often forced to look at artworks from obscure angles with tilted heads and craning necks. These photographs intimately express the dynamics of vision with its vertiginous and disorienting optical illusions. Through the use of close-ups, which are intended to impress the proximity of subject to the viewer, and acute camera angles these photographs assimilate looking in this environment, and dislocate the frontal viewpoint generally associated with viewing art. […]

After buying a ticket for the Caravaggio e i Giustiniani *exhibition at Palazzo Giustiniani—where the extraordinary crowds mean that the museum can only accept advance bookings—I had just enough time to squeeze in the* Velasquez *exhibition at Palazzo Ruspoli before returning to take up my place for Caravaggio. Palazzo Ruspoli, in the central shopping district of Rome, houses temporary blockbuster exhibitions. From its entrance a steep staircase ascends directly from the chaos of Rome's streets and ends abruptly at the ticket office. From there the visitor threads their way along a narrow corridor where there is a desk offering audio-guides, included in the price of admission. Too preoccupied with time to queue for the guide I strode past into the gallery. On entering the dimly lit room, painted deep red for the occasion, I realised at once the consequence of neglecting the audio-guide. A room brimming with viewers confronted me, yet there was complete silence. Every single visitor was wearing an audio-headset. They were engrossed by the glowing paintings and their accompanying commentaries, all reciting the same sequence of words at different intervals and in different languages. This eerie silence was disturbing at first, as the viewers shuffled along, taking their cues as commanded by the voice in their earphones. Difficult to disrupt the flow of the commentary that dictated the time and sequence of viewing, they were aurally isolated from their companions for the duration of the visit. There were no murmurs of adulation, no critiquing the subject, no intimate tête-à-tête. Their engagement with Velasquez was imbued with historical and biographical details the curators and historians that collaborated on the production of the audio-guide directed their gaze.*

Even more disconcerting were the surveillance monitors that were displayed at eye level at the entrance to each room of the gallery. Although positioned for security the viewer was both instantaneously caught and viewed on CCTV, a strange "separation" unlike staring in a mirror, you could see yourself looking at other things.[25] Here you could observe yourself entering the rooms, and see yourself in the context of all the other viewers. How peculiar this felt to be pictured in front of Velázquez, caught in a web of gazes just as Foucault had described of the Velázquez painting, Las Meniñas.[26]

After this curious and somewhat disturbing visit I rushed back to Palazzo Giustiniani where I was thrust again into an experience dictated by the museum. Negotiating the gallery in groups, viewers must file past the works as prescribed by the museum guides while being bombarded by their extensive monologues. Urged forward by the crowd, I swayed between awe and anguish as the route through the gallery provided no opportunity for the visitor to retrace their steps for a second glimpse.

I recite this tale of rushing from one museum to another and back again for two reasons. Firstly, it is indicative of the type of cultural consumption in most major Italian museums today. And secondly, because it encapsulates many of the ideas that have been brought forth throughout this project: that studies in history, museology, art and cultural history, cultural tourism and technology all intersect with the viewer and their own complicated subjectivity, vision, interpretation and experience. It evokes the crowds, booking systems and rapid tours that are part of cultural tourism, the re-used historic spaces that create an enriched context for viewing, the blockbusters and audio-guides that have become synonymous with current museology, and the voiced texts that are the culmination of generations of historians. In addition to this, the CCTV monitors that are intended to enforce appropriate behavior in the museum, are a constant reminder not only of the exchange of glances between viewers, artworks and museum staff, and the theories of vision that lie behind all this looking, but more significantly that the viewer is not seen as an individual but as part of a crowd, a small cog in this great visual culture machine.

Though Velázquez is neither a Renaissance artist, nor Italian, Palazzo Ruspoli, like Palazzo Giustiniani, is an historic Italian residence now converted to a present-day public gallery. Moreover, it is this particular type of encounter that so intrigues me. Both the Velázquez and Caravaggio exhibitions call attention to the

contemporary experience of viewing, and how our engagement with art is directed by museums. They also demonstrate that the guiding voice, be it live or recorded, does remedy in part my concerns with the speed of viewing. [...]
In this project, both visually and theoretically, I have examined not only the surface of things—paintings, furniture, architecture—but also what lies beyond their surface, the abstract and ephemeral notions such as looking, seeing, learning, understanding, knowledge, information, authentic, aura, fetish, the Other, experience, liminality, myth, history and time, all ideas without physical form, invisible concepts that come together in the museum to create an ever varying, transitory and often inexplicable encounter. This being so, what could be more appropriate than the voice, another intangible and fugitive medium to account for the objects present in the museum. Spoken texts that can either productively occupy or overload another of the viewer's senses. The eyes, ears, mind, skin and nostrils are bombarded in each Italian museum encounter.

Notes

1 William Ivins regards the artist's solution to the "mathematical problem of perspective" as the "rationalization of sight" and considers it to be one of the most significant events of the time. William M. Ivins, Jr., *On the Rationalization of Sight* (New York: Da Capo Press, 1973), 7-8. [Editor's note on the footnotes. Footnote citations in all these excerpts have been made uniform to the Chicago Manual of Style, with the caveat that the citations in the originals vary widely and not all have complete bibliographic information. In general, English and Australian scholarly citations vary much more widely than American citations, and there is no uniform standard. The different degrees of completeness of citations reflect differences in the original texts. Readers interested in pursuing the subjects discussed here are urged to get copies of the full theses from the respective institutions. —J.E.]
2 Meinhardt, "The Sites of Art: Photographing the In-between," in *Louise Lawler: An Arrangement of Pictures,* translated by Fiona Elliott (New York: Assouline, 2000), unpaginated.
3 Susan Best, "Merleau-Ponty and an Ethics of Vision," conference paper at the 25th Annual International Conference of the Merleau-Ponty Circle, George Washington University, 14-16 September, 2000, unpublished.
4 Bryson,"The Gaze and the Glance," *Vision and Painting: The Logic of the Gaze* (London: Macmillan, 1983), 93.
5 de Bolla, "The Visibility of Visuality," in *Vision & Textuality,* edited by Stephen Melville and Bill Readings (London: Macmillan Press Ltd., 1995), 285.
6 This is what Bryson refers to as "scotomise," scanning rather than seeing. Cited by Stuart Hall in *Representation: Cultural Representations and Signifying Practices* (London and New Dehli: SAGE, in association with The Open University, 1997), 65.

180   Jo-Anne Duggan

7 Crary further divides the act of looking into another two categories of "observer" and "spectator" to better contend with the nuances of viewing: namely that "observer" signifies something more than merely looking, and that "spectator" could imply a more "passive onlooker." Both of these terms appropriately describe the idea of the "engaged viewer" and that of the "distracted viewer" within the museum environment. Crary, *Techniques of the Observer: On Vision and Modernity in the Nineteenth Century* (Cambridge, MA: and London: MIT Press, 1991), 5.

8 Crary, *Suspensions of Perception: Attention, Spectacle, and Modern Culture* (Cambridge, MA and London: MIT Press, 1999), 50-1.

9 Roger Cardinal discussing Barthes" "The Third Meaning," in "Pausing Over Peripheral Detail," *Framework* 30, vol. 1 (Coventry, England: University of Warwick Arts Federation, 1989), 30.

10 Crary, *Suspensions of Perception*, 60.

11 Vivian Sobchack, "What My Fingers Knew: The Cinesthetic Subject, or Vision in the Flesh," paper given at the conference Special Effects/Special Affects: Technologies of the Screen, Melbourne, March 25, 2000, unpublished.

12 Ibid.

13 For more on the senses refer to Sobchack, *The Address of the Eye: A Phenomenology of Film Experience* (Princeton, N.J.: Princeton University Press, 1992).

14 Baudrillard, *Fotografien—Photographies—Photographs: 1985-1998* (Ostflidern-Ruit: Hatje Cantz Publishers, 1999), 130.

15 Marks, *The Skin of the Film: Intercultural Cinema, Embodiment and the Senses* (Durham and London: Duke University Press, 2000), 22.

16 Marks, *The Skin of the Film*, 162-3.

17 Marks, *The Skin of the Film*, 23. Interestingly Marks cites Berenson's assertion "that the quality most essential to painting [for Florentine Renaissance painters] was "the power to stimulate the tactile consciousness" (165).

18 Bryson, *Vision and Painting*, 121.

19 The idea of tracing the path of the viewer's gaze on paintings has also been undertaken in the exhibition "Telling Time" at the National Gallery in London, in conjunction with the Applied Vision Research Unit at the University of Derby. http://ibs.derby.ac.uk/gallery/updates.shtml, accessed 11/12/2001.

20 Professor Margaret Livingstone of Harvard University quoted in, "Mona Lisa smile secrets revealed," no author cited, *BBC News Online*, http://news.bbc.co.uk//2/hi/entertainment/2775817.stm, accessed 18/2/2003.

21 James Elkins, *The Object Stares Back: On the Nature of Seeing* (San Diego: Harcourt Brace, 1997), 99-100.

22 Bryson, *Vision and Painting*, 93-6.

23 Ross Rudesch Harley, "Motion Landscapes: A Video-Essay On Panoramic Perception," DCA thesis, University of Technology, Sydney, 1999, unpublished, 32.

24 Harley, "Motion Landscapes," 52.

25 Leader comments, "when we see ourselves on CCTV…There is a separation of the look, the emergence of our look as an object, outside us." Leader, *Stealing the Mona Lisa: What Art Stops Us from Seeing* (London: Faber and Faber, 2002), 142.

26 Foucault, *The Order of Things: An Archaeology of the Human Sciences* (London: Tavistock Publications Limited, 1970 [1966]), 3-16.

13

Sue Lovegrove

"The Unsolidity of the Ground" is the title of Sue Lovegrove's PhD thesis, written at the Australian National University, in the School of Art, in 2002. Lovegrove is a painter, and her art, along with a report of her research, comprised two-thirds of the thesis. The other third was the dissertation component.

The subject of her dissertation was an analysis of a painting called *Big Yam Dreaming* (1995) by the Aboriginal artist Emily Kngwarray. (A digital image of the painting is available at www.dreamweb.nl/emilypics.htm.) "My central argument," she writes,

was that Aboriginal desert women's paintings are informed by all aspects of daily life and that includes everything that goes on around them; the "humbug" and constant pestering for money by family members, substance abuse, domestic violence, sorriness (deaths in the community), hunting, visits to country, caring for family, socializing as well as the influences and aesthetic interventions that occur at the art centre. All are equally important activities that occupy peoples lives and are important in determining what paintings look like and what cultural meanings are encoded in them. Just as Aboriginal paintings are intended as representations of sacred Dreaming stories and as conceptual maps of an artists affiliation to particular sites, they could also be described as genre paintings, representing stories of everyday life and domestic existence.

Lovegrove's painting concerned "notions of representing the land" and especially "areas of Central Australia which are Anmatyerre and Arrernte clan lands":

My relationship to this part of the country is driven by a deep passion and love which is detached from any desire of belonging or ownership. The paintings are about finding ways to represent a "philosophy of being" without projecting one's desire or ego onto a place. I have attempted to paint about an intimate experience of

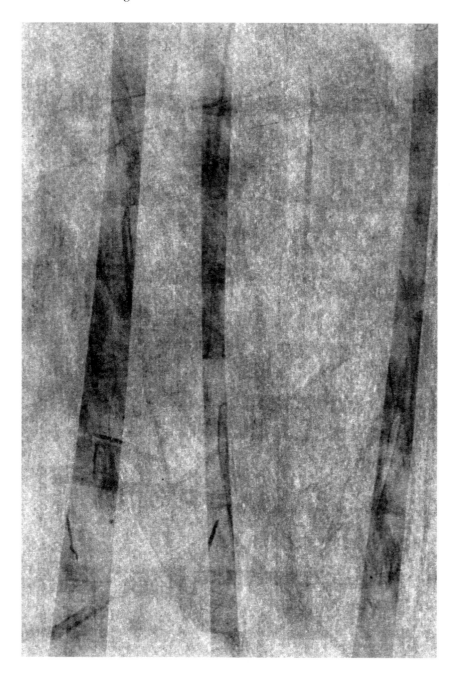

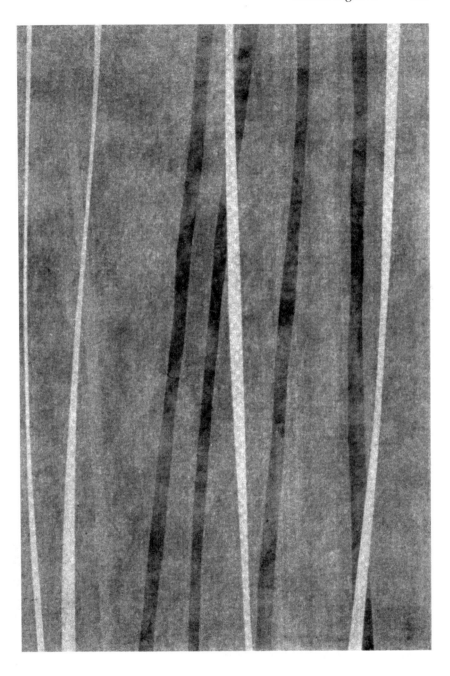

the land that reflects an embodiment of sensations felt and experienced, as well as what is seen. Things appear and disappear in ambiguous spaces, partially veiled in white. Thoughts flicker, and images hover at the periphery of one's perception, suggesting what could be described as an aesthetic of the glimpse. The feeling perhaps of holding a place in one's memory, not just looking at it. I aimed to evoke a natural rhythm of movement through the process or performance of painting, similar to the rhythm of breathing or walking. A quiet, involuntary, marking of time.

The title of the final series of paintings is *To Hear the Earth Breathe.*

I asked Lovegrove how she imagined the relation between her paintings and the Aboriginal works she studied. She wrote:

I've been a bit slow to respond to this because to be honest I don't think I really answered that in the thesis. This I think was partly because of the format that Canberra School of Art set with the dissertation as a separate entity to the studio work and partly because my research was on Aboriginal art (as opposed to European art). There is a great deal of sensitivity in Australia to non-Aboriginal artists being influenced by Aboriginal art due to past history where artists have misappropriated Aboriginal imagery and spirituality, albeit with sincere intentions. Aboriginal people are acknowledged as being the custodians of specific stories relating to an individual's totemic relationship to sites and ancestral beings. This means that only specific individuals have the authority to paint images relating to those narratives. Because of this, my dissertation became a study in anthropology and cross-cultural theory that was quite seperate to the evolution of my own paintings.

However, my motivation and viewpoint throughout the research was as an artist rather than as a theorist, and what I hoped to do was understand how an Aboriginal woman might perceive the land around her and how she might perceive the pictorial space of the canvas. It was really an investigation in what determines Aboriginal aesthetics. This was important for me as an artist because I wanted to think about ways of painting the landscape that didn't rely on the European models of perspective and naturalism: for example describing ways of being in a place, moving through it, the rhythm of walking or glimpsing things rather than holding the entirity of a view in one's gaze. Also considering the concept of a vertical orientation to space—what is above and below the ground, rather than a horizontal viewpoint. To find different models of perception isn't an act of appropriation, but rather an acknowledgment of the cultural convergences currently taking place in contemporary Australian art. It may also be perceived as twenty-first century primitivism. The studio report was really a second piece of research, that ranged freely over personal narratives, Eastern philosphy, Australian colonial history, Aboriginal bark painting and Aboriginal women's desert painting.

The Canberra School of Art model of the PhD requires two bodies of research, and to me [that meant] one supports and informs the studio practice, and the other is an entirely theoretical piece of research that stands alone, also contains "original thought," and also informs the studio practice. [...] From my own point of view, although at the time I may have struggled with that extra load, I learnt so much more as a result. I loved every minute of it and was very grateful that the dissertation was outside of me, the artist, as it made the writing of quite complex cross-cultural issues a lot easier. It is a shame however that my dissertation is always the part that gets the most attention. For me it is my paintings that are the most important outcome.

Excerpts from

"The Unsolidity of Ground"

by Sue Lovegrove

1: The Sound of Painting

In the process of painting a canvas, painting up bodies or painting the ground, the sounds that happen—either as song, casual conversation, extraneous sounds or the silences are all an important part of the social experience in some way and thus inform the experience of painting and, potentially, contribute to different layers of meaning. To consider a painted canvas without the aural possibilities of experience doesn't acknowledge the important social and kinship relationships between people that are reinforced through the activities of painting, whether that be on canvas, skin or the ground.

When I visited communities in Central Australia I had the opportunity to watch several women painting. At Ikuntji art centre, Haasts Bluff, I witnessed Narputta Nangala, a senior Pintupi woman, sing as she worked, sometimes for several hours. It was a low sound that arose from deep within her body, as if it came from the earth itself. It was a private and quiet song that seemed to be for her personal benefit only as she sat slightly separate from the others. The song was not projected into the space of the room but was just loud enough to slip out of her body, spilling along the ground as if to hover just above the canvas before disappearing into the surrounding space. The song was integral to Narputta's experience of remembering her country and family in the process of painting. For Pintupi women at Ikuntji, painting was a vital expression of homesickness or loneliness since many of the women were isolated from their country 800 km to the west. Rodney Gooch told me that he also witnessed Emily Kngwarray singing in a barely audible, deep rhythm while she painted. As part of his employment at CAAMA [Central Australian Aboriginal Media Association], Gooch recorded many of Emily's songs. In 1988, when a collaborative project of batik cloth, *A Picture Story*, was being documented, Emily apparently pointed out the story in her cloth and sang the songs for *Alhalkerre* while beating the rhythm with her hands.[1]

I also witnessed women communicating in sign language while they painted. Another time when we were all, women, children and dogs, piled into the "troopy" on a hunting trip, there was a lot of very excited discussion over crowbars, who was coming and who wasn't. The sound of women and engine noise was deafening, making it impossible to understand anything that was going on. One of the women, Anmanari, then started signing to me something that I understood as, "this is how life is, this is what it's meant to be." I interpreted her message as an expression of unmistakable pleasure and joy. Signing appeared to be part of everyday communication for all kinds of ritual, personal and practical reasons.

Silence is also maintained in the presence of important sites, in ceremony and during "sorry business." (Sorry business is the term used for everything related to death.) When discussing matters of ritual importance, sound is reduced to whispers or forbidden altogether, necessitating the use of a complex sign language.[2]

To visit a "sorry camp" is to witness another sound not normally heard in daily life. It is a spine chilling wail emanating from the shadows of women sitting in the dirt around small camp fires, their bodies smeared in white ochre.

While women paint up their bodies in *awelye*, (women's sacred ceremony), they also sing the appropriate songs pertaining to the subject of the ceremony. The singing is not always continuous, nor is it lead by any one particular individual. The number of repetitions of the song, maybe as many as thirty times, seems to be determined by the mood of the women present rather than any strict protocol.[3] Similarly, when an action, either the painting up or the dancing of a ceremony takes longer than the song, then the song is repeated until the action is completed.[4] The importance is placed on the interaction between the song and the activity of painting or dancing, not the song alone. The song validates the design being painted.

The rhythm of traditional song is called *tracking*.[5] The song usually starts in a strong voice, then begins to dissolve and dissipate as the breath runs out. Just as the sound begins to fade into the distance, the voice then reappears again up close. This cycle is repeated over and over into a continuous sound which echoes patterns of movement, of walking across the land. The rises and falls in the song emulate the rises and falls of the country in a rhythm and cadence similar to that of walking, that is again reflected in the rhythm of painting. The song, being a series of repetitions, has no beginning and no end, but is suggestive of a series of accumulations.[6]

In a similar way, Arandic languages have an elastic capacity to expand and contract, incorporating larger patterns of movement or action, thereby linguistically articulating a person's relationship to their surroundings through the pattern and rhythm of speech. The effect of this makes every part of the trace of movement simultaneously present in speech. For example, the description of the trace of an animal incorporates its rate of progress, where it stopped, where it was agitated and where it ate, in an accumulation of syllables that express the complexity of the action taking place. This kind of grammar transfers the emphasis from the actor and the act to the action itself.[7]

Arandic songs (in translation) are often descriptive of the subject's appearance or the pattern of its movement. For example Strehlow's translation of a phrase in a song cycle referring to a ritual pole goes something like this, "the pole towers upwards."[8] The repetition of this phrase, along with other phrases describing the pole's function and how it appears, acts to reinforce the ancestral power associated with the pole. The phrases do not carry meaning through invocations of praise or authority as hymns or chants might do in a European context, but through the repetition of description.[9] In this way the desired continuity of ancestral power is achieved through an accumulation of the same phrase.

Similarly, the repetition of a painted line on canvas or the repetition of the same form on different canvases, may serve to fulfill this role of instilling ancestral power in images. This concept is echoed in the repetitions of marking the canvas or the accumulations of lines in *Big Yam Dreaming*. [See the image at www.dreamweb.nl/emilypics. htm. –J.E.] In a way, the spatial resonance of Anmatyerre painting could be seen to expand or contract depending on what size the canvas is, incorporating more or less material as required. This would explain the numerous representations of "Yam Dreaming" that Emily painted, where she has adapted the composition of lines to suit the scale of the canvas. This way of perceiving the meaning of images located in a repetition of performance causes some anxiety amongst a non-Aboriginal audience who constantly seek evidence of originality and inspiration as a bench mark of artistic brilliance.

2: The Social Space of Painting

The subtlety and importance of the social and kinship relations was not clear to me until I actually visited desert communities. Whenever I interacted with women, whether discussing a painting, going hunting, or doing anything, the women's relationships with each other were always stated either indirectly or directly. The hierarchy of who was present determined who sat where and paintings were always explained to me first in terms of who was present at the time, who was participating, or who else had ritual affiliation to country. Paintings also could not be talked about in the presence of the "wrong" people.[10] The paintings were always considered in their social and kinship context before any other ancestral or ritual meaning of the story was mentioned.

While I was at Ikuntji art centre, Haasts Bluff, I assisted the art adviser, Kate Podger, with the stocktaking of all the paintings for the end of financial year. This meant that I was able to see a lot of the early works on paper from the mid 1990's as well as catalogue many of the paintings completed while I was there. Cataloguing paintings involves documenting the story, title and giving the work an accession number.

When I asked Narputta about one particular painting, she responded by describing it as a "long time" painting from "old days." She then spoke at length of her "pass-away" (a local term for a deceased person) sister, Tatali Nangala who was one of the leading women artists working for Papunya Tula. I understand that Tatali was an important sibling to Narputta because apparently as a young child Narputta was separated from her family and spent some time living near Alice Springs. It is likely that Tatali may have taught Narputta many of the stories of country from her father's and mother's sides. The two women painted together at Kintore, where their country is located, near Lake MacDonald. When Narputta saw this particular painting, it brought on a wave of "sorriness" and grief for her "pass-away" sister and at the same time for her father's country, the site where her sister is now buried. She proceeded to sing her country, both her own song and her sister's. Narputta then went on to tell me how important it is for her to return to this country to look after her sister's grave.

Narputta asked every day whether she had enough money in the bank for a Toyota. Unfortunately, every day her money was handed out by herself, or the adviser on her behalf, to someone else, as is appropriate in family obligations. As a consequence she will probably never save enough for a car and if she does her sons will more than likely disappear with it anyway. But she was desperate to get that Toyota in order to return to her country to look after her sister's grave. The Toyota in this context, is an important aspect of western influence that enables people to reclaim their mobility and access to country after thirty years of coerced living in distant government organised communities. The potential acquisition of a car seemed to be an important motivation for Narputta to paint.

The emotions that Narputta expressed on seeing this "long time" painting and the social meanings in the foreground of her mind, including her need for a Toyota, appeared as the principal source of meaning for her. Second to this was the ancestral narrative of *kukardi*, the sand goanna travelling under *tali*, sandhills.

There is a belief amongst non-Aboriginal people that painting serves the purpose for Aboriginal people to "keep country strong" in their minds, as a way of remembering country and that painting can somehow stand in for ceremony. This may be so, but actually, I found it to be the other way round—that painting was an expression of loneliness for family and country and provides a means of earning money in order to visit relatives and country. One activity doesn't replace the other, just assists in its potentiality.

Narputta also mentioned *kuminjayi* Strocchi in relation to the painting. Marina Strocchi was the non-Aboriginal art adviser between 1992 and 1997, who set up Ikuntji art centre and who played an important role in taking senior Pintupi women back to their country at Kintore in 1994 to do a collaborative project. *Kuminjayi* is a term usually used in place of a person's name when they are deceased. Marina Strocchi is not deceased, but lives in Alice Springs. When Narputta spoke of the painting she also remembered Marina with fondness and some "sorriness" at missing her. She expressed a longing to see her non-Aboriginal companion who was as important to the painting's story as anyone else at the time. Narputta may have used the term *kuminjayi* in this context as a precaution because she didn't know if Marina was still alive, but even so, *kuminjayi* seemed to take on richer and broader meanings. Instead of being an expression of an erasure of a person's presence so as not to arouse any unnecessary grief, it became an expression of personal longing and in relation to her sister Tatali, an expression of deep "sorriness'. In a way the concept of *kuminjayi* could be understood as "sorriness" itself.

This made me think of "sorriness" as an important social meaning in many contemporary desert paintings, as "sorry business" (the term used to describe everything related to death), happens frequently in contemporary life and affects everyone in the community. I am not suggesting that there is a specific "sorriness" to each painting but that it is there as another layer of meaning, another condition that influences the immediate environment in which images are painted. Every time I have visited an Aboriginal community there has been "sorry business" either about to begin or just finishing. While I was at Utopia, there had recently been an alcohol related suicide shooting. Most of the business that took place at the art centre while I was there was about "payback" and who should be considered responsible for the suicide. Everyone is drawn in to these interpersonal relationships because that is what holds the social fabric of the community together.

At a place like Papunya there can be a murder or stabbing every week. The whole community is often in perpetual motion, moving between "sorry camps'. Then there is further violence in "payback" rituals, potentially causing more deaths. I'm not calling in to question the morality of "pay-back," just reinforcing the point that trauma as a result of high levels of violence and death is a very visible and dominant part of contemporary life and must impact on the production of the paintings. Women artists also invariably become involved in and are the victims of alcohol related domestic and sexual violence.

The experience of sorriness is also part of *Big Yam Dreaming*. I am not suggesting that this is directly related to how the painting was produced, although inevitably there must have been grief and trauma in the background of Emily's life somewhere, but that sorriness is evident in the way the painting is perceived by Emily's family. When Gloria Petyarre and Violet Petyarre visited the Queensland Art Gallery to view Emily's retrospective exhibition, what they were seeing in the paintings was their "pass-away" Auntie. When Gloria sang her song and Emily's song in front of the paintings, one aspect of what she was doing in this activity was expressing her own sorriness and grief that her Auntie's paintings represented for her. The painting's meaning for Emily's family was essentially social and kinship based. This also indicates the way meanings can change alongside the painting's history, quite independently from meanings an artist might have intended. Thus it is likely that *Big*

Yam Dreaming has quite different meanings for Emily's family now, than it did in 1995 when she painted it.

3: "'Make 'im Flash One'"

While increasing the quantity of work produced, the adviser also has to ensure the quality of work is maintained to guarantee sales. The ability to discern "good" and "bad" Aboriginal art is fundamental to the whole business. This is done by art advisers working closely with the artists by directing the aesthetics of colour choice, composition, markmaking and in some cases subject matter. The aim is to educate the artists on how to make a painting that will sell, to "make 'im flash one" (a term I heard Pintupi women use to describe making a good painting). Simultaneously the adviser works the industry by selling the paintings with stories of traditional relationship to country, reinforcing the idea that the work cannot be understood beyond the surface by the uninitiated, thus perpetuating the perception of an Aboriginality based on mysticism and the "secret sacred'. Stories are presented in this context as the mark of authenticity that states the Aboriginal origin of the work and that suggests it is about people's relationship to country, and not abstract painting.

During my experience at art centres, most of the discussions I had with the art advisers were about our subjective opinion of what was good and bad Aboriginal art and what kinds of advice to give artists. Many of our suggestions invariably were based on European concepts of visual language: the use of positive and negative space, contrasts of pure or complementary colours and composition. However, what seemed to be happening on the canvases was not at all predictable and often moved outside European conceptions of pictorial space. What might be described as an aesthetic of the "unexpected" often took place—something closer to a visual anarchy where there appeared to be no rules.

From my experience, women's relationship to colour, for example, appeared quite random and chaotic. There seemed to be a general sense that the more colours the better as far as the artists were concerned. It was an aesthetic based on what women described as the "prettiness" of colour. When left to their own devices the Pintupi women at Ikuntji often used lots of bright colours in a patchwork arrangement of dotting that all joined up. The women clearly enjoyed using a large number of colours together, pinks, greens, yellows and reds all combined into the one field. This joy of colour has often been linked to the artists" celebration of the wild flowers that are abundant after rain. Mitjili Naparulla describes her painting,

"Putipulawu yila Mitukatjirrla, Flowers around Mitukatjirri', she says "Bloom, I wasn't sure what to paint, so I put some flowers, put different colours. I did it myself, good colours!" quoted in Ikuntji Paintings from Haasts Bluff, 1992–94.[11]

This is an idea that no doubt has truth to it, but I am inclined to think that it is more a product of the symbiotic relationship between the market and artist. It is most likely that art advisers made the visual connection to flowers in their need to legitimise the profusion of colour demonstrated in the paintings into a cultural context and their need to explain the paintings in terms of a literal representation of culture. It would not be "authentic" enough to say they were "abstract paintings of colour'. Subsequently the artists may have adopted the story of the "colour of flowers" as a way of developing new images in which they celebrate their love of colour and that don't rely on the representation of culturally sensitive material. Both of these scenarios are important and valid.

During Emily's career, she was often celebrated for her "extraordinary gift" for colour. I suspect that some misreading is occurring here too. Often titles of her work are suggestive of the changing seasons and abundance of flowers after rain. For example *State of My Country* 1991, or *After Rain* 1990. I am wondering who was responsible for the titling of these paintings and whether she actually had any say in it. According to Rodney Gooch, Emily's response to colour was often to say "that's pretty." I doubt that it had much more significance for her other than that. He also said that her personal preference was actually for soft pink ochre colours not the bright colours for which most of her paintings are admired.

On the occasions when I was able to go hunting with women, their attention was turned towards their aim of procuring food from the land. They never once separated themselves from the environment to look at country in a visual aesthetic, or to admire the visual beauty of it. If they took notice of flowers it was for what that country might yield or what it might tell them in terms of the presence of other things less visible—perhaps witchetty in the roots. There was one memorable moment when hunting with the women at Ikuntji. We were so engrossed in searching and digging for witchetty that when we emerged back at dinner camp all the women had yellow blossoms from the Acacia in their hair. It looked quite beautiful and comical at the same time, a kind of fanciful desert hair-do. When I commented on the blossoms they looked at me blankly as if I was stupid and got on with the important business of eating.

The cultural meanings of colour and material (natural ochres) are often closely connected to the place of origin or source of that colour. This association with place is often incorporated into the meanings generated by the use of the colour or material. For some Pintupi people red ochre from Karrku Mountain is called *karrku*. The use of that colour in ground or body painting signifies the place of origin, the mountain. Contemporary materials of acrylic paints and canvas exist outside this semiology and therefore remain free of association and cultural meaning. This increases the possibilities of use and as a consequence often manifests as a profusion of colour occurring simultaneously on the canvas.

When colour is free of association and meaning it appears as a condition that could almost be described as a colour "blindness'. This blindness would result from being flooded with colour free of any context or semiology, and an inability to see colour for its separate chromatic possibilities. This anarchic perception of colour perhaps also mirrors Aboriginal people's relationship to "otherness', that is non-Aboriginal people and all that is associated with the non-Aboriginal world. They have an ability to use and adapt resources available without recourse to their intended purpose or meaning. This approach encompasses anything from cars (the humour of Bush Mechanics), to money, housing or food. It is an aesthetic philosophy that reflects the temporality of "the moment'. Just as one thing (colour or material) is used, another can easily replace it since meaning or importance (in a painting) is not contingent on its presence.

The analogy is easily transposed onto Aboriginal people's relationship to material objects and possessions. What is available is used for what ever purpose required, it doesn't matter who it might apparently belong too (that's usually the white person!) or what it is meant for. It is a practice that continually baffles non-Aboriginal people and frequently causes concern when things used are abandoned where ever they are, like the rubbish that engulfs communities and the vast amounts of painting money that just seem to disappear into the sand, here one minute gone the next.

At Haasts Bluff there has been an interesting adaptation of commercial oxides that can be bought cheaply in large quantities from hardware stores in the form of cement colouring, replacing traditional ochres for ceremony. Natural ochres are iron oxides, so essentially the material is the same only it no longer carries the association to the place of origin. The "collecting" of the ochres from town is now relegated to the non-Aboriginal worker. Oxides have the added advantage of being strong "pure" colours and so have increased ancestral power associated with them. Such strong colours are hard to find in the natural environment locally.

This relationship to things as dispensable and adaptable presents an aesthetic possibility that is in contradiction to how non-

Aboriginal people might like to perceive Aboriginality. These co-
lourful paintings are sometimes hard to sell. They aren't always easy
to look at. The visual effect can sometimes be quite confusing as the
colours obscure any structure that the painting might have. They
slip outside the market's expectations of Aboriginal art and what
non-Aboriginal people might want to decorate their homes with.
The whole purpose of their production was for a non-Aboriginal
market, so inevitably some intervention has to take place in order
for them to be desirable to the consumer.

In these situations the art adviser mixes some new colours and
suggests some editing to reduce the palette. From my observations
of women artists they demonstrate a very strong understanding of
the graphic possibilities of extreme tonal contrasts, which relates
to their experience of body painting. Body painting utilises alternate contrasting colours of white or ochre on dark skin to create a
dynamic effect which shimmers. The brilliance and luminosity of
white is also associated with the ancestral power and energy of *al-
tyerre* (the sacred Dreaming). When given a limited palette of a high
key colour, usually white or a pale tinted ochre, with a low key or
strong colour on a dark background, the women invariably came
up with an image that utilises the contrast of tonal opposites in a
rhythm alternating between light and dark.

When the rhythm and pattern predominates in the graphic quality of the image, instantly spatial relationships begin to occur, creating a visual order out of what was previously chaotic. The nuances
and idiosyncratic events of every day life become part of the work.
Slops and drips fall on the canvas in odd places, a dog walks over
it and the wind catches the corner flipping the canvas onto itself all
adding up to the effect that "looks" like the art of another culture.
It is an instant winner and guaranteed to sell. Since linear paintings
by women have now become associated with body painting, they
are effectively authenticated in terms of a "traditionalist" reading
of Aboriginality, even though what is really being communicated
is a performed idea of what Aboriginality might be. In the process a cultural authenticity is constructed that has some relation
to Aboriginal people's visual language but also aspires to satisfy
non-Aboriginal aesthetic and political interests. These paintings are
really about the contemporary forms of life and interventions that
people live with and negotiate on a daily basis. In this they could
be described as contemporary Aboriginal genre painting—the art
of everyday life.

To read Katungka Napanangka's painting (next page) in terms of contemporary life the story goes something like this: Katungka is a Pintupi woman who lives at Papunya. She only recently started painting at Ikuntji art centre after her mother Katarra Nampitjinpa passed away last year. Katungka's husband Pastor Murphy drives her to Haasts Bluff every day so that she can paint at the art centre. As a less senior woman, she mostly works outside on the verandah with two or three other women. Katungka paints stories relating to her country, *Intiti* near Kintore. The story in this painting is about *kuniya*, carpet snakes who hide in holes in *tali*, sandhills.

The colours were selected by the art adviser, two complementary colours, yellow ochre and dioxazine purple with white. The painting was made flat on the ground. Katungka started by painting the parallel lines, the *tali*, from the bottom, then she worked the left hand side of the canvas and then the right hand side. She painted the two sides on different days causing a seam to run through the centre of the painting where the lines meet. The top left hand section was developed in response to one of her earlier paintings that had a similar lacy effect. It was suggested by the art adviser that she leave the dark purple of the background at the top and bottom as a kind of framing device that utilises the negative space and provides some contrast with the high key ochre and white. The dark patches in the lacy section were going to be filled in with white, only I suggested they might look better left purple, as "holes." The next day Katungka had a "tummy" ache so the painting was hurried along and the lacy pattern changed quite dramatically. The following day it was suggested by the art adviser that she might tidy up some of the purple "holes" so that they were neat.

In my interpretation, the changes of mood and concentration according to whatever else was happening in Katungka's life are important in the reading of this image. Also the involvement of non-Aboriginal people, including myself, affected the final result. This should not be thought of as negative, just an extension of the symbiotic relationship between artists and outsider that I have been elaborating. In the same way, Albert Namatjira learnt a European watercolour technique from Rex Batterbee to paint his country. I would argue, however, that Katungka's painting is richer and more interesting if it is considered as a representation of the relationship between Aboriginal and non-Aboriginal people and an expression of the joys and struggles of contemporary life, in whatever forms that might present. The background story of *Intiti* is also important but not necessarily the focus or primary source of meaning.

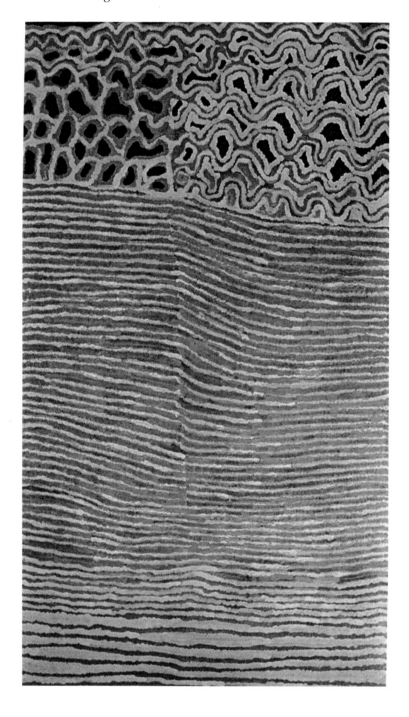

Notes

1 Anne Marie Brody, *Utopia, A Picture Story* (Perth: Heytesbury Holdings, 1990), 17.

2 Ted Strehlow, *Aranda Traditions* (New York: Johnson, 1968), 115.

3 Richard Moyle and Slippery Morton, *Alyawarra Music, Songs and Society in a Central Australian Community* (Canberra: AIATSIS, 1986), 55.

4 Moyle and Morton, *Alyawarra Music*, 55.

5 Stephen Mueke, *Textual Spaces* (Sydney: UNSW Press, 1992), 52.

6 Paul Carter, *The Lie of the Land* (London: Faber and Faber, 1996), 64.

7 Carter, *The Lie of the Land*, 64.

8 Ted Strehlow, *Songs of Central Australia* (Sydney: Angus and Robertson, 1971), 112.

9 Strehlow, *Songs of Central Australia*, 284.

10 Anne Marie Brody, *Utopia, A Picture Story* (Perth: Heytesbury Holdings, 1990), 14.

11 Marina Strocchi, *Ikuntji, Paintings from Haasts Bluff, 1992-94* (Alice Springs: IAD, 1994), 106.

14

Frank Thirion

"Circular Continuum: The Depiction of Historical Time in the Art
of Paddy Fordham Wainburranga" is the title of Frank Thirion's
dissertation, finished in 2004 at the Australian National University's
School of Art. Thirion's studio practice was concerned with the
concept of "Cultural Measurements'; it was complemented by his
research into the indigenous Australian Rembarrnga artist Paddy
Fordham Wainburranga[1]. Thirion was interested in revealing how
history is recorded cross-culturally, and whether "there a distinctive indigenous notion of time," one that "follows a circular continuum," that informs the "accounts of historical events in the
Wainburranga paintings."
    "I would have to say," he writes, "that my meeting with the art-
ist Paddy Fordham Wainburranga in 2002 remains one of my most
memorable experiences. Paddy has a considerable public profile
having been collected by all the major national galleries and institutes in Australia [...] and internationally. His generous recounting
of stories suppled me with an extraordinary insight into his paintings and how history can be constructed from the Rembarrnga
point of view." Thirion's own studio experience in the School of Art
was just as important, and "extremely useful to my art practice."
    Several of Thirion's paintings, such as his Paysage de Sel (Salt
Country), done in 2002, are made with salt. It is intended to suggest
an desiccated landscape seen from above. "Salinity," Thirion says,
"can be interpreted in part as the consequence and the by-prod-
uct of generations of unsustainable farming practices, a heritage of
colonisation and the result of dispossessing the traditional own-
ers of their land." The dots are references to Aboriginal painting
as it is practiced in Central Australia. "This particular influence is
neither generated by post-modern appropriation practices of the
late 1980s," Thirion remarks, "nor is it to be seen as a form of misap-
propriation of indigenous art. The colours used in the dots are similar

to those colours first used by early colonial painters in rendering the Australian landscape." And he adds that the "map-like quality of the dots" also refers to Western culture's desire to "contain and apportion property."

Another painting, Gecko Cat (2003), is a floor installation made of 730 individually cut-out shapes of geckos. Thirion intends it "to illustrate the ecological damage Australian feral cats do to the native fauna." In conceptual terms, the 730 geckos represent the

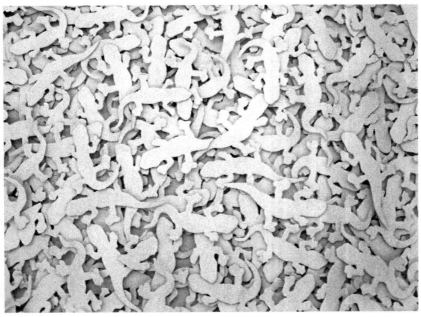

consumption of one feral cat in a year, if it only ate two geckos per day. According to current research, the total population of feral cats in Australia is estimated to be between 3.8 and 12 million. The density of the feral cat population varies with each season and is related to reproduction. The impact of these feral predators on the wildlife populations poses a significant threat to a great number of native species. For example, the stomach contents of one feral cat caught in the Lake Eyre area of South Australia showed that it had eaten 24 Painted Dragons; 3 juvenile Bearded Dragons, 3 Earless Dragons, 3 Skinks, 1 House Mouse and a Zebra Finch in a single meal. Contrary to popular belief, feral cats in Australia are not noticeably larger than their domestic counterparts. The average typical weight of a feral cat is 3.4 kg. The work dramatically illustrates the pressure some ecological systems are under. [...] The three-dimensional work can thus be read to parallel the consumption by European settlers with their unsustainable appetite for land.

In 2007, Thirion sent me an update, with this sad notice:

I am saddened to inform you of the passing of Paddy Fordham Wainburranga last year. He was unwell for a number of months and his general health deteriorated rapidly. I gave him a copy of the Printed Project book with the image of Coffin Box[2]. I recall at the time that he was very pleased to see this specific work in print. Although Paddy was a prolific artist, the Coffin Box painting was an important work that recounted the traditional cultural practices of his Rembarrnga people. The painting, along with thirty-eight other culturally significant works, were tragically lost to him in the 1998 Katherine floods. Because the paintings exist only in photographic form, Paddy wanted me to know the stories attached to them, so that the cultural history could be maintained for a younger generation. I know that Paddy would have liked the idea that his cultural knowledge is to be extended to a wider audience.

Excerpts from

"Circular Continuum:
The Depiction of Historical Time in the Art of Paddy
Fordham Wainburranga,"

by Frank Thirion

Wainburranga's representation of mortuary rituals is seen in the bark paintings called Coffin Box[3] (1980s) [illustrated here] and The Sick, the Dying, the Mourning[4] (1989). [...] Both paintings depict the same Dupun/Lorrkon ceremony rituals. [...]

The Coffin Box painting [is...] a far more complex system of representation. The main iconography is entirely painted in white and decorated with red and yellow ochre dots. The principal use of white in this image alludes to its level of importance. Traditionally, this technique was used by the Rembarrnga in the creation of rock art imagery like that seen in the Cadell River area. Wainburranga defines "one colour" paintings as the "old style" suggesting images painted monochromatically have a presence connecting them to the Dreamtime continuum.

Unlike The Sick, the Dying, the Mourning the figures are painted directly onto the untreated bark surface. In this visually busy poly-scenic narrative, Wainburranga has created a generic pictorial form to represent the many characters appearing in the story. Men are depicted in various occupations: musicians, dancers, holding tools or spears, some carrying a dilly bag on their backs. The feature distinguishing the sexes is that the women are depicted with breasts. Children are also depicted, among the mourners. On the left-hand side, at the bottom of the picture, is the only image that alludes to an aged person. This is where the pictorial narrative starts. In this first compartmental border we recognise the familiar image of the old blind man led by his son to the ritual site as depicted in The sick, the Dying and the Mourning.

Really, that old man they've been taking. Leading with a stick and take, him back to place. See that long one? Yes, they've been taking. We call that Jimbajumbuk[6]. That's how the old man die. This one where old man bury, that's where they leave him. That's why they've been dancing now, now they've been take him. Coffin box here now they've been

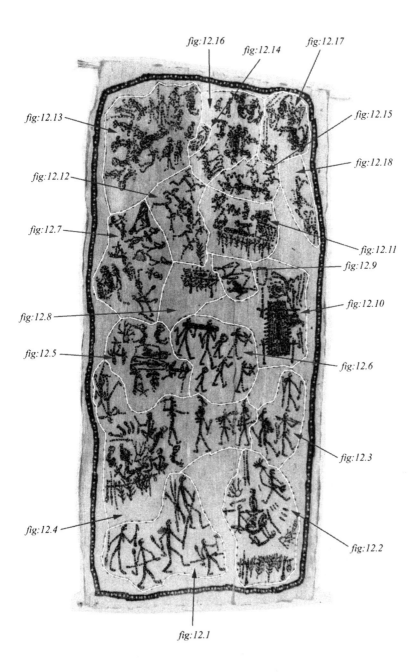

fig:12.16   fig:12.14   fig:12.17

fig:12.13

fig:12.15

fig:12.12

fig:12.18

fig:12.7

fig:12.11

fig:12.9

fig:12.10

fig:12.8

fig:12.5

fig:12.6

fig:12.3

fig:12.4

fig:12.2

fig:12.1

bringing, they've been dancing here. Righ there (stabbing paper with his finger for emphasis). Yeah. This is the place for dead people. They've been go taking him and cover him. They're organised here. Yeah. This is the place they're dancing now. Corroboree. Yeah. History, dancing for dead people. This is the place. They've been leaving this coffin box. They've been sending him up and leave him. This is a place for dead people. I know. It's a, a Dupun Lorrkon place. Yeah, two names, Dupun Lorrkon. Coffin box.[7]

There are a number of defined activities taking place throughout the painting; each compartmental border depicts an event relating to the ceremony. There is a continuous narrative structure in place within the painting, but it would be ambiguous and inaccurate to attempt to plot all the movements of each individual figure to illustrate the structure. Figures such as a musician, dancer, and even an elder may not be the same particular individual from one section to the next. But there is one individual who is the prime focal point of the narrative: the deceased. His presence depicted in varied forms can be observed and followed throughout the Dupun/Lorrkon ritual. His death is already known at the beginning of the narrative, as we see the old blind man been led by his son to participate in the funeral rites. This first activity is observed taking place at the bottom of the painting on the left-hand side.

The reading of the Coffin Box painting does not follow the circular pattern discussed in Wainburranga's previous works. In this painting the illustrated narrative follows a route which begins at the "bottom" left of the painting and ends at the "top" right of the picture where the story ends. The pictorial narrative commences with the bordered compartment numbered fig:12.1, and is read from left to right to fig:12.2, and then moves up to the neighbouring compartment above fig:12.3 and continues in reverse order, right to left to fig:12.4. The pictorial order snakes through the painting until it reaches the last top bordered compartment at fig:12.13 where the painting must then be rotated 180 degrees to be read from a right to left. In this work reference to the cyclical pattern is implicit in the subject matter which is the ceremonial activities associated with the life and death cycle. [...]

Each compartmental border in the painting is an episode in time, and they may encompass different spans of time; while some represent a number of hours within one day, others imply a much longer duration. In (fig:12.8) we see the depiction of the body of the deceased left to decay on a platform for a number of months. The bones are finally removed and placed in the hollow log (fig:12.10).

The activities contained in the Dupun/Lorrkon painting are as follows:

Fig:12.1 The old blind man been lead by his son with three others to participate in the funeral ritual.

Fig:12.2 A campsite where a ceremonial activity is talking place. There we see the old man with his stick nearby on the ground with three others engaged in songs with another is seen dancing.

Fig:12.3 The group of men travel with the old man being carried on the shoulders of his son.

Fig:12.4 There are Fourteen figures in this compartmental border. The old man and his son are greeted by a woman, while other figures are seen sitting around a campfire mourning the deceased. He can be seen lying on the ground near the humpy. A hunter is returning to camp with a goanna. Other bush foods such as yams are present.

Fig:12.5 The body is prepared to be taken away to a new location. Clap stick are played by three musicians, a weeping mourner is seen sitting on the ground while someone standing is adding wood to the campfire.

Fig:12.6 The mourning party leaves for a new site, led by the clap stick musicians followed by a party of mourners. The body, wrapped in large bark sheets, is carried by two men holding spear throwers.

Fig:12.7 Fourteen figures are represented in this area. A large number of musicians is depicted around a campfire, participating in a corroboree. Three other figures appear to be mourning women.

Fig:12.8 The body is placed on a bush platform and left to decay.

Fig:12.9 Two figures are seen collecting the bones, on the ground is a small bark sheet for the remains to be carried in.

Fig:12.10 Two figures walk to a new site. One is carrying the remains.

Fig:12.11 There are six figures in this compartmental border. Three are musicians; one is dancing. Two other figures (perhaps the same individual) are seen preparing the bones. One is painting the bones and the other is placing them in the hollow log.

Fig:12.12 The figures in this section are depicted "upside down" in relation to the figures discussed so far. This is the consequence of Wainburranga rotating the painting. Five men wearing armband adornments perform a ritual dance. One individual has a decorated pole while another is holding an object.

Fig:12.13 This section contains the largest group of figures involved in a corroboree, there are 19 men sitting around an object. One figure appears near the depiction of food items.
Fig:12.14 Bush foods.
Fig:12.15 Six figures. Three are carrying the hollow log while the other three are dancing.
Fig:12.16 A large group of Fourteen figures. Two are holding the hollow log, six are musicians with three sitting and three standing to the side, four are dancing and two are just sitting on the ground with one of them holding a spear-thrower over his head.
Fig:12.17 This image is also painted "upside down" in relation to the orientation of other figures in the work. It has seven figures in it and their activities are unclear. Two appear to be women, one sitting on the ground, the other behind her in a pose reminiscent of fig:12.2 (with the old man sitting on the ground and another behind him with his arms on the others shoulder).
Fig:12.18 This image is also "upside down" to most of the figures in the painting and shows two men walking. […]

In the Coffin Box painting the generic human forms and their activities exist in an undefined pictorial space. Figures are depicted sitting, dancing, walking, even "upside down" in what appears to be a pictorial void. But this void is not the depiction of emptiness; it may be interpreted as the depiction of I suggest the Dreamtime space, the Dreaming realm itself. In Wainburranga's depiction of the Dreamtime space, the pictorial "void" stands for the Dreaming realm where remembered temporal events are also depicted. In other words, Dreaming stories, as well as historical events, are remembered on the same physical plane in the present.

Evidence of Dreaming events occuring in a time shaped by ancestral beings can be witnessed in the environment today; and the transformation of the physical world and of its totemic animal forms continues to exist in the present. The very material on which bark paintings are made has its beginning in the Dreamtime. These are organic materials which follow a physical cyclical pattern of growth, decay and regrowth. This would support the conceptual notion that the physical bark surface of a painting which depicts Dreaming events of the past and invokes them in the present, will already be infused with the eternal existence of the Dreaming.

In discussing the art of the Yolngu people of Arnhem Land, Morphy explains their ability to transform the surface of the bark painting. Through a process of cross-hatching a shimmering brilliance (bir'yunhamirri) is revealed. In conjunction with ritualised ceremonial activities, the painting surface evokes the ancestral past into the present as this "quality of shininess is the power of ancestral beings incarnate in the object." Morphy further describes these paintings as having the ability to create "a depth of field for the Dreaming". The surface of the painting works to activate a "spiritual realm', a sacred connection into the Dreamtime present. Moreover, in reviewing the Yolngu's concept of the "sacred" (madayin) Nigel Lendon says "for the Yolngu there is no circumstance in time and space where the present of the madayin may not be invoked"

In discussing the Yingapungapu sand sculpture(s) associated with Yirritja mortuary rituals, Morphy explains the manifestation of the restricted mardayin ("sacred law"). He notes, "As a manifestation of the ancestral past, it exists outside of time. In interpreting the paintings, people continually switched from one perspective to the other, from ancestral past to present practice." This switching from the ancestral past to the present suggest a circular pattern is taking place in the cognitive process of ritualised activities.

The theme of the Coffin Box painting illustrates how the indigenous notion of time operates in a cyclical continuum. The Coffin Box painting elaborately details the many traditional mortuary rituals undertaken by the indigenous people of Arnhem Land. The subject matter dealing with death and ceremonial remembrance is a common theme within Rembarrnga art. Departing from human existence to reincarnation as a totemic spiritual essence is a feature of the cyclical construct of Rembarrnga belief. By representing a remembered event the subject is ritualised as an element of the continuum rather than a finite end in itself. These ceremonial activities continue to exist today. The events occupy a temporal space in living memory; the recent past is remembered as a place in time. The act of remembering becomes a ritualised entity in itself. That is, in Wainburranga's remembered past there was an actual "old blind man" who participated in the ritual he depicts. The old blind man now becomes an allegory of life and death. A generic depiction of the old man appears in both paintings.

The Dreaming events of the past are brought forward into the present through oral renditions that are remembered. In such a way, I suggest, the old blind man becomes fused into and part of the "Dreamtime present'. In other words, the recent past, which is remembered, becomes an element in the depiction of the Dreaming. This "Dreamtime present" can be seen depicted in all of Wainburranga's paintings.

Notes

1 [For a picture of the artist and sample images, see www.fairdinkumab-originalart.com/paddy.html. –J.E.]

2 [*Printed Project* is the first form of this book; see the note in the Introduction. — J.E.]

3 Coffin Box is one of a number of bark paintings created the early 1980s and was damaged in the 1998 Katherine flood. The painting exist[s] only as a photograph and had (at the time) no information to accompany it. Wainburranga revealed this painting's narrative to me on being shown its image.

4 [The painting is executed in] natural pigments on eucalyptus bark. [Its dimensions are] 96.5 x 145.0 cm.

5 See E.J. Brandl, *Australian Aboriginal Paintings in Western and Central Arnhem Land: Temporal sequences and elements of style in Cadell River and Deaf Adder Creek Art* (1973). The rock art paintings examined in the Cadell River area are identified by and associated with the Rembarrnga and Ngaglbon people who both lived at the bowana (river) location. These two linguistically affiliated groups share social and cultural bonds with each other. Plate XIV show a painting created by Mandarrg a Rembarrnga man (born around 1915). His rendition of "The Rainbow Snake" in the one -colour style was painted around 1965. p.124. There are strong style similarities between these paintings of this area and of those painted by Wainburranga.

6 Jimbajumbuk: it is not clear if this word is the name of the "stick" or is associated with death.

7 Wainburranga interview, tape L side-b 27/09/2002.

8 Howard Morphy, op.cit., 1998., p.188.

9 Ibid., p.198.

10 Nigel Lendon, "Beyond Translation: Learning to Look at Central Arnhem Land Paintings" in Morphy, *Outside In: Research Engagements with Arnhem Land Art* (2001), 20. *Madayin* also spelt *mardayin*.

11 Brandl, *Australian Aboriginal Paintings*, plate XLII, p.152. Figure 31 is part of the schematic depiction of the mortuary ceremony; [see p.] 22.

15

Ruth Waller

Technically, Ruth Waller doesn't belong in this book, because she has an MA, and not a PhD: but the quality and interest of her work make it relevant. (It is also a rejoinder to less rigorous doctorates, because she manages much of the detail and thoroughness of a PhD in an MA format.) She is also included here because she is one of the best examples I know—at either MA or PhD level—of the *use* of art history to further an artistic agenda.

Waller entered the MA program in the Australian National University School of Art in order to focus on moments in art history that she thought could inform her art practice. She recalls that she "thoroughly enjoyed the challenges of developing a body of writing developed out of a process of the sustained scrutiny, analysis and interpretation of pictures." It was "a process of interrogating my own enthusiasm, of finding ways to account for an intuitive sense of connection to paintings from a time and culture quite remote from my own." That formulation seems especially apt: it shows how the history of art, including its research protocols and interpretive methods, can be understood as a support for painting practice.

"As my research developed," she explains, "I was fascinated to find myself immersed in the late medieval world-view," and she began to think about "how painters gave visual form to theology. While this naturally involved investigating the narratives depicted and the pictorial devices employed in relating these episodes, I was also led to consider how the late medieval painter might have thought about the nature of perception itself and the role of painting within this devotional cosmology."

Some of her attraction to the material turned on theology and representation, and some on formal properties. In particular, she says she has "long enjoyed the transitional or hybrid qualities of the compositional/spatial relations of late medieval painting." She was "delighted," then to discover an historical subject that "seemed to

thematically parallel or exemplify the formal fascination these pictures held for me." Thhat subject turned out to be the moment in
which a miraculous intervention into "worldly time and space" is
used by the late maedieval painter to show the "intersection" of the
transcendent and the mundane. "I have to admit," she adds, "I also
found the fabulous stories they depict highly entertaining."

Because Waller's own art practice was directly influenced by
her research, I have put her paintings at the end of this chapter, following the excerpts.

Excerpts from

"Miraculous Scenes From the Altarpieces
of Siena and Florence of the Fourteenth and Fifteenth
Centuries,"

by Ruth Waller

This thesis focuses on a selection of paintings depicting saints performing miracles. These are all small panels extracted from altarpieces from the fourteenth and fifteenth centuries. Some of them
are wing panels from polyptychs; most are predella panels. All of
the painters whose work I have chosen to discuss are Sienese with
the exception of Fra Angelico, who brought the Sienese influence
to the Florentine altarpiece. My thesis is that these paintings are
characterised by particular pictorial devices which structure them
as visual allegories significantly representative of the changing intellectual and devotional culture of the late medieval period. The
artists whose work will be the subject of this study are the Sienese
painters Guido of Siena, Duccio, Simone Martini, Ambrogio and
Pietro Lorenzetti, Sassetta, the Master of Osservanza, Sano di Pietro,
Giovanni di Paolo, and the Florentine painter Fra Angelico.

My fascination with predella narratives began in Florence,
when I first came across Fra Angelico's depiction of the miraculous
leg transplant performed by the saints Cosmas and Damian, now in
San Marco. I had no idea what story lay behind this exquisite little
panel which was once part of the San Marco predella. Who were
these characters hovering over this sick bed, and how or why had
they come to be attaching a black leg to the body of a white man?

I began to notice other small and miraculous pictures. In the Louvre I watched many people stop, their curiosity sparked by Sassetta's small panel of *The Blessed Ranieri* who swoops in on a cloud, like some medieval superhero to free the poor from prison. In the Uffizi, in a panel painted by Ambrogio Lorenzetti, a small boy is strangled in the street by a winged, claw-footed and reptilian grey figure in peaked cap and cloak, while inside a house the same child rises up, drawn from his death-bed by rays emanating from a hovering haloed saint.

Despite their small size and marginal status these little panels seem to hold a strange attraction [...]. I found myself first enchanted by the apparent clarity of intention in the construction of these worlds in miniature, designed so specifically to serve the devotional purpose of each painted episode, and simultaneously frustrated by my inability to identify the players, to unravel the sequencing of events or interpret them.

Having puzzled thus over so many of these little pictures, I began to search out their narrative content through sources such as de Voragine's *The Golden Legend*, compiled around 1260 (a source commonly used by painters at this time) and George Kaftal's extraordinary modern catalogue of the *Iconography of the Saints in Tuscan Painting*. But I knew that simply unravelling these narratives would not explain why, as a painter, I found them so compelling. There was something about the structure of these pictures that intrigued me. I tried probing them in the studio. I made studies from them; I tried emptying them of their original narratives and looking at their spatial structure. This revealed little more than just how significant the relationship between each narrative and the structure of the picture spaces in which they take place appeared to be.

It is important that, as a painter, I acknowledge that my fascination with this period in painting also reflects my interest in the issues of modernism and beyond. With painting's adventures in the undoing of the unified perspectival field, post-Cézanne, there has been a renewed interest in the pre-Albertian picture space. The modern eye takes pleasure in and sympathizes with the apparent discontinuities, the lack of unity of space and time in these pictures, and with the strange and particular quality of precariousness which we experience in their pictorial structure. Their townscapes and built structures often recall a rather jerry-built stage set. This resonates with the deeper sense of the precariousness of human life implied in these scenes of everyday misadventure. This quality is, I suspect, structured into these pictures by those pictorial devices which allude to the experience of the provisional and contingent nature of worldly circumstances.

These pictures are however evidence of a significant rebirth of interest in painting's ability to conjure an illusion of the visual world, which came after a period of hundreds of years during which that was considered inappropriate and irrelevant distraction for the painter whose work was to serve the principles of Christian worship. Late medieval painters like Duccio, Simone and the Lorenzetti brothers demonstrate a growing interest in delivering back to us a sense of the world finely observed. They develop systems of oblique projection and empirical perspective which they apply very inventively in constructing narrative pictorial spaces—interior and exterior spaces, intimate and vast spaces, views of nearby and distant places. Fra Angelico and Sassetta do apply vanishing point perspective to their pictorial design but perspective here remains in the service an overarching allegorical pictorial structure and purpose. For the modern viewer at least, we do not experience the illusion that we as viewers inhabit the space of these paintings. Certain pictorial devices, certain conventions, hold us in a kind of suspension, outside the frame. In one sense it is as if we experience the progress of the narrative more through the mind's eye of a reader than through the eye of a body which might physically experience the space. On the other hand this fascination, the "push-pull" we feel in front of these pictures, is also surely a product of our experience of the history of painting.[1] The modern viewer, having seen the post-Renaissance heights of the painting as a unified field of perspectival illusion, can feel the early stages of its "pull" in these little pictures. And yet, through the history of Modernism, we have seen painting release itself from illusionism to investigate the expressive potential of its own vocabulary and processes, and thus confront us in so many different ways with its own materiality and objecthood, "pushing" us out to enjoy it in its flatness.

This is an interesting and pleasurable point of entry into the visual culture of another time and place, which may help explain the attraction such material holds for us today. However, in focussing on these paintings of miraculous events, I have tried, rather, to consider them in the context of late medieval theology and hagiographic culture. Having found no references to any records which may give us evidence as to how these painters thought about the problems of religious narrative painting, I have developed my analysis with reference to secondary sources. It is thus via Eco, Huizinga and Price's *Medieval Thought* that I was alerted to the pervasiveness of allegory in the medieval world and have come to consider these paintings as demonstrating an allegorical vision. Discussions of allegory in medieval literature and theology by John Freccero and Peter Heath and Panofsky's conclusion to *Perspective as Symbolic Form* prompted me to consider ways in which allegory, which Northrop Frye has referred to as a "structuring principle of fiction"[2] might operate as a structuring principle in devotional narrative painting. In all this, I have tried to develop my thesis in a way which reflects my research process as a painter. This is to say, my focus is on identifying the particular pictorial devices these painters employ in their structuring the imagery of miraculous narratives as allegory and illustrating the significance of saints and miracles in late medieval religious culture. Thus my investigation of the subject of miracles and of the issue of their representation in these panel paintings, will be through close observation and comparison of pictures, informed by the consideration of the aspects of the art historical, intellectual, devotional and exegetical culture of the day. [...]

> Behold how the Divine Wisdom lies hidden in sense perception, and how wonderful is the contemplation of the five spiritual senses in the light of their conformity to the senses of the body.
>
> St Bonaventure (1217-74)

In a culture where the world itself had been for centuries seen as pervaded by allegory, devotional narrative painting can be seen as more than merely a vehicle for allegorical narratives, painting can be seen as a modelling of allegory itself. Further, painting might be seen to operate at this time as a field for the allegorical interpretation of vision itself, constructing vision as a modelling of revelation.

Duccio's depiction of *Christ Healing the Blind Man*, now in the National Gallery in London, exemplifies this principle while representing Christ as the master upon whose example the lives of the saints who follow are modelled. The divine gifts of sight and revelation are simultaneous and one and the same, and we apprehend this allegorically as we witness this principle demonstrated in the world. Let us consider how theology comes to be expressed through the allegorising of vision at this time.

In his essay, "Dante's Medusa: Allegory and Autobiography," John Freccero begins by describing St Augustine's conception of language:

> For St Augustine, language provided the paradigm for all human understanding, for it seemed to derive timeless truth from an utterance in time. This mediation between time and eternity made language, the word, a perfect symbol of the relationship of God to the world. Christian reality was ...

like syntax, time pressed into the service of eternity. History was the unfolding of God's word in time. The elements of history, men and events, were as syllables linked together, striving towards closure and significance, the end term which, in Christian language, was the Word made flesh.

In the thirteenth century, the Franciscans bring new interpretations to the significance of "the Word made flesh". Franciscan theology has a tremendous impact on the ways in which painting is conceived as a devotional art in the late Middle Ages and actively fosters a vernacular culture of religious teaching and celebration. David Jeffrey sees the key to this in the Franciscan interpretation of Christ as having been sent by God into the world in order to glorify all of creation.

In the life of Saint Francis, we see self-conscious re-enactment of episodes and lessons from the life of Christ and a demonstration of the principle of God's identification with all of creation. Jeffrey emphasises the influence of Franciscan friar, Bonaventure, whose theory celebrates sense perception as the first of the four lights of knowledge. Here again we see the world conceived in allegorical terms, but, more than this, perception is allegorised as a modelling of revelation and of the union of the soul with God. Jeffrey summarises Bonaventure's position:

If we consider the medium of perception ... we shall see therein the world begotten from all eternity and articulated—made flesh, in time- because of generic, specific, or symbolic likeness to the Creator. Words inhere in the Word: in language and in vision the processes of creativity are analogous to the formulations of the Creator. When the contact between organ or faculty and object is established, there results a new percept, an expressed image by means of which the mind reverts to the object. The exercise of sense perception reveals, accordingly, the pattern of human life. But in the delight ... is opened the union of the soul with God.

This is allegory in the anagogical mode—whereby both our direct visual experience of the world and our devotional imaging of it are interpreted as revelatory.

Let us take Augustine's idea of language as "time pressed into the service of eternity" and, in the light of Bonaventure's theory of sense perception, apply it to painting where both time and space may be pressed into the service of eternity. The picture space becomes

a kind of "sacred geography," to borrow the term Salvatore Settis
uses to describe the experience of pilgrimage:

> Religious geography ignores landscape and defies histo-
> ry. the fabric of valleys, mountains and rivers, passes and
> bridges, the ship on the sea, are all points along the line of a
> journey towards the holy place. Cities and castles can act as
> reference points or stopping places; but a map showing the
> precise lie of the land is not only "technically" impossible, it
> is not even desirable. What does it matter how wide a river
> is? Few even counted the days spent on the road....
> The place where the pilgrim encounters the sacred is by
> its very nature indefinable, its real history is irrelevant to
> it. What is important is that tradition should confirm the
> sacredness of the place, the more intense presence of the
> divine, with authority, always relying on basic stories which
> need no verification, episodes from the life of Christ or one
> of the saints.
> Faith in the ominpresence of God outside space and time
> is thus wedded. paradoxically, to the quest for some privi-
> leged contact with him located in a sacred event.[3]

It is in this spirit that I begin to investigate the visual syntax of
allegory, first by considering the greater scheme of the altarpiece
and then proceeding to discuss particular features of allegorical
narrative design and key examples. [...]
Through the late medieval pictorial eye we witness narratives
played out over time within pictorial structures which imprint them
with a theological design. This design operates at the macro level in
the organisation of the altarpiece as a gestalt, as a configuration of
images of varying sizes and shapes. A polyptych combines a number of pictorial conventions: iconic portrait panels of single figures,
panels of groups of figures (often the Virgin and saints) in compositions which conceptually and formally represent an intersecting of
the iconic with the narrative, and the narrative panels which are the
subject of this study. The polyptych altarpiece thus delivers us the
simultaneous apprehension of an entire system of images, while
across this system, and within each of these panels, we experience
the representation of time and space in many different ways.
An excellent example of this is the *Beato Agostino Altarpiece* by
Simone Martini, painted in 1324 and now in the Pinacoteca in Siena
[shown in outline here]. Let us consider the specific relations of the
narrative parts to the whole in this beautifully preserved polyptych.

It is evident and significant that each of the episodes depicted in this altarpiece takes place in or around Siena. If we begin at the upper right hand panel and move anti-clockwise, we are being led from a scene in the country outside Siena, in to the wolf attack just outside the town walls, further in to an urban street where the balcony accident occurs, and finally (right though the wall) into a Sienese domestic interior. This locational "zooming in", leading usthrough a sequence of episodes in the life of this city, both demonstrates the omniscience of the divine gaze and at the same time localises it. This constant, the divine presence, is metaphorically represented by the repetition of the gold leaf sky and by the recurring presence of the Blessed Agostino, signalled always by that gold disc, the halo, tooled with radiating patterning.

Simultaneous with this apprehension of the geography of the sequencing of these outer narrative panels and the relationships between these scenes, we see them in relation to the central portrait panel. Compositionally these events are designed with strong architectural obliques which seem to radiate from the central figure of Agostino, however, the narrative action in each scene draws toward him in its resolution, each victim (and each viewer) being delivered by their rescue literally and allegorically closer to him.

The figure of Agostino stands tall, holding a bright red bound volume of his *Constitutiones* of the Order. His feet, concealed by his robes, are just above the bottom edge of the picture. His head, centred in the multifoiled arched frame, is tilted slightly to our right as he listens to a small angel, speaking into his right ear. The downward swoop and the small scale of the angel's body echoes that of Agostino in his interventions in the side panel scenes. On either side of the Beato and reaching to shoulder height, are trees with dense dark clumps of foliage. Three multicoloured birds perch in these trees while a fourth a plain brown bird sits on the ground a little behind. This setting alludes to the Augustinian identification with the hermitic tradition, as do the portraits of St Anthony and St Paul in the rondels on either side. The horizon is set very low, leaving four-fifths of the surface given over to the luminous gold leaf ground.

The picture spaces within which these events are shown as taking place combine devices of empirical perspective with continuing use of oblique projection. As a means of drawing the entire structure together the major structural orthogonals in each narrative scene converge towards the central panel which thus serves as both a compositional and a spatial axis. Compositionally there is a rough symmetry in these obliques which radiate from the saint's portrait, while spatially major architectural structures are projected from a series of (perspectivally irregular) vanishing points within this central panel.

Simone Martini's description of the play of light in this work reveals more about the world of Beato Agostino and the ways in which paintings were designed as visual theology. While forms are modelled, as if lit by a directional light source, the direction of this light is not consistent or unifying across the picture, but rather acts as a guide to our narrative and episodic reading of the scene. Forms are thus lit, but they do not cast shadows. The role of gold leaf in this work is simultaneously one of colour and of light, of precious materiality and symbolically, of an other worldly immateriality. Built structures are constructed tonally, in that each plane has a distinct tonal value, but rarely do these surfaces appear to be internally modulated in any way by local light or shadow.

Equally, colour relations are designed to guide us in our reading of these scenes. Red and green are the key colours in relating these narratives one to the other. The red lozenge shape of Agostino's book acts as a focal point for the system of reds, pinks and terracottas which highlight the action through the wing panels. These reds are complemented by tertiary greens and dark blue greens in the garments of the less significant characters, and expanses of tertiary greys and soft earth browns in the description of landforms and architecture. In the Medieval period colour tended to be modelled from its purest strength as its darkest value, into highlights by the addition of white. Here we see this approach broadly persists, though with a limited introduction of some darker tonal modelling. Colours act also as keys to these episodic narratives, enabling us, in a pictorial world where there is little differentiation in appearance between individuals, to readily identify each separate character in their sequential representations in the drama as it is played out. [...]

It is an essential characteristic of any figurative painting which employs devices of spatial or volumetric illusion that we experience simultaneously a compositional configuration of shapes or motifs on the picture plane and our reading of the picture space as a three-dimensional location for the pictorial action. Our perception of the picture is a simultaneous apprehension of a compositional gestalt and a spatial modelling of a pictorial world. In paintings designed with allegorical purpose this relation can be seen to be charged with particular resonance. [...]

This quality of a significant and sympathetic compositional relation between the pictorial design given to the action in each scene, and the structures of the world within which these events take place, which I have termed *compositional consonance*, is particularly engagingly and inventively developed into the picture space by fourteenth century Sienese painters such as Duccio, Simone Martini and the Lorenzetti brothers, and continues to characterise Sienese predella narratives into the late fifteenth century in the work of Sassetta, Giovanni di Paolo and Sano di Pietro. While the Sienese resist the pursuit of scientific perspective championed by their Florentine rivals, they do increasingly explore devices of pictorial projection. Using a variety of devices of scale, spatial and volumetric projection and empirical perspectival effects, in concert with managing pictorial light and colour to serve devotional narrative, the Sienese design their picture space allegorically as an intersection of the worldly and the divine. The picture space is constructed as a moralised, theological domain within which the hagiographic narrative is projected into allegory. In this sense, the device of echoing the shapes, forms and dynamics of the narrative action with the features of the architectural or landscape setting, while bringing formal coherence to a composition, can also be considered as having semantic implications. Those towers, trees and pathways which so often assist in our reading of an episode by signalling key characters and events, also imply a deeper allegorical intention. Revelatory events appear consistently to enjoy a significant consonance with the features of their architectural or geographical location. It is as though God's intention, God's design, is delivered to us by being metaphorically modelled, sympathetically structured into the world.

Whereas, in the thirteenth century, this sympathetic structuring occurs as a device of compositional design on a single plane, in the fourteenth century the picture plane and the picture space are engaged in a constant exchange of motifs and features charged with allegorical purpose. Symbolic relations within the narrative are thus signalled across space and time, while being delivered for our simultaneous apprehension on the picture plane. While these scenes are structured spatially and compositionally to model the narrative as a passage of time, they also manifest the narrative and present it as a design outside sequential time and habitable space. This pictorial matrix, signalling that the narrative has a higher purpose, is an example of allegory in the anagogical mode.

Further, in the same city (of Siena) a mother had a boy who
fell off a certain balcony which was in need of repair; and
a large plank fell down on top of him. She commended the
boy to Agostino; and by grace of God and merits of the saint
the plank hovered in the air for such long time that it ren-
dered certain the escape and safety of the boy.[4]

This rescue takes place in urban Siena. A small boy is falling
head first into the street from an upstairs balcony. A dislodged timber panel is falling down on top of him. The mother watches in
great distress, her hands grasping her headscarf as she leans over
the balcony rail. Even before the child hits the ground Agostino
sweeps to the rescue, delivered again by the small cloud which
serves as the vehicle for his rupturing of earthly space and its physical laws by this posthumous appearance. The halo, a flat gold disc
with its radiating tooled patterning, is unaccountable to the rules of
perspective illusionism. It acts also to signify Agostino's interces-
sion as an intervention of the symbolic divine space of the gold leaf
ground within the worldly life of the streetscape.

According to the contemporary record quoted by Martindale,
Agostino miraculously suspends the fall of the plank, causing it
to hover midair for such time as to enable the boy to land safely.
He simultaneously gestures his blessing. The rescued child stands
upright, unhurt in the centre foreground, as the turning point of
the action. He is steadied protectively by one man while other witnesses to the miracle reach out to touch him and offer prayers in
thanks.

As in the first of these panels the arch is a recurring compositional motif here, echoing the arched shape of each frame of the
altarpiece and the trefoil forms within them. The arch of Agostino's
body, leading back to the figure of the mother, and the arch formed
by the witnesses clustered around the child, are obvious instances
of this. Smaller arcs are described by the struts which hold up the
balconies. These architectural supports metaphorically echo the
saint's catching and delivery to safety of the falling child. The drama of the fall is also emphasised directly behind the child by the
strong vertical of the doorway, and the dark descent of the stair-
way within; while the ascension of the saint (and of all the faithful
) seems implied by the ladder-like structure of the door which appears to lead from the ground upward to his halo. Its gold coloured
horizontal beams parallel the angle of the hand of benediction.

There is also a formal echoing of the cloud shape in the upturned
skirts of the falling victim, however the mundane and gravity-

bound nature of the child's fall is evident in the downward thrust of the arms and the desperate kicking of small feet.

Again the built setting for this narrative appears to "deliver" the story to us: figures being consistently translated into or reinforced by architectural motifs. Windows seem to witness events: the face-like quality of the balcony from which the mother leans is particularly striking. As in the panel directly above, in which a child is rescued from wolf attack, the picture space is constructed as a street receding at about forty- five degrees to the right, which leads our eye in and out of the central portrait panel, connecting us back to the bearer of the Augustinian Constitutiones and to Christian doctrine.

Examples of Ruth Waller's art practice

Waller's program of study was in art theory, and so it did not involve a studio component. Nevertheless, her studio practice during the period was directly influenced by her thesis.

"During 1998-1999," she writes, "I made a series of paintings using the compositional and spatial structures of late medieval narrative pictures and stripping them of their narrative figurative content, enjoying the spatial tensions of their construction and exploring whether they retained some vestigial narrative implication. In other pictures I introduced figurative elements cross-referencing predella narratives with my own imagery."

In one such picture, a scene from the life of St Francis is "reduced to the shell of a narrative, exploring the pictorial tensions of architectural motifs and a illusionistic devices against a painterly flatness." Waller says that when she first began looking at predella panels, she was curious to see how their compositions served their devotional narratives. "I decided to empty these scenes of their original narratives to see what remained. At the same time I was making a series of still life paintings of old gloves. The two series intersected with pictures like this, where the glove enters the picture space of a Fra Angelico Visitation scene. As you can see it features the small child who falls from the balcony in Simone's Beato Agostino altarpiece."

She concludes: "It seems to me vital that graduate study is driven by a deep passion for one's subject. I have never tired of these miraculous predella panels. They continue to give me great pleasure whenever I encounter them."

Notes

1 Hans Hoffmann, "The Search for the Real," quoted in Dore Ashton, *The Life and Times of the New York School* (London, 1972), 82.

2 Northrop Frye in Peter Heath, *Allegory and Philosophy in Avicenna* (Philadelphia, 1992),198. David Jeffrey, "Franciscan spirituality and vernacular culture" in *By Things Seen*, edited by Jeffrey (Ottawa, 1979), 150.

3 Settis, "The Iconography of Italian Art, 1100-1500," in *History of Italian Art*, edited by Giulio Einaudi, transalated by Claire Dorey (Cambridge: Cambridge University Press), 128.

4 Martindale, Andrew, *Simone Martini* (Oxford: Oxford University Press,1988), 212.

16

Christl Berg

Berg's dissertation, "Tracings: A Photographic Investigation into Being in the Land," was intended to find a "photographic language" adequate to her experience of landscape. She argued that "the conventions of landscape photography are largely based on the concept of "looking at" and rely on the monocular lens of the camera" and on linear perspective, producing "a distancing, totalising view" associated with Cartesian perspectivalism. She used "touch-dependent methods," theories associated with Heidegger and Merleau-Ponty, and works by Richard Long, Hamish Fulton, David Stephenson, Tokihiro Sato, Nikolaus Lang, John Wolseley, Karl Blossfeldt, Harry Nankin, and Susan Derges to articulate her sense of "intimate physical engagement with the land."

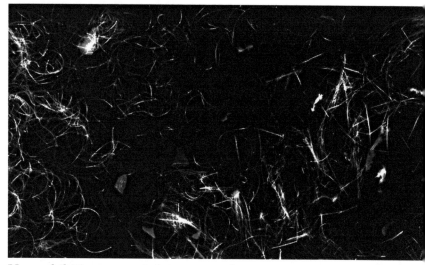

Her exhibition occupied two complementary spaces, one leading into the other. In the first was a large photogram frieze, almost 20 meters long, which included a text wall. She says the space was dimly lit, "immersing the viewer":

> The frieze referred to movement in space and time, accumulated experience, and in its low, long linear positioning invited the viewer to look into it, to move with it and to ponder. The white traces of objects scattered on dark ground suggested layers of events.

The facing wall had a line of wall text "in small white vinyl lettering on pale grey, loosely spaced, directly adhered to the wall. The text intended to further allude to a multi-sensory experience and read: *calls cries laughs woes float slide shift settle ground songs sighs move linger time tremble fall hover drift.*"

The second exhibition space was well-lit. It housed a collection of 187 scans of "finds": "remnants collected from the land and the foreshore." Berg's intention in this second space was "to decipher the land by creating visual phrases and relationships from fragments. The viewer was invited to look close, to examine and to marvel at the richness of forms, structures and textures."

She describes the project as a combination of words and images:

> My investigation has resulted in two bodies of photographic images and text. The images represent traces of fragments

from the land, imbued with personal experience. The text makes reference to the idea that the ground is the repository of stories, of linear and cyclical time. Both the material quality of the images and the text and their arrangement in the gallery space are important.

My original contribution to the field rests on how I have employed the two seemingly disparate technologies of the photogram and the digital image to materially engage with a natural environment, and to translate this experience with the use of two-dimensional components into a three-dimensional gallery environment.

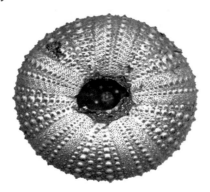

Excerpts from

"Tracings: A Photographic Investigation into Being in the Land"

by Christl Berg

I started this project with the intention to find a way of engaging with the Tasmanian landscape that would result in a visual communication of the experience of being in the land, rather than looking at landscape. I wanted to refer, with caution, to a "natural" environment. Simon Schama, in his book *Landscape and Memory*, states that there is, on the whole of the earth, not a single natural system that has not been substantially modified by human culture and that "it is this irreversibly modified world ... that is all the nature we have."[1]

However, I believe I have found a place (and there are others) where in this present period nature, at an elemental level, is mostly left to its own devices and can follow its "own compulsions,"[2] alongside and over layers of traces of cultural impact. The balance here has shifted from the hegemony of humans to a predominance of other than human life forms. As a human, I am a visitor and I feel that I can tap into this current "natural" system.

Remnants from the cyclical workings of nature's compulsions have informed my contemplations and have provided the material for the construction of my visual language. The language I have devised is based on a phenomenological approach to transcribing and transpicturing the experience of being in place in time—of *Dasein*, in Heidegger's terms.

I have argued, that by refraining from using a photographic camera and the monocular vision of the camera, and accordingly a Cartesian perspectivalist perception and representation of landscape or the environment concerned, I have been able to employ the photographic medium in a more experiential manner. My way of constructing my visual language has relied on my physical presence in the land and on a comprehensive sensual experience. The working methods I have used have been based on walking, observing, touching, collecting, recording, deciphering, and assembling. The work has evolved from an intimate personal connection with a place without directly referring to myself. My chosen place has been Maria Island.

When friends first took me to Maria Island quite a number of years ago I expected naively to find a "genuine" Australian natural environment. These expectations were soon dispelled. While the exoticism of herds of kangaroos grazing in bright daylight and freely foraging emus impacted strongly, I also found myself transported back to childhood experiences in the country in Germany: willow groves, pine trees, a lonesome magnolia, jonquils and daffodils; strolling over gently rolling grassy hills. The restored and dutifully labelled "historic" buildings and the equally interpreted ruins completed this Arcadia at the end of the world.

The at once thrilling and disturbing encounter of the alien and the familiar and the sense of time and space warping, which this initial visit had provoked, took me in 1999 for an 8 weeks residency to Maria Island. Those weeks of much solitude, walking, silent working and occasional talking to animals, plants and wind, as well as working trips to the island since the residency, have prompted me to locate my PhD project on and about Maria Island. [...]

While there are many designed walking tracks on the island, large areas of the terrain allow random wandering and rambling. An area of a square kilometre can reveal remarkable riches and easily occupy a day of working—walking, looking, observing, notetaking, collecting. Standard cartographic representations where land essentially exists as a two dimensional surface become questionable.

Part of my deepening relationship with the island is a better understanding of its geographical and geological position in relation to the rest of Tasmania and an appreciation of the histories of the island which have been recorded over the past two hundred years. These histories have left traces and I connect to and use these traces in my work in a selective manner.

Early explorers' accounts describe in both words and images first encounters with the topography, the flora and fauna; and meetings with the Aboriginal inhabitants. Colonization occurred with the establishment of penal settlements during two periods in the first half of the 19th century, and the two short lived but illustrious industrial periods as well as phases of farming in the times between.

With the declaration of the island as National Park a gradual evaluation of the remnants of these different historical periods has taken place. Buildings and ruins are being maintained and form an important aspect of the attraction for visitors. However, these landmarks occupy only a small portion of the island.

National Park rangers monitor the population of some introduced animal and plant species to assist, as it were, the island in finding its new ecological balance. I sense my experience of the island as witnessing the closing period of a cycle. The turbulence of events over the past two hundred years has calmed; has become history that is being reflected upon. Projections for "new developments" for the island loom on the horizon.

[I am especially fascinated by the] records from the Baudin expedition, [and especially] eight days in February of 1802 around and on Maria Island. Reading Francois Peron's journal entries, I can picture the described location, I can associate with the excitement and the apprehension of discovery.[3] Yet an often intense blanket of melancholia mediates my excitement when I am on the island. I will not meet representatives of the old culture nor their burial sites. I may crouch against the white painted cairn at Return Point to shelter from the southerly wind and look across to Lachlan Island (formerly Isle de Repos) and imagine a reed canoe coming towards me.[4] I can stand at Bloodstone Point and sense the ritual importance this place had in the past as a major location for the collecting of ochre.[5] But, the closest I will get to that past is stumbling over the odd midden.

My mission is not to discover and explore a new continent for the aggrandisement of king and country and the progress of humanity — yet, I am conducting a kind of mapping; attempting to decipher a snippet of Australia, now. The buildings and their remnants do not interest me for this work. My method of recording concentrates on the land and particularly the ground. I like to believe that the ground is a repository for history and memory, and the residues of plants and animals which I gather bear witness. [...]

The project belongs, broadly speaking, to the field of landscape representation and land art. More specifically it relates to that field of interpretations of the land, nature, and the environment that aims to communicate a participatory relationship. I have identified what I consider to be strategies to effect this communication and have examined works by artists which reflect the application of these strategies. Accordingly, my visual context encompasses works that rely on the artists' physical involvement with a natural environment, interpreted through a range of media including drawing, painting, photography, print making, text and installation art. [...]

One must refuse neither the vertigo of distance nor that of proximity; one must devise that double excess where the look is always near to loosing all its powers.[6]

There is a particular thrill connected to travelling through an unknown countryside and meeting the unexpected. I mean, coming around a corner or over a crest and there—gasp—the view. Grand, amazing, wonderful, glorious, moving, awesome... Sometimes when traversing areas of Tasmania, including places that I have been to before, I still get those moments of astonishment; and I love them.

When I first arrived [at Maria Island], those moments had a different significance. They were generally on the awesome side because I felt confronted by a view that was unfamiliar, without comparison. Occasionally I think about what would have happened if I had been the kind of photographer who stops and "takes" the picture, the view. What would I have been able to "capture" and how would it have influenced my experience then and now. What would those pictures look like? Would they show the gasp?

It seems to have taken me seventeen years to *really* arrive. Only four years ago did I start to contemplate dealing with the landscape in my work. And yet, regardless of where I have lived, feeling connected in a physical way to my place of residence has always been very important. I do not think that photographing landscape renders a place necessarily more familiar or makes it more like "home." But the fact that it had not occurred to me to make my new place my object of investigation as an artist puzzles me. I can think of three reasons to explain this fact: One, psychologically speaking, I carried a great deal of luggage with me, which needed to be sorted first. Two, landscape photography is burdened with so many clichés that the thought of photographing landscape never surfaced. Three, it has indeed taken me until recently to have the courage to be here, to admit to *Dasein*.[7]

Even if I could produce an image of the grand, wonderful or awesome view and the gasp, it would not convey *Dasein*. My aim is to transfer to two-dimensional surfaces *experience*, which is based on my bodily presence and a range of sensory perceptions in the landscape or rather, parts of land on Maria Island. Experience is the key word and it does not readily align with flat pictures.

Searching for an appropriate way for the photographic medium to transpicture *Dasein* is the core challenge of my project. I have formulated this in my project proposal in the following manner:

> *Much historical and contemporary landscape photography employs a perspectival, distancing view of the landscape.*
> *I propose to investigate means to photographically represent the landscape, which communicate the experience of an intimate reciprocal relationship with a natural environment.*

In order to support the claim in the first sentence, and the proposition in the second, I [...] aim [...] to find a theoretical field within which I can locate my visual work. I will examine different modes of perceiving and representing, which can be related to shifts in philosophical thinking within a contained period in Western culture. I intend to identify a basis of thinking to which I can refer throughout the exegesis. The examination will be brief and purpose-guided. [...]

Between 1630 and 1650 Rene Descartes wrote and published his three scientific treatises, including the text *Optics* in which he extensively examined the nature of vision. He stated:

All the management of our lives depends on the senses, and since that of sight is the most comprehensive and the noblest of these, there is no doubt that the inventions which serve to augment its power are amongst the most useful that there can be.[8]

It has been remarked that "Descartes was a quintessentially visual philosopher"[9] and "Cartesian perspectivalism" has been considered as the most dominant scopic regime of the modern era in Western culture with precursors to this mode of philosophical thinking dating back to Greek antiquity.

The telescope and the microscope, invented around the end of the 16th century, were amongst the inventions Descartes referred to. However, it was the camera obscura that became the emblematic visual apparatus for Cartesian perspectivalism. The camera obscura, the dark room with an aperture on one side through which the bundled rays of the sun project an upside down image of the outside world on the opposing wall, became an object of increasing fascination during this period. The camera obscura had been employed earlier by artists including Leonardo Da Vinci as a drawing aid. Descartes' philosophical position has often been compared to that "of a perspectivalist painter using the camera obscura to reproduce the observed world."[10]

The area of the visible world encompassed and projected onto the back wall of the camera obscura depends on the size of the aperture in relation to the dimensions of the dark room. The projected area is always limited by calculable confined parameters. It is also always only that part of the visible world which directly faces the aperture. The camera obscura has a fixed view.

In addition, both the camera obscura and its more sophisticated daughter, the later modern photographic camera, have monocular vision. The voyeurism of the peephole has been compared to that of the camera; one peering in, the other gazing out, both distancing from and objectifying the seen. As Martin Jay comments: "The camera eye, as monocular as that of the peephole, produced a frozen, disincarnated gaze on a scene completely external to itself ...'[11] [...]

Peter Fuller discusses perspectival space as a "loss of affective involvement'[12] and John Berger wrote:

The convention of perspective, which is unique to European art and which was first established in the early Renaissance, centres everything on the eye of the beholder. It is like a beam from a lighthouse—only instead of light travelling outward, appearances travel in. The conventions called those appearances *reality*. Perspective makes the single eye the centre of the visible world. Everything converges on to the eye as the vanishing point of infinity.[13]

The static gaze that is exclusively *seeing*, has been conceived as space- rather than time-based, as the gaze of simultaneity, "the frozen "take" of a transcendental, atemporal viewing."[14] And Martin Jay refers to an essay by Hans Jonas:

Sight he contends is preeminently the sense of simultaneity, capable of surveying a wide visual field at one moment. Intrinsically less temporal than other senses such as hearing or touch, it thus tends to elevate static Being over dynamic Becoming, fixed essences over ephemeral appearances.[15]

In the tableau, the perspectival theatricalised scenographic painting, space takes preeminence over time. The viewer is placed at the centre of monocular vision and is instantaneously given the "full intelligibility of the scene."[16]

The employment of perspectival representation thus focuses the eye, eliminates all "extraneous" perceptions and steels the gaze. The distancing of subject and object, of the scene and the beholder and of the sense of sight from other senses, can be argued to be at the core of most modes of landscape representation from the Renaissance to today.

Having briefly outlined aspects of Cartesian perspectivalism relating to my project, I will now shift my attention to the phenomenological approach to visual representation.

Thinkers from the 18th century onwards have questioned the pre-eminence of sight as the noblest of the senses. Aspects of the intense examination of the position of sight and vision, which started around the turn of the 20th century, can be related back to Rousseau's and Diderot's time of the 18th century. Rousseau recognized the need for linguistic mediation in his quest to penetrate beyond appearances to reveal an essential truth. Besides the necessity of signs he placed great emphasis on the importance of music. And like Diderot, he preferred the festival over the theatre as participatory event. In the festival the division between actors and spectators, inherent in the nature of theatre, could be abolished. Michael Fried, in a book published in 1980, discussed the "absorptive" as opposed to the "theatrical" modes of painting in the context of Diderot's work.[17]

With the expansion of a broad range of technological visual inventions, such as photography, film and television, the critical examination of the reign of vision over other senses has accelerated. Jean Louis Comolli commented: "… [D]ecentred, in panic, thrown into confusion by all the new magic of the visible, the human eye finds itself affected with a series of limits and doubts." [18]

What then were some of the main questions asked in response to the scopic regime of the modern era and the pre-eminence of the eye?

The development of phenomenology has been attributed to a number of philosophers. Husserl and Heidegger in Germany, Merleau-Ponty and Sartre in France have been named as key figures in the evolution of the shift of thinking away from Cartesian perspectivalism and the ocularcentrism of the enlightenment.

Differing and at times opposing views on some aspects of phenomenology have produced specialised discourses. For my purpose I will extract elements from phenomenological thinking that suit my argument and make sense in comparison to Cartesian perspectivalism. Here is a brief excerpt from Merleau-Ponty's *Phenomenology of Perception* that addresses the question: What is phenomenology or the phenomenological world?

> The phenomenological world is not pure being, but the sense which is revealed where the paths of my various experiences intersect, and also where my own and other people's intersect and engage each other like gears. It is thus inseparable from subjectivity and intersubjectivity …[19]

Husserl, Heidegger and Merleau-Ponty worked on unifying time and space from the standpoint of direct, pre-conceptual experience, trying to arrive at a modality of awareness where the spatial and the temporal are one, or both at once.

In the mode of Cartesian perspectivalist thinking, time and space are completely separate entities. Space and spatial representation have predominance. Space is seen by the atemporal gaze of simultaneity. The tableau, the theatricalized scenographic painting has been one of the manifestations of this manner of understanding the world. Time, according to this understanding, exists in a linear mode only.

In the concept of the glance, as opposed to the gaze, the beholder and the beholder's body undergo an incarnated viewing process. In terms of visual representation, the gaze has been related to the perspectival scenographic view, whereas the glance can be associated with the frieze, which "promises *its* intelligibility to a viewer in binocular vision along a line."[20] The frieze involves a sense of narrative, of development into which intersecting paths and events can be woven. The glance acknowledges the temporal dimension of sight, the flux of sensation in experienced time. The frieze invites the viewer to become a participant by his/her own physical movement.

In Heidegger's writing, the qualities of the glance can be extended to what he calls *Umsicht* (circumspect vision). Here the viewer is within and not outside the visual arena. "... [H]is horizon is limited by what he can see around him. Moreover, his relation to the context in which he is embedded is nurturing, not controlling.'[21] In Heidegger's words: "Letting something be encountered is primarily circumspective; it is not just sensing something, or staring at it. It implies circumspective concern.'[22]

The attitude of circumspective concern can be seen to constitute the core of ecological thinking, of caring about a natural environment which includes humans. Merleau-Ponty points out: "The world is inseparable from the subject, but from a subject which is nothing but a project of the world ... The subject is being-in-the-world.'[23]

This reciprocal relationship expressed in "the being-in-the-world" finds a different set of resonances in James Gibson's writing about what he calls the "visual field" and the "visual world," which he explores from his position as psychologist. Gibson starts with this basic distinction: "The visual field has boundaries whereas the visual world has none ...'[24] Gibson supports this statement about the visual field with the example of a drawing by a person drawing himself with one eye closed.

He proceeds to explain: The visual world "extends backward behind the head as well as forward in front of the eyes. The world, in other words, surrounds us for the full 360°, in contrast to the visual field which is confined to about 180°.'[25] Heidegger's circum-spect vision comes to mind.

Further on, Gibson discusses how objects appear to our percep-tion. He states: "Objects seen in the visual field have a "pictorial" quality. A picture is something that can be defined by mathematics and optics ... A picture consists of a projection of objects in three dimensions on a plane of two dimensions.'[26] This description reso-nates with the application of perspectival principles to visual repre-sentations and the assumption of a homogenous, regularly ordered space.

Continuing with Gibson's assertion, in order to look at objects in the visual world the observer has to move in the world, to come into the required proximity of the object. The observer becomes an embodied participant. The frieze then could be considered as an approximate representational tool for the visual world.

Gibson used an analogy which I find interesting and to which I will return when discussing photographic methods later on. He reflects on how we perceive objects and he uses the example of a round plate. Within the system of the visual field, the plate would be represented as an oval, according to principals of linear perspec-tival vision. The plate becomes a purely seen projected shape. In the visual world, however, the plate is seen and represented as round through an awareness of surface texture, implying touch. Here, "sight is ecologically intertwined with the other senses to generate the experience of "depth shapes"."[27]

I have highlighted the following distinctions in my selective examination of Cartesian perspectivalist thought and phenomeno-logical thought: The gaze versus the glance; the distanced objective viewer versus the embodied seeing participant; and the predomi-nance of space and separation from time versus a unity or simulta-neity of time and space. Martin Jay singled out three changes which the move away from ocularcentrism has effected: "The first con-cerns what can be termed the detranscendentalization of perspec-tive; the second, the recorporealization of the cognitive subject; and the third, the revalorization of time over space."[28]

In the above discussion the three identified differences are not separate entities. They interconnect continuously and unavoidably. This leads me back to Dasein. Dasein as being-in-the-world, being open to the world and the connection of being to time or temporal-ity. To quote J.L. Metha in his text about Heidegger's philosophy:

The being of Dasein himself, it may turn out, lies in tem-porality and an "analytic" of Dasein may yield a way of understanding time that is deeper, more primordial ... The analysis of Dasein is thus the path to be gone over in order to arrive at the meaning of Being.[29]

In the next part of the exegesis I will discuss artists and artworks which have influenced my manner of working, in order to define a wider field of arts practice into which I can place my own current project. References to the theoretical context will be made in an "applied" mode.

Notes

1 Simon Schama, *Landscape and Memory* (London: Fontana Press, 1995), 7.

2 John Szarkowski, *American Landscapes: Photographs from the Collection of the Museum of Modern Art* (New York: MoMA, 1981), 5.

3 See Peron: "Voyages de Decouvertes aux Terres Australes—Maria Island" in *Baudin in Australian Waters*, edited by J. Bonnemains (Melbourne: Oxford University Press, 1988).

4 Return Point on the West Coast of MI marks the place of shortest distance between Lachlan Island and Maria Island. Aborigines used Lachlan Island as a stopover place on the sea journey across Mercury Passage from mainland Tasmania to Maria Island.

5 Bloodstone Point is an outcrop of Tertiary Laterite at the south-west end of the northern part of Maria Island. Aborigines had collected ochre there for ceremonial purposes over centuries.

6 Jean Starobinski in Martin Jay, *Downcast Eyes: The Denigration Of Vision In Twentieth Century French Thought* (Berkeley, CA: University of California Press, 1994), 20.

7 [...] Metha, in *The Philosophy of Martin Heidegger* (New York: Harper and Row, 1991) 52, explains: "Dasein ... is Heidegger's technical term for man in his aspect of being open to Being." Accordingly, Dasein includes the awareness of being in time; it indicates the simultaneity of space and time. As a German, I relate to the word Dasein and its multi-layered meanings, inseparable from its evocative and powerful sonority.

8 Rene Descartes, *Discourse on Method, Optics, Geometry and Meteorology*, translated by Paul J. Olscamp (Indianapolis, IN, 1965), 65.

9 Jay, *Downcast Eyes*, 69.

10 Ibid.

11 Ibid., 127.

12 Fuller, *Art and Psychoanalysis* (London: Writers & Readers Publishing Co-operative, 1980), 87.

13 Berger, *Ways of Seeing* (London: British Broadcasting Corporation, 1972), 16.

14 Jay refers to Norman Bryson's "suggestive terminology" in *Downcast Eyes*, 152.

15 Jay refers to the essay *The Nobility of Sight* by Hans Jonas in *Downcast Eyes*, 24.

16 Jay quotes Bryson in *Downcast Eyes*, 104.

17 See Jay, *Downcast Eyes*, 98.

18 Jean-Louis Comolli, "Machines of the Visible," in *The Cinematic Apparatus*, edited by Teresa de Lauretis & Stephen Heath (London: Macmillan, 1980), 122.

19 Maurice Merleau-Ponty, *Phenomenology of Perception*, translated by by Colin Smith (London: Routledge, 1962), xx.

20 Jay quotes Bryson in *Downcast Eyes*, 105.

21 Jay, o cit., 275.

22 Jay quotes Heidegger in *Downcast Eyes*, 275.

23 Maurice Merleau-Ponty, op cit., 409.

24 James Gibson, *The Perception of the Visual World* (Westport, CT: Greenwood Press, 1974), 27.

25 Ibid., 28.

26 Ibid., 33.

27 Jay, op. cit., 4.

28 Ibid., 187.

29 Metha, *The Philosophy of Martin Heidegger* (New York: Harper and Row, 1971), 33.

17

María Mencía

The ambitious title of María Mencía's PhD is "From Digital Poetry to Digital Art: Image-Sound-Text, Convergent Media, And the Development of New Media Languages." She says that the thesis comes from her work as a professional artist, and her "concern with issues of language and communication, particularly, the investigation of ways [to] arouse emotion and rational thought at once through language." For her, visual poetry provokes both rational and emotive understanding, and she conceived the thesis as a way of expanding visual poetry by the use of new technologies. "With the digital medium," she writes, "the main elements of visual and sound poetry—image, sound and text—can now be incorporated into the same piece of work."

In her thesis abstract, Mencía sets out a series of questions aimed at the production of "new media languages" in which "pre-linguistic and linguistic maintain their symbiotic identities" by attending to "the area in-between":

- How to transfer the main concepts from Visual Poetry to Digital Art?
- How does computer technology transform image, sound and text to create new media languages?
- What is the role of the author, reader, writer, producer in these new interactive textualities of image, sound and text? How has this affected the new conventions of reading, looking, producing, using and thinking?
- What does the digital add to the interactive texts of Visual Poetry? What new meanings and processes of thinking, understanding and interpretation are appearing?
- In which way do new technologies enhance the collaborative nature of practice?

She aims to challenge the viewer (whom she also calls the "viewer/listener/user") with "an interface of signs from different languages and semiotic systems: the visual (still and moving images), the audible and the linguistic."

Excerpts from

"From Digital Poetry to Digital Art:
Image-Sound-Text, Convergent Media,
And the Development of
New Media Languages"

by María Mencía

In this [third] chapter I investigate the area of the in-between that is created by interweaving visual, phonetic, and linguistic areas of meaning: "Image-Text, Phonetic-Text and Semantic-Text." I explore the new media languages (communicative systems) originating in the in-between, where, by mixing different sensory models (visual and auditory), and motion, together with the illusion of "semantic" meaning and the interaction of the user, the emotional and the linguistic meet in a form of symbiosis. To develop these concepts I start by questioning notions germane to Visual Poetry: the blank space of the page, reading and viewing conventions; the page/interface and the inability to hold the whole Image-Text. As well as these notions, there are a series of questions which investigate the production of the interactive digital work entitled Another Kind of Language: How can these principles be applied to Digital Work? Why apply them? How are multi-linear, de-centering narratives and multi-layered structures formed in digital media? What meanings are created from these inter-textualities of Image-Sound-Text in convergent media? What does interactivity bring to the work and what is the role of the reader/viewer/user/author?

Another Kind of Language is an interactive piece made in Flash[1]. It consists of three different layers: the user can travel from one surface to another by clicking on the buttons: A (for Arabic), C (for Chinese) and E (for English), found on the white screen that appears when the project is open. Each surface is blank until the user rolls the mouse over it, revealing still and moving images, which appear and fade away, and triggering phonetic sounds from each respective language. The images are related to the visual representation and cultural background of each language: the English layer

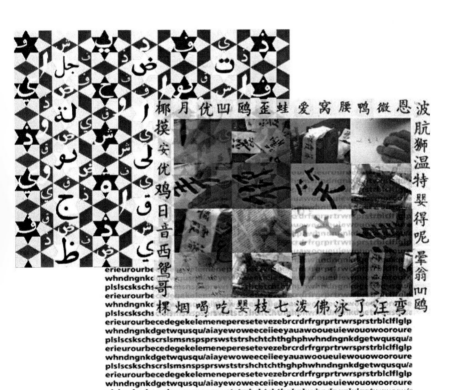

displays the written form of the phonemes, against the blank back-ground—the white page. The writing is visible but not legible and I have used black and white colours as a reference to the white page and black printed ink. In the Arabic layer there are letters embedded in what looks like a tile design. I wanted to bring their visual quality into the surface as this alphabet has such a strong visual quality, and is often incorporated into architecture[2]. The Mandarin layer is composed of animated images which are triggered by the movement of the mouse. As Chinese is an ideographic language, I wanted to explore this quality by using moving images like short narratives underneath the white page.

The sound layers are formed by the "meaningless" phonetic sounds of three different languages: English, Mandarin and Arabic. They were created by speakers of these languages, who sang and pronounced combinations of phonetic sounds commonly used in each linguistic system. The notion of meaningless phonetic sounds interested me, since, according to Saussure, these sounds are not supposed to have any meaning. Their function is to differenti-ate two words; they have a differentiating/distinguishing value[3]. Jakobson agrees with [Saussure] when in Six Lectures on Sound and Meaning (1978), he writes:

> We have arrived … at the view that phonemes, phonic ele-ments by means of which words are differentiated, differ from all the other phonic devices of language, and from all linguistic values in general, in that they have no posi-tive and fixed meaning of their own. Of all sign systems it is only language properly so-called, and within this it is words, which consist of elements which at one and the same time signify and yet are devoid of meaning[4].

I find this paradoxical, signifying aspect of phonemes fascinat-ing. They are the key signifying units and yet they don't have any intrinsic value. With them I am questioning the semiotic and sym-bolic aspects found in this process of signification where they refer to language and yet are outside language in their isolated units. I try to shift them into a different semantic context to transform them into entities with the potential for full linguistic and emotive signification. It is as if I want them to be recognised for their im-portant function in the signifying process; to raise them to the level of appreciation they deserve; transforming "meaningless" phonetic sounds into full entities in the non-linear structure of the commu-nicative process.

When choosing the languages, as well as their sounds, I was interested in the differences between their respective visual and aural elements, reading patterns (right to left, left to right, top to bottom) and linear and non-linear qualities as explained above. The experimentation with the direction of reading patterns is a strong component of Visual/Sound Poetry, and I wanted to transfer this experimentation into a digital artistic/linguistic/poetic form. The reading patterns of Visual/Sound Poetry are partly enforced by the empty spaces between words which are as significant as the words[5]. When the poem is read aloud these interludes are completely semantic, visual, silent components of the performance. When reading a visual poem for the first time the reader struggles, searching for meaning—which line, which word next—until he/she realises the conventions are different here and lets go of the old ones to experience the new. With Another Kind of Language I try to involve the user via the mouse to reveal the linguistic images and sounds and provoke in him/her similar queries. When the work has been exhibited the users have brought to my attention their interest in understanding the individual sounds, and their attempt to make a coherent sentence, message or something syntactically linear; to find a language that communicates; the urgency to freeze the image and see it as a whole; to relate the sound to the image; and to find a coherent sense[6]. These inquiries demonstrate the linguistic and visual conventions users bring with them and the piece gives them the opportunity to challenge these conventions in favour of more open, multiple readings. [...]

Visual Poetry seeks to revolutionize the concept of writing, reading and looking. We are able to recognise references, as for instance certain typographical characters or different systems but the process of putting pieces together occurs as in a puzzle but the puzzle never becomes resolved. We recognise independent meanings and try to put them together. Although these processes exist in conventional poetry, they become more evident with Visual/Concrete poetry because the association between the parts of the poem is an essential component in the formation of meanings and interpretations. Thus, the reader/viewer is invited to decode the visual and verbal message by participating in the structure of signification that controls the piece, although this does not mean that by putting these pieces together a stable transparent meaning is found.

The practice of reading/looking/listening reproduces the act of creation; it requires a participatory commitment from the viewer-reader. Carline Bayard in The New Poetics in Canada and Quebec, From Concretism to Post-Modernism (1989) states:

Concretism demands that the attention of poet and reader-listener be focused on the material components of the poem. It is the interrelationship of these elements and their perfect coincidence with their semantic message which produce a concrete poem both in time (performance) and space (on the page)[7].

Concretist texts deconstruct the systems of typography, layout, spelling, syntax and metrics by avoiding old rules and inventing new ones. Emerging digital work equally creates new parameters, perhaps because it is still in a process of discovery or perhaps because the versatility of the medium accommodates all kinds of visual, aural and linguistic codes. Among some of the concretist texts we find syntactical ambiguity, discontinuity and omissions to the point of depriving the reader from reading. In Mallarmé's Un Coup de Dès (1897), there is a tension between legibility and illegibility, meaning and loss of meaning. On the other hand, in some poems we find different reading patterns, which provide various multiple texts instead of one, as for instance, with many of bill bissett's visual/concrete poems where the reader becomes the creator by choosing the different combinations. White spaces might give the impression of discontinuity when there is none. In some of the poem-collages, the structure of sentences is destroyed. In other texts the grammatical structures offer so many combinations that they become comparable to geometrical variables. The absence of punctuation allows for a variety of structures, depending on the reading order adopted by the reader. A simple visual law in these texts is that the eye tends to read first what it can immediately decipher, then slowly interprets the other letter puzzles. Bob Cobbing, in Changing Forms in English Visual Poetry, quotes from Ionesco: "Integration alone is not enough; disintegration is essential too; that is what life is, and philosophy; that is science, progress, civilization."[8] This is what concrete poetry does in my view: there is a constant integration, fusion and disruption of the elements named above, and the reader moves from the position of the viewer to that of the writer, to the reader again and so on, in a random order but following a simultaneous reaction.

All these aspects of textuality, narrative and the notions of the reader and writer which are found in Visual Poetry I consider to be antecedent to hypertextual narratives and new forms of communication on the Internet. The non-linear, layered characteristics of Visual Poetry: the space between words—which creates the spatial, material and now, virtual, word—the coalescence of the visual and linguistic within the same system; its interactive quality and the independence of the reader in choosing in a text free from the bond-age of the line and the classic readerly text. These are now all bases for hypertext. Espen Aarseth's definition of non-linear structure in Cybertext: Perspectives on Ergodic Literature is as follows:

> A non-linear text is an object of verbal communication that is not simply one fixed sequence of letters, words, and sentences but one in which the words or sequence of words may differ from reading to reading because of the shape, conventions, or mechanisms of the text[9].

With hypertext narratives the boundaries of image and text have become blurred, encouraging the reader to participate and become the viewer-reader-writer-producer-user. Network communication is established through links and via shifting navigational paths. Non-linearity has become an important factor in recent critical thought. Conceptual systems founded upon ideas of centre, margin, hierarchy, and linearity have been replaced with those of multilinearity, nodes, links, and networks as discussed by Landow, Derrida and Barthes. Barthes in S/Z differentiates between two kinds of texts: the readerly (lisible) and the writerly (scriptable). The readerly is the classic text, based in communication and an ideology of exchange.

> This reader is thereby plunged into a kind of idleness—he is intransitive; he is, in short, serious: instead of gaining access to the magic of the signifier, to the pleasure of writing, he is left with no more than the poor freedom either to accept or reject the text: reading is nothing more than a referendum[10].

The writerly text resists established reading and is "the novelist without the novel, poetry without the poem... production without product."[11] He explains how in this case the reader becomes a producer of the text rather than a consumer. I associate this textuality described by Barthes to the printed text (readerly) and electronic hypertext (writerly). The blocks of text that composed the hypertext would be what Barthes describes as lexias, and which are connected by links, multiple reading paths which as Landow in Hypertext 2.0 states, "shift the balance between reader and writer."[12] Landow points out that hypertext changes the experience of reading, writing and text signification, reconfiguring the role of the author and authorial property.

Derrida's non-linearity would be the notion of textual openness, intertextuality and de-centred narratives as he describes in Of Grammatology (1976); without a focused point, a beginning or an end. Gregory Ulmer considers the displacement the user experiences when using the text, as one of the main features of hypertext. Ulmer contends in Applied Grammatology (1985) how Derrida's texts already reflect the workings of electronic media. His book Glass, according to Landow, has all the characteristics found in hypertext narratives: it is a printed hypertext which in fact appear at the same time as the personal computer.

Di Philadelpho Menezes in his paper Interactive Poems: Intersign Perspective for Experimental Poetry, discussing digital communication, states:

> By increasing the potentiality of non-linear and de-centred contemporary literature, hypertext changes the conception of text and writing, thus transforming the role of the author and the possibilities of literary education. This new ethic of technological texts must be considered even when we go out of textuality and enter hypermedia programmes, a further development of hypertext, where non-verbal (visual and sound) signs are joined. Hypermedia facilitates working with experimental poetry as hypertext does literary works.[13]

In the experimental digital art/poem Another Kind of Language [...] the viewer can travel along the surface clicking on specific buttons which take them somewhere else: experimenting with a displacement of mutable points and direction. This creates a shifting: from the contemplation of the viewer to the participation of the user, through reading, looking, listening and interacting. The user is the creator of compositional images and sounds. There is the trace of the author but the work exists thanks to the user. The roles have shifted.

Notes

1 Interactive Macromedia programme. See Mencía, www.m.mencia.freeuk. com.

2 The fondness to employ script, as a decorative element in Islamic culture, is in part attributable to the proscription of graphic representation, in particular of the human form. Instead of religious icons, sentences from the Koran are used in the representation of God. This encourages the use and development of the beautiful calligraphic nature of the Arabic language.

3 See Saussure, *Course in General Linguistics* (1995).

4 Jakobson, 1978, 69.

5 As with Mallarmé's *Un Coup de Dès,* 1897.

6 This information has been gathered through speaking with the participants. I did not consider recording these comments at the time, due to the spontaneous nature of the interaction.

7 Bayard, *The New Poetics in Canada and Quebec: From Concretism to Post-Modernism* (1989), 84.

8 Cobbing, *Changing Forms in English Visual Poetry* (1998).

9 Aarseth, *Cybertext: Perspectives on Ergodic Literature* (1997), 41.

10 Barthes, *S/Z* (1974), 4.

11 Barthes, *S/Z*, 5.

12 Landow, *Hypertext* 2.0 (1997), 25.

13 Menezes: www.geocities.com/Paris/Lights/7323/philadelpho.html, accessed 02/02/09.

18

Uriel Orlow

Uriel Orlow says that his thesis and his art practice were "quite separate (although related)": the thesis did not aim to provide a theoretical framework for the practice, but had "its own remit." The practice-based and research-based components of his PhD "share concerns and questions about medium, image, time and narrative." Both are case studies, "focusing on different kinds of paradoxes in order to intervene critically in debates around medium-specificity, image-temporality and the representation of history." The thesis is a study of Chris Marker's film *La Jetée,* and the practice-based component—the artwork—is a multi-screen video-installation about a Holocaust archive in London. Orlow explains the connections this way:

> One of the key hypotheses and propositions of this PhD project can be summarized as follows: *A work of art has a particular power of sustainable critical intervention in theoretical debates and their resultant positions of knowledge and meaning.* Belonging to a different order from these debates, i.e. to a second order complexity (that of symptomatic over-determination and concealment) which eludes complete revelation, knowability or measurability, an artwork is beyond the total reach of epistemology and can thus provide a *sustainable source* for critical intervention in the production of knowledge and meaning. The focus of the PhD is a notion of contradiction understood as the *critical motor* of a work of art; one which, paradoxically, effects an interruption or pause in the dialectical progression from one position of knowledge or meaning to another.
> This critical/paradoxical power of intervention is *particular* to a work of art; it can be conceived of only in terms of a specific work and cannot be deduced for art in general. For,

such a deduction or generalization would by virtue of its mechanism force the particular work of art—as an example of works of art in general—into an epistemological order (that is, reduce it to a complexity of the first degree) and thus master or absorb its critical power which consequently ceases to be *effective* and *sustainable*. This means that the *case-study* is the format of choice for an engagement with the particular critical power of a work of art in relation to specific theoretical positions of knowledge and meaning.

In the Introduction to his thesis, Orlow expands on this idea:

Whilst making use of film and photography theory, as well as philosophy, psychoanalysis and literary theories, the thesis does not claim to have advanced knowledge in all of these disciplines (the advancement of, or an original contribution to, a discipline of knowledge is one of the main criteria traditionally defining PhD research). Rather, I am engaging in these specialist discourses as an artist who is thinking about a work of art. The proposition of the thesis is that a work of art is not only explainable by, or inscribed in theoretical debates but can itself advance or contribute to them. My work, then, becomes that of a mediator or ambassador, shuttling back and forth between the work and the discursive contexts it is engaged in and contributes to: settling ideas in the work and extracting criticality from it.

Because the art component of Orlow's PhD takes some explaining, I have excerpted parts of his documentation first. Afterward, I give some passages from his thesis.

Excerpts from

The documentation for *Housed Memory*
(the practice-based component of the degree)

by Uriel Orlow

Housed Memory is a multi-screen video-installation comprising eleven hours of video about the Wiener Library in London.

The Wiener Library is the world's oldest Holocaust memorial institution, archive and library. [...] It specialises in contemporary European and Jewish historiography, especially the rise and fall of the Third Reich, anti-Semitism, racism, the Holocaust, World War II, the survival and revival of Nazi and fascist movements and post-war Europe. The Wiener Library's collections comprise books, periodicals, press archives, original documents, eyewitness accounts, unpublished memoirs, a photo and video archive and artefacts [for a total of] 60,000 books, 10,000 document collections, 2,500 runs of periodicals, 10,000 photographs, 1,200 eyewitness accounts, [and] 100 unpublished memoirs.

Housed Memory explores the status of an archive/library such as the Wiener Library by raising questions about the signification and significance of its collections. By approaching the historical, political and emotive specificity of the Wiener Library's collection on various levels, *Housed Memory* operates as a kind of agency—relating the diverse material, practical, methodological, conceptual and personal aspects to each other and to the viewer.

[The first and principal portion of *Housed Memory* is a nine-hour video, which "constitutes a video archive of all the contents" of the Library]. An audio archive consisting of recorded conversations with all staff at the Library reflecting on their work with, and their relationship to, the collections, is interwoven with the visual archive.

An endless but discontinuous tracking-shot reveals and records, shelf by shelf, the document that is the archive itself, portraying the contents of an extensive historical, political and cultural archive which are otherwise only visible to the archivists who work in the Library. In so doing, the camera takes on the role of an historical witness and the video itself becomes an independent and excessive documentary. *Housed Memory* steadily produces a sense of the unknowable which is nevertheless a felt presence: an emanation which accumulates from the material evidence gathering which constitutes the archive's tireless work of memory.

Instead of showcasing individual items and their disturbing facts or images, in this work the entire collection is shown. The tracing of the outer layer, the sheer material surface of the collection which itself is not directly accessible to the public (only by the intermediary of a catalogue and ordering system) produces a different balance between transparency and opacity, between access and inaccessibility, as well as opening up questions around the relationship between the singularity and content of each item held and the totality and meaning of the collection as a whole; a totality which is at once contained and made elusive by the video.

[The nine-hour video is one part of the art practice component. A second is *Inside the Archive*, a silent 30-minute looped video.] This video consists of a series of photographic stills which take the viewer through the interior of the Wiener Library. Moving through the different spaces of the archive, the image lingers on minute and banal details, foregrounding material conditions of the archive.

[The third part of the artwork is *The Wiener Library, London*, a 90-minute video with sound.] This video further investigates the relationship between locale, structure, organisation and meaning of a collection such as the Wiener Library's. This work shows the exterior of the Library building in a London street. Scrolling over this everyday image are thesaurus entries which allow the collection to be searched by way of keywords, that is provides an associative access to and overview of the collection, rather than taxonomic or diachronic organisation of it. As such the Wiener Library is shown as both an urban environment, and as a historical and hermeneutic map. The constancy of the everyday image on one layer is contrasted by the insistence of the fragmentary textual scrolling which overlays it with a darkly evocative refusal of representation.

Excerpts from

"Time+Again: Critical Contradictions in Chris Marker's *La Jetée*,"

by Uriel Orlow

Chris Marker's short film *La Jetée*, made in 1962 and released in 1964, inhabits a peculiar place in post-war European cinema as well as his own oeuvre. Even though it is mostly known to (an ever increasing number of) initiated cinephiles, *La Jetée* is regarded as one of the bright stars in the sky of European auteur-cinema. Moreover, being the only fiction-film made by this prolific and influential documentary film-maker (who is also a writer and photographer), *La Jetée* shines out of Marker's politically engaged oeuvre. Above all though, *La Jetée*'s singularity and continuing spell is due to the intriguing nature of its story and image-apparatus. The fascination of *La Jetée*'s plot stems at once from the narrative simplicity of its tragic love story as well as from the philosophical complexity of its

time-travel paradigm. *La Jetée's* representational apparatus is simi
larly compelling, with its unique, near-exclusive use of beautifully
shot photographic images, stills presented in the cinematic contex
of a film and thus affirming a paradoxical kind of medium. The two
paradoxes–that of the double-death and that of the photographic
film–are the main focus of the thesis and are explored in relation to
larger debates and using a number of pertinent theoretical models
    [...] In the first instance, as a montage of still photographic im
ages, *La Jetée* conjures up a pre-history of cinematic movement and
the latter's pre-conditions. As such it points to cinema's fundamen
tal association with (or indeed the core provided by) photography
namely, its being based on what Deleuze calls the *any-instant-what
ever*,[1] which was made possible in modernity. For, whereas the pre
modern representation (or illusion) of movement was an idealised
synthesis of positions which themselves are immobile (and eter
nal), i.e. a *reconstitution* of transcendental poses or privileged in
stants, the mechanics introduced by modernity (not only the shut
ter mechanism of the camera, but already the mechanism of the
engine itself) allows for an extraction and then a *recomposition* of
instants from a mechanical succession of any-instant-whatevers (as
opposed to controlled transitions or poses). On this level there is no
distinction between photography and cinema: the shutter mecha
nism of both allows for the capturing of any-instant-whatevers. So
cinema in the first instance differentiated itself from photography's
single pictures by recomposing or re-assembling the many more
(but very similar) snapshots taken by the film-camera; that is, by an
operation which could be termed *primary montage*; an assemblage
which works between one photographic frame or photogram and
the next by putting them together. Deleuze calls the movement-im
age that cinema produces in this way, the *image-moyenne*, the inter
mediary image that appears *between* one image and the next, that
is, in their interval.[2] Even though this primary conception of cinema
(through montage) produced cinema's moving images, the visual-
technological invention of such images was not yet accompanied
by a conceptual innovation (i.e. did not yet produce a conceptually
new *kind* of image), and thus in some sense still lacked medium-
specificity, since photography had already invented the represen
tation of the *any-instant-whatever*. Deleuze describes how this kind
of cinema went "no further than the movement-image, that is, an
image composed of photograms, an intermediate image endowed
with movement. It was therefore still an image corresponding to
human perception, whatever the treatment to which it was subjected by montage."[3] In other words, this first kind of cinematic image
was, on the whole, still constrained by spatio-temporal coordinates

and had not yet tapped into the potential of cinema, its power to deterritorialise space and time, and by extension, to deviate from human perception which has a "natural" tendency to territorialise, to align space and time.[4] Deleuze thus asks: "But what happens if montage is introduced into the very constituent of the image?"[5] or in other words, what happens if montage no longer just serves the purpose of producing an intermediary movement-image, but aims at the cinematic photogram or frame itself, thus evacuating movement from the interval between two frames? What happens when movement is absent, or illogically present as in the still movement of the repeated frame? Moreover, what *exactly happens* in *La Jetée*?

La Jetée's relegation of "normal" cinematic movement to zooms, dissolves and fades which are added to apparently immobile images, not only aims to expose the smallest cinematic unit, the frame or photogram, the stillness at the heart of the alleged cinematic illusion of movement, thus enhancing the dichotomy between movement and immobility, but rather points to a fundamental cinematic *power*; that namely of the *variation* of movement, of cinema's power to slow movement down (even to its degree zero) or in turn accelerate it.6 Furthermore, rather than exposing the alleged illusion of movement in cinema, the production of a moving image through immobile frames—*photogrammatic montage*, by repeating the same frame rather than linking it to the next, exposes *the illusion of the illusion*; the illusion of immobility. For, the still image in cinema, the photogram, is fundamentally no less in motion than the moving image and thus undermines the very opposition between movement and immobility. Deleuze describes such photogrammatic montage in two different ways, as flickering montage or hyper-rapid montage: "Flickering montage: extraction of the photogram beyond the intermediate image, and of vibration beyond movement [...]. Hyper-rapid montage: extraction of a point of inversion or transformation (for the correlation of the immobilisation of the image is the extreme mobility of the support[...])."[7] So instead of confirming a *dichotomy* between immobility and movement, which in turn provides the basis for an opposition between photography and cinema, the photogrammatic image in cinema shows that immobility and movement are irrevocably linked to each other, that movement is at the heart of every immobility, and that immobility as such, is a *variation* or *deviation* of movement, but not its opposite.[8] Indeed, rather than opposing cinema and reminding it (and us, the viewers) of its photographic base, the *photogrammatic logic* in *La Jetée* actually promotes the cinematic, namely this power to vary or deviate movement, which could be thought of as the "true" conceptual invention of cinema. I will repeat myself: Photography had already invented the *any-instant-whatever*, the snapshot, the image taken in a fraction of a second and already embodying the potential re-assemblage, re-animation of any-instant-whatevers. Indeed, photographs are themselves always already in motion. While on a deep, imperceptible, molecular level, there is no difference whatsoever between the movement in photographs and that in cinema, that of moving particles, visibly there is of course a difference, but this is not a difference in kind (quality), but rather one in degree (quantity). As has been pointed out, the photogram, like all photographs, shows the degree zero of movement, rather than its opposite. So if there is a *real* difference between photography and cinema, that is, a difference in kind (a qualitative difference) it stems not from movement itself (i.e. from quantity/degree), but from cinema's power to variate or deviate movement, its power to change movement qualitatively.

So *La Jetée*'s almost exclusive use of the photogram or re-filmed photograph neither represents a regression / reversion of cinema to photography (its progenitor) nor an opposition of cinema and photography on the basis of movement (or its lack). Instead, paradoxically, the photogrammatic image, which *apparently* deviates so much from cinema's norm (movement), exposes exactly as such, as deviation, cinema's medium-specificity; a medium specificity which is, however, not understood in terms of the status of the image (as object or vis-à-vis its reference or perception), but rather in terms of its power to change movement, to emancipate itself from (natural) movement and thus act upon (human) perception itself. Deleuze writes:

> The frame is not simply a return to the photo: if it belongs to the cinema, this is because it is the genetic element of the image, or the differential element of the movement. It does not "terminate" the movement without also being the principle of its acceleration, its deceleration and its variation. It is the vibration, the elementary solicitation of which movement is made up at each instant, the *clinamen* of Epicurean materialism. Thus the photogram is inseparable from the series which makes it vibrate in relation to the movement which derives from it. And if cinema goes beyond perception, it is in the sense that it reaches to the *genetic element* of all possible perception, that is, the point which changes, and which makes perception change, the differential of perception itself.[9]

As already demonstrated in the introduction to *Still Film*, the second part of this case-study, *La Jetée* does not just employ the photogram, but by being composed almost exclusively of photograms, takes the *photogrammatic logic* to its extreme. The initial perplexity of this unique (unprecedented and unrepeated) position between the photographic and the cinematic can now be explained. It is the very closeness to photography which paradoxically allows *La Jetée* to *conceive* of itself as cinematic; that is, conceiving of cinema's *qualitative* difference to photography, while at the same time dismissing a quantitative pseudo-difference (based on movement or its lack). This is what *La Jetée*, what the photogrammatic in cinema theorizes and shows so powerfully—a difference that, in measured terms, is so slight yet has a huge, perhaps unmeasurable, impact. The minute, sometimes almost imperceptible vibration which accompanies the photogram in cinema changes its "photographicity" fundamentally, catapulting it into the cinematic. The minute but crucial difference produced by the photogrammatic in *La Jetée*, as Deleuze rightly indicates in passing, can be thought of in terms of the notion of the *clinamen*, which (along with Epicurean philosophy in general) is described by Lucretius in *On the Nature of Things*, like this: "Sometimes, at uncertain times and places, the eternal, universal fall of the atoms is disturbed by a very slight *deviation* - the *clinamen*." He insists that ""if it were not for this swerve, everything would fall downwards like rain-drops through the abyss of space. No collision would take place and no impact of atom on atom would be created. Thus nature would never have created anything."[10]

If it is a deviation, however slight, which, at the heart of linear movement, initiates change and produces the new, then the photogrammatic makes exactly this visible *as image*. For, the projection of a "still" image, through its *apparent* immobility, allows for the slight vibration, the slight swerving which is part of every image in cinema, to become visible. If it is this clinamen, this vibration or deviation from linear (natural) movement, whether that movement produces a still or a moving image, which is the *differential* of cinema, and thus produces a kind of medium-specificity, this is a medium-specificity which is neither simply epistemological (empirical or logical), that is, situated only in the apparatus of the image, related to the mechanical projector which produces the vibration, the slight swerving of the image in cinema, the deviation from its linear unfolding, nor is its remit exclusively hermeneutic (phenomenological or psychoanalytical). Rather, it operates somewhere between the epistemological and the hermeneutic, on perception itself, which takes place both in what is seen ('objectively') and in the seer (subjectively).[11] As such the clinamen, the deviation changes both the image (from the photographic to the cinematic) as well as perception itself, by "forcing" it to come to terms with this new *kind* of image.[12]

To be sure, the photogrammatic is only the seed of this new kind of image, not its point of *origin* but its *genetic* element. However, by applying the photogrammatic logic with unprecedented and unrepeated consistency, *La Jetée* produces out of this genetic element a cinematic work which *realizes* and *theorizes* its own cinematic potential, its cinematic power, that of the deviation from linear movement, and consequently of its emancipation from spatio-temporal co-ordinates — for it is linear movement which links time and space, which of course is also mirrored in the time-travel narrative (a conjunction or doubling which will be addressed in the conclusion). But what are the implications of this emancipation? What kind of temporality does *La Jetée* produce beyond the spatio-temporal co-ordinates?

[…] Here it is time itself that becomes *directly* visible *as image*, in this new kind of image which is emancipated from movement; but it is a fundamentally contradictory time. It is neither derived from movement (in the world), nor does it originate in the "soul" (intentionally), but rather it must be thought of as a "third" time. Deleuze roots this "third" time in Kant, even though my argument and that of *La Jetée* (as well as partly Deleuze's own) is that this time might be conceptually thinkable, but practically only becomes *realized* through and in this new kind of image, which becomes its symptom: "Time has shaken off its dependency on all extensive movement […]. Time also does not depend on the intensive movement of the soul — to the contrary, the intentional production of a degree of consciousness within the moment is what depends on time. With Kant, time ceases to be *originary or derived*, to be become pure form of interiority, which hollows us out, which splits us, at the price of a vertigo, of an oscillation that constitutes time: the synthesis of time changes direction by constituting it as an insurmountable aberration. "Time gets unhinged'."[13] And this is exactly what *La Jetée* shows us, produces, invents, and suffers: a deviant, irrational, illogical time, a third time not just in the gap between universal and lived time, but a time which itself produces and is produced in the gap. *La Jetée*'s protagonist is travelling through this gap. It is only because he embraces this gap, while being hollowed out by it, only because he is able to conceive of time as neither universal nor strictly personal, but rather as fundamentally contradictory itself that he can make his contradictory journey into time. And it is the photogrammatic which shows us this journey as image, which is the symptom of this time, the image as gap and hinge at once; a vertiginous image of time, which itself is out-of-joint.

Notes

Deleuze, *Cinema 1: The Movement-Image* (London: Athlone, 1992), 3-8.

2 This has led to the very paradagim of the movement-image, that is the action-reaction dialectic whose interval is inhabited by the affection image. Cf. Deleuze, *Cinema 1*, 56-70.

3 Deleuze, *Cinema 1*, 82.

4 Henri Bergson, *Time and Free Will: An Essay On The Immediate Data Of Consciousness*, translated by F. L. Pogson (London: Allen and Unwin, 1971).

5 Deleuze, *Cinema 1*, 82.

6 Deleuze locates the first instances of this cinematic power in *Crazy Ray* (Clair, 1923), and *Man with a movie camera* (Vertov, 1929), which, with its series of photograms, can be considered as a strategic predecessor of *La Jetée*. He writes that montage which is no longer oriented at the image interval (in order to produce movement) but at the image itself "designates the point at which movement stops and in stopping, gains the power to go into reverse, accelerate, slow down" (83).

7 Deleuze, *Cinema 1*, 85.

8 The proclamation of movement at the heart of all things is certainly as old as the pre-Socratic philosophers. More recently, it was Bergson that reminded us, again and again, ever since his doctoral thesis *Time and Free Will* (which, incidentally, was published in 1895, the same year as the Lumière borthers invented the cinématographe) that everything is in motion and that immobility therefore is an illusion, which can be exemplified by two trains running parallel to each other and at the same speed and thus creating the impression for their respective passengers that neither train moves. Curiously Bergson was vehemently opposed to cinema as he regarded its movement as false movement (therefore contradicting himself). See *Creative Evolution*, translated by Arthur Mitchel (London: Macmillan, 1911), especially the last chapter. For a discussion of Bergson's position on cinema see Paul Douglass: "Bergson and cinema: friends or foes', in *The new Bergson*, ed. by John Mullarkey (Manchester: Manchester University Press, 1999) and of course also Deleuze, *Cinema 1*.

9 Deleuze, *Cinema 1*, 83.

10 Lucretius, *De Rerum Natura*, translated by R.E. Latham (New York: Penguin, 1951), 66. The Epicurean/Lucretian indeterminism of matter had long been rejected by science's deterministic efforts. Only recent developments in physics which acknowledged undeterminable (and uncaused) slight swerving in the declination of atoms, have re-attributed the notion of the clinamen importance. See, for example, Nobel Prize-winning physicist Ilya Prigogine's *Order Out Of Chaos*: "The clinamen, this spontaneous, unpredictable deviation, has often been criticised as one of the main weaknesses of Lucretian physics, as being something introduced adhoc. In fact, the contrary is true - the clinamen attempts to explain events such as laminar flow ceasing to be stable and spontaneously turning into turbulent flow. Today hydrodynamic experts test the stability of fluid flow by introducing a perturbation that expresses the effect of molecular disorder added to the average flow. We are not so far from

the clinamen of Lucretius!" Prigogine and Isabelle Stengers, *Order out of Chaos* (New York: Bantam, 1984), 141.

11 Cf. Bergson's notion of perception which is in things, and the image which is something between a thing and a perception. *Matter and Memory,* translated by Nancy Margaret Paul and W. Scott Palmer (New York: Zone Books, 1991), especially chapter 2.

12 Analoguously, the new *kind* of image which photography gave us was that of the *any-instant-whatever*, which wasn't perceptible before.

13 Deleuze, "Foreword" in Eric Alliez, *Capital Times*, translated by Georges Van Den Abbeele (Minneapolis: University of Minnesota Press, 1996), ii-iii.

19

Phoebe von Held

Von Held's dissertation, called "Alienation and Theatricality in Brecht and Diderot," considers Brecht's concept of alienation by a reading of Diderot's *Paradoxe sur le comédien* and *Le Neveu de Rameau*. Her aim, she writes, is to "enlarge and differentiate our understanding of alienation." Her reading is not a study of the influence of Diderot on Brecht, but an analytic investigation of the "conceptual difference and contrast" between texts written in two historical periods. She means it to call into question "the ideological and aesthetic assumptions underlying Brecht's concept of alienation." The concept of the actor's self-alienation leads, in the two writers, to very different conclusions. "In fact," von Held suggests,

> alienation leads to an effect of recognition only once the spectator has recognised himself caught in a situation of aesthetic delusion. Whereas for Brecht "distance" is an essential notion in his formulation of the alienation-effect, an aesthetic of alienation derived from Diderot would instead be based on the notion of intimacy.

Brecht's concept of self-alienation "depends on a temporality of stasis and is vision-based," while Diderot's "explores the aesthetic experiences of processual time and favours the medium of sound." The earlier writer emplots alienation as a means of questioning moral precepts, "introducing a notion of critique dependent on ethical self-interrogation"; the later writers " aims to sharpen the spectator's political consciousness, thereby instigating resistance to the alienated conditions of capitalism."

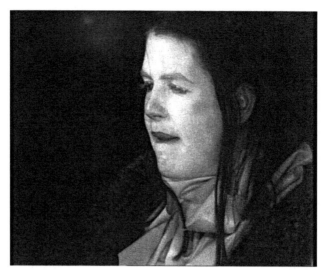

NEPHEW: That mask! That mask!

Having a mask made to look like him!

Above all that mask makes me suspicious.

I would give one of my fingers to have thought up that mask.

PHILOSOPHER: If I were you, I would jot these things down on paper.

It would be a shame if they were lost.

NEPHEW: Do you seriously believe

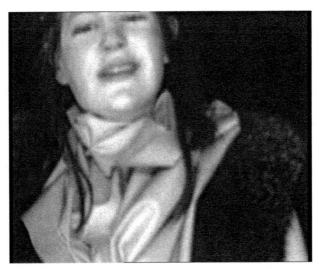

that the story of the dog and the mask should be
written down anywhere?

Excerpts from

"Diderot's Paradox of Alienation:
Critique and Affirmation of Communication in
Le Neveu de Rameau,"

By Phoebe von Held

Von Held wrote this to introduce her excerpt:

Alienation is a theme presented in Denis Diderot's *Le Neveu de Rameau* in a variety of different forms, incorporating some of Rousseau's core ideas around alienation and even anticipating important aspects of Marx's theory of alienation. It is explicated as a structure that vacillates between a human condition rooted in sociality, and a Marxist form of alienation that is changeable since it is based on an inequality in material possession, in the fetishistic constitution of money, in the idiotisms of language and in the automatism of action. In sum, Diderot proposes in *Le Neveu de Rameau* a critique of alienation at the level of the theme.

The following text is a section from my dissertation that introduces the question of how Diderot relates the problem of social and psychological alienation to his own literary aesthetics, in particular to the dialogical style typical for his writing. How is Diderot's thematic critique of alienation negotiated with a literary aesthetic? For, if Diderot – similarly to Rousseau and Brecht – exercises a critique of communication and even language, he does so without sacrificing the pleasures of expression. In this he is diametrically opposed to Brecht's aesthetics of alienation. Communication is explored in literary terms in a way which inflates tendencies towards alienation and by a celebration of the communicative contact with the other, regardless of its potential delusional implications.

Critique of communication as a form of alienation is articulated in *Le Neveu* in so far as it represents a narcissistic structure in which the participants become inevitably entangled once they exchange words and actions. The communicator is incessantly under pressure to perform for the other, never presenting his authentic natural being but offering only appearances which he believes the other to expect. Any communicative act must be fundamentally flawed by an erasure of truth. Rousseau connects this communicative form of alienation with the notion of theatricality. A sociology marked by lying, obscurity, anonymity and appearance is implemented with the origin of social interaction, and most incisively with the birth of language. The historical progress of culture and civilisation heralds nothing positive, but implies a profound movement towards human alienation and social conflict. The result is a social universe in which the notions of alienation and theatricality become inextricably linked and are furthermore connected with the problem of inequality in material possession and social status.

Le Neveu deals with all of these manifestations of alienation, albeit in an a-systematic manner. No hierarchy is built around the way in which they are articulated. Alienation experienced by a theatricalised subject who performs for the other and encounters others" theatricality coexists with the phenomenon of material alienation. Alienation, deriving from the abstract yet absolute exchange value of money, coincides with the social tendencies towards automatisation. Through these various layers of a non-unified theory of alienation pierces an urgent call for human dignity and individualism.

In the field of textuality, a textuality which stands out as thoroughly dialogic, the question of alienation reappears again, this time within an intimate conversation between reader and text. In the dialogical extension of the contents is rooted a certain paradox, which is highly productive in creating an epistemological methodology of alienation, at once dialogical and subjective. This paradox emerges from a contradiction between a critique of alienation postulated from within the text and the treatment of dialogue, which could be said to affirm alienation. Dialogue is explored and unpacked with breathtaking dexterity in all its riches and exuberance. Despite the pejorative assessment of language leading to a world of deception and appearance, Diderot neither stops communicating nor representing communication with unabashed expressive naturalism. Whereas Rousseau draws the necessary consequences from his analysis of alienation by searching for authenticity in solitary existence and "solilogical" forms of communication, Diderot remains communal in his aesthetics, implementing the psycho-social dynamics of the dialogue as one of the key structures of his writing.

As Jay Caplan writes in his conclusion to *Framed Narratives*, "rather than lament the human tendency to mistake fiction for reality, or deplore the "effeminate" position one thereby comes to occupy (these are Rousseauist gestures), Diderot positively delights in doing so. [...] Unlike Rousseau, Diderot does not feel the need to be alone in order to be him-self. On the contrary, he only feels himself when "alienated" in dialogue, represented or real. [...] It doesn't occur to him – as it does to a Rousseau – that identifying with the representation of a suffering heroine might make him less likely to help someone who really was suffering.[3]

Whereas Brecht, in keeping with Rousseau's politics of anti-identification drew aesthetic consequences from his critique of social alienation, by numbing the illusionistic capacity inherent to language or dramatic representation, Diderot stays within the corrupt medium, uncoiling in his aesthetics communication's dialogical and thus alienating powers[4].

Whereas both Brecht and Diderot announce a critique of illusion, appearance and alienation at the level of the theme, Diderot, in terms of aesthetic solutions stays within a paradox. Brecht's concept of aesthetic *Verfremdung* clearly functions as a critique of alienated conditions. Diderot instead throws into contradiction intention and method. As a result, two very opposite aesthetics can be observed. Brecht draws all the necessary consequences and aims to prevent his aesthetics from continuing to multiply notions of alienation, appearance and illusion. This aesthetics of alienation will imply a tendency towards minimisation. Communication and expressiveness are interrupted and muted so that a break can be put onto the seductively absorbing appeal communication exerts on the reader or spectator.

In the same way as Roland Barthes in *The Third Meaning* defines the chosen gestures of Eisenstein's film as devoid of polysemous meaning, reduced to signify the specific, the chosen, the intentional, realist, non-figurative art, in general could be said to undertake a liberation of language from its expressive excesses. A minimalism of highly specified signification becomes characteristic for modernist aesthetics, and especially for Brecht's. Hand in hand with an economy of minimisation that throws into marked relief political urgencies, expressiveness, eloquence, dynamics, and above all, the overriding constituent of all those aspects, naturalist illusionism are exorcised. Represented communication can no longer communicate like in real life. It must signal its very difference, its potential to interrupt the continuities of an alienated reality.

For Brecht, no self-contradiction troubles the relation between political thought and aesthetic practice. A political project against alienated social conditions clearly demands an aesthetic which does not delude, alienate or seduce. But since aesthetics cannot help communicating, communication can only be represented in a tamed version, stripped down to its essential signification. It is divested of its drive to create expression above and beyond the limitations of a reduced form of content and intent. It becomes inhibited in its exuberant tendency towards otherness, in its inclination to perform towards and for the other.

On the contrary, for Diderot it is precisely the dialogical dimension of language which is explored in all its complexities. The performative relation between "I" and "you" which is profoundly permeated with the notion of illusion becomes one of the key principles of the Diderotian text. The Brechtian continuity between a critique of alienation and its political reflection on aesthetic theory is thus cancelled. Despite a complex texture of causalities drawing links between alienation implied in communicative action, exploitation within the master-slave relations, the depiction of self-alienation through automation, mental illness, and imagination, Diderot insists on naturalistic communication and its deceptive and illusionistic capacity. If one of Diderot's main characteristics can be found in his enthused sociability, *Le Neveu*, despite its thematic anti-alienation agenda, is entirely consistent with this enjoyment in dialogical rapport. Diderot creates a dialogic fervour which puts the reader directly in touch with the presence of his thought, the movements of his mind, the sense that here is someone speaking now, someone who addresses us, someone who will not let us escape from the labyrinthine movements of his mind, who draws us closer into the intimacies of his own presence. What is apparent is precisely the need for a communicative partner, a dialogical other, despite the fact that at the level of thematic representation, the Nephew (one of the two protagonists) can only speak despicably of the other and his pantomimic distortions.

Diderot's naturalistc aesthetics revolves around the figure of an interlocutor, an other, who sets into motion and gives reality and "realism" to his form of expression, someone who is there to acknowledge, to believe, or to question his imaginary representations almost in the sense of Bakhtinian "answerability."[6] If the author indulges in communication in contradiction to his protagonist, the Nephew's satire of communication, he does so to come into touch with this other, even at the cost of an illusionistic kind of identification. The power of illusion is thus celebrated with utmost virtuosity. The other as someone who is courted with performative genius, who is to be won over, convinced and hypnotised, becomes an indispensable figure in Diderot's scenario of writing fiction[7]. If the Nephew is self-ironic about his conflation of social and artistic skill, such self-irony extends directly to the representation of the text at large. *Le Neveu* becomes an inverted mirror of the Nephew's satirical propositions of an anti-alienation theory.

But this cynicism behind an exchangeability of aesthetic and social representation, involving the invasion of illusion into the realm of sociality, is not the only characteristic of Diderot's dialogically inclined literature. Jean Starobinski, in "Diderot et la parole des autres" has shown in a number of texts, reaching from Diderot's translation of L'Essai sur le mérite et la vertu, to *L'Essai sur les règnes de Claude et de Neron*, to *Est-il bon? Est-il mechant*, to the *Eléments de Physiologie, Le Rêve d'Alembert*, and also touching briefly on *Le Neveu*, that Diderot's tendency to allow for exteriority is typical for his writing and indeed his philosophical conception of consciousness[8]. Diderot's concept of speech, defined as a medium that is in itself other, whilst including the speech of others, determines the author's own process of thinking and writing. In the *Eléments de la Physiologie*, Diderot proposes that exteriority imprints itself on and prints the structures of our consciousness,

> Je suis porté à croire que tout ce que nous avons vu, connu, entendu, aperçu, [...] jusqu'à la multitude des voix humaines, à la mélodie et à l'harmonie de tous les airs, de toutes pièces de musique, de tous les concerts que nous avons entendus, tout cela existe en nous à notre insu[9].
> (I have come to believe that all we have seen, known, heard, perceived, [...] from the entire range of human voices to melodies and harmonies of all the airs, all the musical pieces and all the concerts we have heard, all of this exists within ourselves in our unconscious.)[10]

Diderot entrusts his consciousness to exteriority. As in the *Paradoxe*'s postulations on expression, the self's interiority is constantly opened up to exteriority, to the point where it becomes itself a structure of otherness. Contrary to Rousseau who suggests that such exteriority annihilates the self, for Diderot there is no threat involved in the exteriorisation of the self. Rather, the self nourishes itself upon exteriority and is situated in a constant dialogue with otherness. As Starobinski shows, this otherness is at the root of the Enlightenment project itself, not only in the sense of exploring scientifically the unknown structures of objects but also in terms of communicating new insights back to a wider public. Language and linguistic symbolisation of objects come from the other and must be given back to the other. The self is situated in a position of constant mediation. It affirms its own centre in a dialogic movement between re-situating itself in relation to the other and trying to re-situate the other. There is no problem in the attempt to make the other identify with one's own position since such identification is only limited to a transitional moment in the other's consciousness. In time the other will surely overcome his identification and re-appropriate the given proposition, replying back and contributing further to the network of communication at large. Part and parcel of Diderot's belief in communication is that he entrusts his dialogic partner as himself with the gift of self-alienation.

Such a concept of a positive, self-affirming form of alienation represents a radical alternative to Rousseau's anxiety of alienation, a form of otherness which threatens to annihilate the self. Diderot allows the self to turn itself inside out, to identify entirely with the other's position, but also to split itself into two to rationalise self-consciously its own communicative externalisations. He treats alienation as a natural condition, a natural medium, within which we move and constitute our identity. This is diametrically opposed to Rousseau's dichotomous approach to alienation as unnatural and parasitic. Diderot's concept of nature, from the outset, is thoroughly pervaded by otherness. There is no possibility of reversing or undoing alienation in total, no longing for a return to a pure state of originality. Diderot rather accepts, utilises, explores and plays with a condition of alienation, which is acceptable by virtue of being irremovably natural.

Hence, Diderot's concept of the self is defined by a willingness to become decentred. In the words of Starobinski, who exemplifies Diderot's "consent to alienation" in the ways in which the latter would trust his editor and friend Naigeon to insert changes even in his most autobiographical writings: "Il s'affirme lui-même, par l'aliénation consentie, le service rendu, le renfort d'éloquence qu'il apporte à une cause commune."[11] (He affirms himself through consented alienation, the service to others, the eloquent support he contributes to a common cause.)[12] This trust in the other as a friend, the very possibility of a "friendly" form of alienation, invokes the possibility of a community and sociability which instead of jeopardising the stability of the self and its collective, promises to enrich the realm of knowledge, communication and culture, at the same time as opening up a potential for political action. These politics, rather than be prompted by a materialist-historical anti-alienation dynamic, would derive from the individual's capability to entrust itself to a form of "aliénation consentie."

Notes

1 Denis Diderot, *Le Neveu de Rameau*, edited by Jean Fabre (Geneva: Droz, 1950)

2 These different themes of alienation in *Le Neveu de Rameau* are discussed in the preceding chapter of the dissertation, "Le Neveu's World of Alienation," 170.

3 Jay Caplan, *Framed Narratives: Diderot's Genealogy of the Beholder* (Manchester: Manchester UP, 1986), 90.

4 On Diderot's anti-solipsist attitude, see Eric-Emmanuel Schmitt, *Diderot: Ou la philosophie de la séduction* (Paris: Albin Michel, 1997), 129-47.

5 Barthes, *The Responsibility of Forms: Critical Essays on Music, Art and Representation*, translated by Richard Howard (Berkeley: University of California Press, 1991), p. 45.

6 See M.M. Bakhtin, "Art and Answerability," in *Art and Answerability: Early Essays by M.M. Bakhtin*, edited by Michael Holquist and Vadim Liapunov, trans. and annot. Vadim Liapunov (Austin: University of Texas Press, 1990), 1-3.

7 Caplan interprets the presence of the addressee as part of a sacrificial economy, where the beholder is to fill in empathetically for the loss of a represented figure. Although this theory is demonstrated convincingly with regard to *Le Fils naturel* and *La Religieuse*, the position of the adressee as a fundamental constituent, seems to me even more fundamental than that. Although the notion of 'lack' might be key to the constitution of an imaginary dialogical partner, such lack, as *Le Neveu de Rameau* shows, is not necessarily based on an economy of sacrifice. Caplan (1985) on Diderot's economy of sacrifice, see his chapter "The Aesthetics of Sacrifice," 15-29.

8 Starobinski, « Diderot et la parole des autres, » *Critique* 28 (1972) : 3-22.

9 Denis Diderot, *Eléments de physiologie*, publiés par Jean Mayer, Paris, 1964.

10 My translation.

11 Ibid., 11.

12 My translation.

20

Brief Conclusions
James Elkins

If you have read the eleven essays in Part One, and sampled the eight excerpts in Part Two, then you have a fairly accurate picture of the state of the studio-art PhD.

You may still be thinking: Okay, fine, but this degree is still a bad idea. It will keep young artists in school more than ever before. It will make it even less likely that they will develop individual voices. There are a lot of great artists out there, you might say, who don't need the PhD—and there's a lot of art that could not have been made in a PhD program at all. People who have taught in MFA programs know the sinking feeling of encountering more purpose-made, over-intellectualized art, whose raison d'être is determined by the institution, whose makers speak glibly about the biennales, the major markets, contemporary theory, and institutional critique. (Dave Hickey is especially good at this kind of complaint.) Surely the PhD will just make more people like that. It's a hot house, green-house kind of idea, too ivory-tower, too shut away from the wider world.

And besides—you may say—how many MFA students are capable of serious research? Or if you don't like the word "research," then how many can write 50,000 or 100,000 words on any subject? And look at what happened in the UK: some PhD-granting institutions are interesting, but many are a kind of prolonged MFA, with students just sitting in their studios another two or three years, producing more of the same art, writing about themselves, navel-gazing, trying to achieve a pinnacle of self-awareness that may or may not make their work more interesting. Those aren't real PhD programs, they're just glorified studios. The students are not guided not by specialists but by their same old studio art instructors.

Those are all legitimate objections. There is no real defense against them. Why persist, then? Why not give up and let the MFA or MA keep their places as the highest formal degrees?[1] Why not be content to set up open institutions like the Jan Van Eyck Academy in Maastricht in The Netherlands, where artists can study beyond the PhD without getting any additional degrees? Why not let artists get degrees in other fields if they think they need them?

Because of market pressure. Every indication is that the studio-art PhD will spread like the MFA after World War II. It will spread slowly in the US, because of the lack of financial incentives, but it will spread, and eventually it will be the degree everyone needs to get teaching jobs. Given that, it seems tremendously important to consider these two things:[2]

1. The impending PhD is a signal opportunity to rethink education. Art schools and colleges can learn from mistakes made in the UK and elsewhere, and institute a genuinely challenging, well-conceived version of the doctorate. For example US institutions can avoid the tortured uses of administrative jargon and the fragile deployment of half-understood theories that mar some existing PhD dissertations. They can avoid the descent into solipsism and interminable self-reflection that infests some studio-art dissertations. They can avoid the unstructured extension of the MFA that is so tempting for newly-implemented PhD programs. They can avoid parroting the sciences, or hopelessly emulating the disciplinarity they see in other parts of the university.

Now is the time to rethink the concept of advanced art education, and by extension, all education that purports to include creative or expressive elements. The studio-art PhD is worth pondering and pursuing because it raises questions about the university that are not raised as forcibly in other contexts. I can think of five areas of questioning in particular. First, the PhD involves a fundamental questioning of the MFA, which has never had a secure basis. As Howard Singerman, Timothy Emlyn Jones, and others have pointed out, the charter of the MFA is not itself a coherent document, and it has never been clear what the degree is intended to accomplish.[3] It is based, so I have argued, on a set of mutually contradictory values that come from different historical sources: late Romanticism, the French Academy, the Bauhaus, identity politics in the 1960s and 1970s.[4] A conceptually clear PhD would require a clearer MFA. Second: the PhD would be an opportunity to do serious work on the always vexed relation between studio art departments and the rest of the university. Studio art departments are always the poor cousins of academic departments, just as art schools throughout the world have only tentative and ad hoc relations with their local universities. (When they have connections at all.) The studio-art PhD is among other things a bid for parity and recognition, so it will entail re-opening the many half-finished conversations about the function of the university, the idea of the university, and the coherence of the university.⁵ Third, the studio-art PhD can be an occasion to revisit the entire question of advanced degrees ("terminal" degrees, in the somewhat startling US term). As Mick Wilson argues in this book, the history of the PhD is hardly a neutral one, and it can be argued that it sits uneasily even in fields where it now seems natural. Fourth, and most interesting to me, the PhD will ask scholars in all fields to reconsider what it means to supervise a dissertation. Nominally, supervision means that the student is guided to a level of competence equal to others in the field; but with the increasing interest in interdisciplinarity, that model becomes weak. (How can a student be expected to be equally competent in two or three fields? What is competence when fields are mingled?) Studio-art PhDs raise such conversations to an entirely new level, because the student is *making* something, and scholarship is—often, as I argue in Chapter 11, but not always—subservient to expression. Fifth, and last: the studio-art PhD creates the possibility for wholly new kinds of interdisciplinary, transdisciplinary, and other unnamed configurations, because it does not add kinds of scholarship to one another: it mingles scholarship with expressive work. For these and many other reasons, the studio-art PhD opens up the most basic dogmas and assumptions of the contemporary university. It is nothing less than a chance to re-conceive disciplinarity.

2. For artists, the studio-art PhD is only useful in a tiny percentage of cases, but those cases are extremely interesting. If, as an artist, you need to know about Lacan, cognitive science, chemistry, or Aboriginal culture, at a professional level—if it will somehow inform your work, if you feel it's necessary to go forward—then the PhD is for you. If you are like ninety-eight percent of artists, you don't need to know any academic field quite that well, and so the degree isn't necessary. For many students, the degree could be actively harmful: it could keep students in the university, or in school, just when they should be out finding their way in the world. It will inevitably produce a scholasticism—a uniformity, an orthodoxy, a conservatism—as every academic discipline does. If your art is, say, Neoexpressionist, then an advanced degree may actually harm your practice by making you aware of historical and critical reasons to doubt your own interests. (I have sometimes advised artists who do expressionist work to drop out of school even before the MFA.) But if your work depends on, say, a feminist critique of psychoanalysis, then the studio-art PhD may be just what you need.

Many artists and scholars are hobbled because they are insecure about theory: they haven't studied enough of it to know quite what they are permitted to say, and so they become timid, and never really join the discourse on their subject. When a student comes to me and says she's just discovered someone like Derrida, and can I please help her to find good books to read, I often say: You have two choices. Either forget about Derrida, and go back to your studio and get on with your art, or else take two or three years and really study him, until you feel you know his work inside out. That advice is intended to avoid the common situation in which a student learns *some* theory, but not enough to really move freely in it, or to use it to make interesting moves. As a result their art, or their scholarship in the case of academic students, becomes timid. For art students, the PhD in studio art should fix that. It can produce genuinely well-informed, professional-level practitioners, who really know the issues and how to intervene in current critical impasses. Such students would do the sorts of philosophically-oriented work that is praised by Rosalind Krauss, for example, in regard to artists such as Marcel Broodthaers. For the small percentage of art students who really *need* to master some body of knowledge, the PhD is not only a good idea but an essential one. The art world is filled to overflowing with half-digested theories, bluster, incoherence, and disorganized, impressionistic writing.[6] In a sense that's the status quo, and it would not make sense to critique it: but in some cases, when particular claims are being made about specific concepts and philosophic positions, then the PhD would be the only place an artist could go to really join the conversation of contemporary visual theory.

MFAs, despite their many virtues, simply do not produce graduates who really know theory. I say that after twenty years teaching at the School of the Art Institute in Chicago: in all that time I have seen no more than a couple of dozen students who were educated at the level of rigor that is expected of, say, philosophy students in major universities. MFA students are routinely given degrees even though they have only a sketchy, somewhat bewildered sense of such things as deconstruction, semiotics, or psychoanalysis. In virtually every case, that just doesn't matter. In a small number of cases—maybe two percent of the general population of MFA students—it really does.

Let's work to raise the bar, and make art education more difficult.

Notes

1 Here let me cite again "A Certain MA-ness," edited by Henk Slager, special issue of *Makhuzine: Journal of Artistic Research* [Utrecht School of the Arts] 5 (2008), ISSN 1882-4728, which has a collection of essays theorizing the MA and MFA.

2 A condensed, polemic version of what follows, which can also serve as a laundry list of points in this book, is my "Ten Reasons to Mistrust the New PhD in Studio Art," *Art in America* (May 2007): 108-9.

3 Howard Singerman, *Art Subjects: Making Artists in the American University* (Berkeley: University of California Press, 1999).

4 My *Why Art Cannot be Taught: A Handbook for Art Students* (Urbana IL: University of Illinois Press, 2001).

5 In addition to the sources cited in Wilson's paper (Chapter 4) see R. D. Anderson, *European Universities from the Enlightenment to 1914* (Oxford: Oxford University Press, 2004). The coherence of the "idea of the university" is addressed, with additional sources, in *Visual Practices Across the University*, edited by James Elkins (Munich: Wilhelm Fink, 2007).

6 I try to analyze this in the "Editor's Afterword to the *Art Seminar* Series" in *Re-Enchantment*, co-edited by David Morgan, vol. 7 of *The Art Seminar* (New York: Routledge, 2008); the essay is an attempt to characterize the exact kinds of disagreement, incoherence, etc., that took place in the seven-volume series.

List of Contributors

Jan Baetens teaches at the Institute for Cultural Studies, of the Katholieke Universiteit Leuven; he has a PhD in French literature. His research on photography is oriented towards the narrative uses of the medium, inter-art comparison, and the cultural dynamics of "high" and "low" (for instance in the field of the so-called "photonovella"). A contributing editor to *History of Photography* and *FotoMuseum Magazine*, he has published (often in French) numrous books and many articles on photography, fiction, and other subjects, for example *Cent ans et plus de bande dessinée (en vers et en poèmes)* (Paris: Collection Traverses, 2007). He has also collaborated on a number of projects with Hilde Van Gelder; see some examples in her biographical note. jan.baetens@arts.kuleuven.be.

Christl Berg is the head of the Printmedia Studio at the School of Visual and Performing Arts of the University of Tasmania. She arrived in Tasmania in 1984 from Germany via a very long working holiday in India. In 1992 she completed an MFA at the School of Art, University of Tasmania in Hobart and in 2003 her PhD at the same institution. Christl has exhibited her photo media based work since 1989 and has held a full-time lecturing position for the past ten years at the School of Visual and Performing Arts,University of Tasmania in Launceston. Tasmania with its remarkable natural environment, its complex cultural history and vibrant contemporary art milieu has become her much loved and appreciated home. Christl.Berg@utas.edu.au.

Victor Burgin, M.F.A. (Yale), is Millard Professor of Fine Art, Goldsmiths College, University of London, and Professor Emeritus of History of Consciousness, University of California, Santa Cruz. He is one of the most distinguished teaching artists of our time, whose cross-disciplinary work bridges media, culture and art. Former Chair in Art and Architecture, The Cooper Union for the Advancement of Science and Art, New York, and Professor of Art History, UC Santa Cruz, Burgin served as visiting professor and artist-in-residence in many countries. His media and conceptual art was exhibited in museums and art galleries worldwide. He is the author of *Thinking Photography, Between, The End of Art Theory: Criticism and Postmodernity, In/Different Spaces: Place and Memory in Visual Culture, Shadowed.*

Jo-Anne Duggan is a scholar and photomedia practitioner whose artistic career has evolved through more than 30 solo and group exhibitions in Australia, Italy, Ireland, and the US. She received her Doctorate of Creative Arts from the University of Technology, Sydney in 2004. Her artwork is held both in public and private collections in Australia and internationally. She has recently been appointed Research Fellow at Victoria University in Melbourne. She has lectured at a number of universities in critical theory, visual art, art history, design, and visual communication. She is an active member of various boards and councils in the arts industry and academic sector. Her contributions to the field of visual arts in Australia have been recognized by awards and residencies received from international, national, state and regional bodies such as the Australia Council, New Work Grant (2005); Arts Queensland Project Grant (2005); and Australian Foundation for Studies in Italy Fellowship (2003).

James Elkins teaches at the School of the Art Institute of Chicago, where he is E.C. Chadbourne Chair in the Department of Art History, Theory, and Criticism. His writing focuses on the history and theory of images in art, science, and nature. Some of his books are exclusively on fine art (*What Painting Is, Why Are Our Pictures Puzzles?*). Others include scientific and non-art images and archaeology (*The Domain of Images, On Pictures and the Words*

That Fail Them), and natural history (*How to Use Your Eyes*). www.jameselkins.com; texts on saic.academia.edu/JElkins.

Timothy Emlyn Jones is a Welsh artist who came to the Burren College of Art in January 2003 to take up the post of Dean and Graduate Director. Prior to joining Burren College of Art in January 2003 he was the Deputy Director of the Glasgow School of Art and before that the Assistant Principal (Academic Affairs) at Wimbledon School of Art, London. His fascination with art education began at Hornsey College of Art as one of the student organisers of the 1968 sit-in, and his subsequent academic career includes a track record of academic innovation that spans secondary through to doctoral levels of education. His research interests are in drawing considered as a process of enquiry. As an artist he has exhibited internationally and he is represented in public collections in a number of countries.

Charles Harrison is Professor of History and Theory of Art at the Open University. His research interests include: theories of art since 1648; theories of modernism in the arts; the work of Art and Language; modern European and American art, with particular interest in art since 1950; the Conceptual Art movement; and considerations of gender in the interpretation of modern art. His publications include *Art in Theory 1648-1815* with Paul Wood and Jason Gaiger (Blackwell, 2000); *Essays on Art & Language* (MIT Press, 2001); *Art in Theory 1900-2000*, with Paul Wood (Blackwell, 2002); and *Painting the Difference: Sex and Spectator in Modern Art* University of Chicago Press, 2005).

Sue Lovegrove completed a PhD at Canberra School of Art, Australian National University in 2002. After 15 years of tertiary teaching she decided to become a full time artist and now resides in Tasmania. Sue has exhibited in numerous group shows and held 10 solo shows in Australia. She is represented by Christine Abrahams Gallery in Melbourne and Helen Maxwell Gallery in Canberra. Sue's artwork is inspired by the natural environment, in particular journeys into wilderness areas. In 2003 she was a recipient of the Australian Antarctic Division Arts Fellowship, which enabled her to travel to Antarctica and Macquarie Island. Sue's current work is investigating the representation of the Southern Ocean and Antarctica through abstraction.

María Mencía is a digital artist and lecturer in Digital Media at Kingston University, London, UK. She holds a Digital Media Art practice-based PhD from The University of the Arts London, a Chelsea College of Art MA in History and Theory of Art, and two degrees one in Fine Art at Camberwell College of Art, London and the other in English Philology at the Complutense University, Madrid, Spain. María has exhibited nationally and internationally, including: *onedotzero*, ICA, London, 2003; ISEA 2002 (Orai), Nagoya, Japan, 2002; and FILE 2002, São Paulo, Brazil. She has participated in the following conferences: ARCO 2004 International Conference in Visual Studies, Madrid, Spain; Digital Surface: Approaches to Current Research in Contemporary Art Practice; Culture 2000 European Union, TATE Britain, London, 2003; BEAP 2002 (Biennial of Electronic Arts Perth), CAIIA-STAR: Consciousness Reframed IV, Australia. www.m.mencia.freeuk.com.

Judith Mottram is Professor of Visual Art at Nottingham Trent University and has been Associate Dean for Research and Graduate Studies in the College of Art, Design and Built Environment since 2004. Before joining Nottingham Trent she was Director of Research for the School of Art & Design at Loughborough University following six years as their Program Leader for Painting. She is a member of the AHRC Postgraduate panel for Visual Arts and Media, a member of the AHRC Peer Review College, and is on the Editorial Board for the Journal of Visual Art Practice and the journal *Color: Design & Creativity*. In addition to her particular research interests in practical questions about the use of drawing, pattern and color, she has contributed to reviews of practice-led research, the compilation of a database of completed art and design doctorates, and discussions on eLearning and subject knowledge in art and design.

Uriel Orlow is an artist, writer and AHRC research fellow in creative arts at University of Westminster, London. He completed a PhD in Fine Art at the University of the Arts, London in 2002. Hi art and research explore the roles language, the image and memory play in structuring our experience. Using a wide variety of media – from video and sound to photography, billboard-posters, text and drawing – he engages with historical sites, body memory, archives and libraries. Orlow's work has been included in exhibitions and film-festivals internationally. Recent exhibitions include *Videoland, Artneuland*, Berlin (2006-7), *Ghosting, Arnolfini*, Bristol (2006), Swiss Art Awards at ART 37 Basel (2006), *Around the World in Eighty Days*, Institute of Contemporary Arts (ICA), London (2006), Extra-Muros, Fri-Art centre for contemporary art, Fribourg (2005), and *Glad to be of service*, ifa-Galerie, Berlin (2005). His publications include *Re: The Archive, The Image, And the Very Dead Sheep* (Double agents: 2004) and a monograph on his work, *Deposits*, published by The Greenbox in 2006. More information at www.urielorlow.net.

Henk Slager is dean of the Utrecht Graduate School of Visual Art and Design (MaHKU) and its professor of Artistic Research. He is on the board of Earn (European Network for Artistic Research). Recent curatorial projects include: *Demirrorized Zone* (De Appel, Amsterdam, 2003), Busan Biennial (curator Theory Program, 2004), *The Intermedial Zone* (Museum Boijmans van Beuningen, Rotterdam 2005), DARE (Dutch Artistic Research Event, several locations, Utrecht 2006), *Shelter 07* (The Freedom of Public Art in the Cover of Urban Space, Harderwijk 2007), and *Flash Cube* (Leeum, Samsung Museum of Art, Seoul, 2007).

George Smith is Founder and President of the Institute for Doctoral Studies in the Visual Arts (IDSVA). Headquartered in Portland, Maine and supported by a worldwide faculty, IDSVA offers online instruction and holds residencies in Tuscany, Venice, New York, Paris, and at Brown University. Among the very first to write an interdisciplinary dissertation for the PhD at Brown, Dr. Smith is an internationally recognized interdisciplinary scholar. He has published widely on relations between literature and the visual arts. His essays on psychoanalytic theory, philosophy, visual culture, and the literatures of France, England, and America have appeared in critical and philosophical journals and collections throughout the U.S. and abroad. See www.idsva.org.

Frank Thirion is a practicing artist who came to Australia from Paris, France in 1967 and currently resides in Canberra. He gained a Bachelor of Visual Arts degree from the Australian National University School of Art in 1999, with First Class Honors and was awarded a University Medal. In 2004 he completed a PhD in Visual Art (Painting) at the ANU School of Art. His art has been collected internationally and acquired by some of Australia's major national institutions. He is continuing with his research on Rembarrnga bark paintings. See current work on frankthirion.com.

Hilde Van Gelder teaches History of Art at the Katholieke Universiteit Leuven. Her photographic research is focussed on photography's contribution to the confusion of the artistic genres in postwar art and on the medium's critical function in contemporary art, especially Belgian art. Her recent publications include *Photography between Poetry and Politics: The Critical Position of the Photographic Medium in Contemporary Art,* edited by Van Gelder and H. Westgeest (Leuven: University Press Leuven, 2008); and "A Matter of Cleaning Up: Treating History in the Work of Allan Sekula and Jeff Wall," *History of Photography* 31 no. 1 (Spring 2007): 68-80. She has collaborated with Jan Baetens on a number of projects, including "Hybridization," a special issue of *History of Photography* 31 no. 1 (spring 2007); "Mediumspecificiteit: terug van weggeweest?," *Context K* 3 (2006): 133-145; and "Petite poétique de la photographie mise en roman (1970-1990)," in *Photographie et romanesque,* edited by Danièle Méaux (Caen : Lettres Modernes Minard, 2006), 257-71. hilde.vangelder@arts.kuleuven.be.

Phoebe von Held completed a PhD in Fine Art at the Slade School of Fine Art in 2001 on "Alienation and Theatricality in Brecht and Diderot." Her work as a theater director/designer includes two productions for the Citizens Theatre, Glasgow: Diderot's *Rameau's Nephew* (1998) and *The Nun* (2002), which she also co-translated and adapted. Currently she is working on a dramatisation of Diderot's *D'Alembert's Dream,* a collaborative project with biomedical scientists from the NIMR and animation artists. From 2002-4 she was a research fellow at the IRS, University of London. She has taught courses on Seventeenth- Century French Drama, Contemporary British

Drama, Site-specific Performance and Alienation and Theatricality. Her publications concern the work of Denis Diderot, dramatic and literary theory, site-specific performance and eighteenth-century studies.

Ruth Waller is a painter, currently living in Canberra, Australia with two tabby cats and a partner who commutes from Cambridge (UK). She is a Senior Lecturer in painting at the Australian National University School of Art. Born in Sydney in 1955, Ruth developed a passion for early European painting while in high school. In recent years, with the benefit of studio residencies in Tuscany and Barcelona and regular trips to the Northern Hemisphere, this enthusiasm has been reflected and investigated in her studio practice. Her most recent exhibition featured a series of paintings made in response to Bruegel's *Dulle Griet*. She is represented by Watters Gallery in Sydney and Helen Maxwell Gallery in Canberra. Her work is included in the collections of the National Gallery of Australia, National Gallery of Victoria, Art Gallery of Queensland, and numerous regional museums and private collections in Australia. See her recent work at www.wattersgallery.com.

Mick Wilson is an artist and critic. From the mid-1990s to 2000 he produced a series of one-person shows and projects including: *Trains Made Mary Vague*, Temple Bar Gallery & Studios (2000); *The Tuilleries Incident*, Hugh Lane Gallery, Dublin (1999); *The Medium's Project*, Temple Bar / various (1998); *Athman Ben Salah: On Loss*, Triskel, Cork (1997); *The Bull/Ox Herding Series: Cruising Masculinity*, Project Arts Centre, Dublin (1996); and *Queerly Heteroclite*, City Arts Centre, Dublin (1995). He recently returned to artmaking with his participation in the group exhibition *Blackboxing* (2007) curated by Tessa Giblin at the Project Arts Centre. He has been Head of Fine Art at the Dublin Institute of Technology; before that, he was director of MAVis and the BA visual arts practice programs at IADT (1998-2004) and an associate lecturer at NCAD, CCAD, IADT and TCD (1991-1998). His PhD was completed in 2006 on the topic "Conflicted Faculties: Knowledge Conflict and the University" at the National College of Art and Design, Dublin.

List of Illustrations

Page 173, top:
Jo-Anne Duggan, *Impossible Gaze #2*. Origin: Room L – The Carrand Room, Museo Nazionale del Bargello. © Jo-Anne Duggan, c-type photographic print, 1m x 1.25m, 2002.

Page 173, bottom:
Jo-Anne Duggan, *Impossible Gaze #15*. Origin: Room X – Appartamento del Re [King's Bedroom], Appartamenti Reali, Palazzo Pitti. © Jo-Anne Duggan, c-type photograph, 1m x 1.25m, 2002.

Page 174:
Jo-Anne Duggan, *Impossible Gaze #1*. Origin: Room II – Sala del Trono [Throne Room], Appartamenti Reali, Palazzo Pitti. © Jo-Anne Duggan, c-type photograph, 1m x 1.25m, 2002.

P. 182, left:
Sue Lovegrove, *To Hear the Earth Breathe, No. 232*, 2001. Acrylic and gouache on canvas, 130 x 90 cm.

P. 183, right:
Sue Lovegrove, *To Hear the Earth Breathe, No. 227*, 2001. Acrylic and gouache on canvas, 60 x 45 cm.

P. 196:
Katungka Napanaga, *[Title Unknown]*, 2001.
Acrylic on canvas, approx. 120 x 90 cm. Courtesy of the Ikuntji Art Centre.

P. 200:
Frank R Thirion, *Paysage de Sel (Salt Country)*, 2002. Salt, acrylic and spray paint on canvas, 180 x 220 cm.

P. 201:
Frank Thirion, *Gecko Cat*, 2003. Salt, acrylic paint on craft board, 150 x 170 cm,
scale ruler enamel paint on wood 5 x 25 cm.

P. 204:
Paddy Fordham Wainburranga, *Coffin Box*, 1980s. Bark painting. Courtesy the artist.

P. 205:
Diagram of Paddy Fordham Wainburranga, *Coffin Box*, 1980s. Bark painting. Courtesy the artist; diagram by Frank Thirion.

P. 218:
Simone Martini, Beato Agostino Novello altarpiece, outline drawing by Ruth Waller.

P. 221:
Simone Martini, *Miracle of the Fallen Child*, from the Beato Agostino Novello altarpiece, outline drawing by Ruth Waller.

P. 223:
Ruth Waller, *After Giotto (The Church in Ruins)*, 2000. Oil on canvas. 140 x 180 cm.

P. 224:
Ruth Waller, *Glove Visitation I (after Fra Angelico)*, 1996. Oil on board, 30 x 35 cm.

P. 225:
Ruth Waller, *The Fall*, 1999. Ink and pencil on paper, 23 x 29 cm.

P. 227:
Christl Berg, *"frieze,"* detail of installation view. Total frieze: 18.5 meters, 12 sections of photograms.

P. 228:
Christl Berg, *"frieze,"* detail of section #5. Photograph, 104 x 160 cm.

P. 29, top:
Christl Berg, *Finds,* installation view.

P. 229, bottom:
Christl Berg, *Find #37,* digital print, 21 x 21 cm.

P. 230:
Christl Berg, *Find #8,* digital print, 42 x 25 cm.

P. 245, top:
María Mencía, *Another Kind of Language,* 2002, installation views. DIFFERENTIA exhibition, PM Gallery, London.

P. 245, bottom:
María Mencía, *Another Kind of Language,* 2002, screen shot.

P. 255:
Uriel Orlow, *Housed Memory,* stills, 2000. Video with sound, 11 hours.

P. 256:
Uriel Orlow, *Housed Memory,* stills, 2000. Video with sound, 11 hours.

P. 266-269
Phoebe von Held, stills from the theater production of *Reameau's Nephew,* adapted and translated by Phoebe von Held and Nina Pearlman, produced and performed at the Citizens Theatre, Glasgow, 1998.

Lightning Source UK Ltd.
Milton Keynes UK
01 February 2010

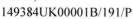